D1291669

THE BONDS OF HUMANITY

The Bonds of Humanity

Cicero's Legacies in European Social and Political Thought, ca. 1100–ca. 1550

CARY J. NEDERMAN

The Pennsylvania State University Press
University Park, Pennsylvania

Library of Congress Cataloging-in-Publication Data

Names: Nederman, Cary J., author.
Title: The bonds of humanity : Cicero's legacies in European social and
    political thought, ca. 1100–ca. 1550 / Cary J. Nederman.
Description: University Park, Pennsylvania : The Pennsylvania State
    University Press, [2020] | Includes bibliographical references and index.
Summary: "Surveys the many different impacts of Ciceronian theories on
    a diverse array of texts and authors between 1100 and 1550, presenting
    a counternarrative to the widely accepted belief in the dominance
    of Aristotelianism in early European political and social thought"—
    Provided by publisher.
Identifiers: LCCN 2019047143 | ISBN 9780271085005 (cloth)
Subjects: LCSH: Cicero, Marcus Tullius—Influence. | Political science—
    Europe—History. | Social sciences—Europe—History. | Ciceronianism.
Classification: LCC JA84.E9 N44 2020 | DDC 320.01—dc23
LC record available at https://lccn.loc.gov/2019047143

The Pennsylvania State University Press is a member of the Association of
University Presses.

It is the policy of The Pennsylvania State University Press to use acid-free
paper. Publications on uncoated stock satisfy the minimum requirements
of American National Standard for Information Sciences—Permanence of
Paper for Printed Library Material, ANSI Z39.48–1992.

In memory of Edd Whetmore (1946–2016)
and
for Annie Wilson Whetmore

To be ignorant of what occurred before you were born is to remain always a child. For what is the worth of human life, unless it is woven into the life of our ancestors by the records of history?

—Cicero, *Orator* 120

We are like dwarfs sitting on the shoulders of giants so that we are able to see more and further than they, not indeed by reason of the sharpness of our own vision or the height of our bodies, but because we are lifted up on high and raised aloft by the greatness of giants.

—John of Salisbury, *Metalogicon* 3.4
(ascribed to Bernard of Chartres)

CONTENTS

While completing the first draft of this book, I found myself driving along the back roads of the Sierra Nevada foothills in the company of a retired employee of the California Department of Transportation named Randy. Randy had spent more than thirty years plowing snow from highways in the winter and then patching up those same roads the following summer. A Sisyphean task, to be sure, but one that kept the rest of us safe. Inevitably, the conversation came around to the question of what I did for a living. I told him that I was a university professor who was on a research leave of absence to write a book. And, just as inevitably, he asked me what the book was about. I explained to him that it concerned the ways in which the social and political philosophy of Cicero was read by early Europeans. His next question was obvious: "Why would you want to bother with that?"

I thought hard for a while on what Randy asked. It would have been easy enough, I suppose, to explain that a professor was expected to do research and write books in order to advance knowledge—which is, of course, our standard response to such queries. But it made me think a little past that pat answer. So I asked him, "Do you care about your family?" "Sure, ya." "Do you care about your friends?" "Ya." "Do you care about your God?" "Yes, sir." "Do you care about your country?" "Of course." "Do you care about your fellow human beings, strangers, whoever they are?" "I'm obliged to." "Tell me," I said to him, "which one of these is the most important?" "It depends. God should come first, I guess, but I love my wife and kids and grandkids, my friends, my country. And I don't want to see other people suffer. It's tough." And I said, "See, that's what my book is about. A bunch of folks who are trying to figure out where their loyalties lie, who know that they have responsibilities to a lot of others in different ways but don't necessarily have any easy answers to how those work out. They were just like you and me. By listening to them, it can make us think." In the end, that's what I am trying to do here.

ACKNOWLEDGMENTS

The composition of *The Bonds of Humanity* has followed a very long and somewhat tortuous route. My interest in Cicero started early. I was absurdly fortunate to study with wonderful undergraduate teachers at Columbia University, especially Herbert Deane and Robert Denoon Cumming, and to be favored with Neal Wood as my doctoral co-supervisor at York University. Neal entrusted me, while I was still a grad student, with reading and commenting on the manuscript of his now-classic book on Cicero's social and political thought. He "sold" me on Cicero at a time when few others cared. So much of where one winds up as a scholar depends upon where one starts.

For too many years, I promised my friends that I would see through to the finish a project that effectively commenced in the mid-1980s. To them, I offer thanks for their patience and encouragement. Among those who have propelled my efforts to complete *The Bonds of Humanity* are (in strictly alphabetical order): Marcia Colish, Ben Fontana, Dean Hammer, Bettina Koch, Jason Maloy, Constant Mews, Walter Nicgorski, Gary Remer, Takashi Shogimen, and the late Paul Sigmund. Sometimes one's fiercest critics prove to be one's most valued teachers, credit for which I assign in particular to Paul Rahe. At a key moment of despair, Nancy Struever stepped in with crucial words of sympathy and uplift. And Gary Remer— bless you, my friend—provided the Blue Baker pastries from afar when I truly needed them (or at least what they signified). These people have enriched my life and my mind beyond measure. I love them one and all.

A Faculty Development Leave granted to me by Texas A&M University during the Fall 2016 term made possible the completion of a first full draft of the manuscript. The award of a fellowship by the Caltech-Huntington Humanities Collaboration facilitated the research for and composition of several chapters. I am deeply grateful to the members of the Caltech-Huntington group for their intellectual encouragement and stimulation: Warren Brown, Jennifer Jahner, Leah Klement, Bettina Koch, and Benjamin Saltzman. Useful suggestions were offered to me along the way by Charlie Briggs, Daisy Delogu, Dan Kapust, Sylvain Piron, Riccardo Saccenti, and

Andrea Tarnowski. I have been favored by my ability to depend upon the reliable and precise research and editorial assistance of an amazing group of Texas A&M doctoral students: Guillaume Bogiaris, Reed Stevens, Tyler Theel, and, especially, Ben Peterson (who saved my hide on more than one occasion). The Political Science Department office support personnel, especially Dede Bright, offered exceptional aid during the long process of preparing the manuscript. The staff of the Interlibrary Loan Department at Texas A&M demonstrated unparalleled readiness to indulge my (sometimes very taxing) requests and needs. Without all of you folks, *The Bonds of Humanity* couldn't have happened.

The Bonds of Humanity also wouldn't exist in its current, proper form without the singular support and advice of my editor at Penn State, Ellie Goodman. From the beginning, she "got" what I wanted to achieve when others didn't, and she escorted me along the path to strengthen the volume in ways that are difficult to specify yet easy for me to comprehend. I have published many monographs with many different presses over the course of thirty or so years, but Ellie stands alone as the editor who has provided keen guidance from first to last. You are the very best, Ellie. Take a bow. The two anonymous reviewers for PSUP were truly founts of wisdom. Both of them compelled me to rethink and recast significant dimensions of the project.

As ever, my greatest debt (an intellectual as well as a deeply personal one) is owed to my long-term partner (now wife) Karen Bollermann, who watched me suffer over the composition of this book, who offered succor, and who (barely) survived to tell the tale. On more than one occasion, I was ready to abandon *The Bonds of Humanity*. On account of Karen's wise counsel, I did not.

Early drafts of chapters in this volume were presented as talks to or conference papers at the American Political Science Association, the Australia and New Zealand Association of Medieval and Early Modern Studies, Dartmouth College, and the University of Minnesota. The audiences at all of these venues were generous with their questions and comments. Some material contained herein initially appeared in print in fragmentary and significantly underdeveloped form over the course of three decades in *European Journal of Political Theory*, *The Historical Journal*, *Journal of Medieval History*, *Journal of the History of Ideas*, and *Political Theory*. In devoting in excess of thirty years writing this book, it's almost impossible to know which parts of it poured out of me in its lines from time to time (thanks, Joni).

As I completed the initial draft of the manuscript, my best friend of forty-five years, Edd Whetmore, died after a long and increasingly debilitating illness. I recognized Edd for his kindnesses often times in the acknowledgments to my previous books, and he has always been around to receive my appreciation. This time—incomprehensibly to me—I must express my gratitude to him posthumously. I share my thanks equally with his wife, Annie, my former doctoral student, who cared for and loved Edd from first to last. *The Bonds of Humanity* is for both of you.

College Station, Texas
January 11, 2019

I have used the following editions, all from the Loeb Classical Library series, for this volume. On numerous occasions, the English renderings of the Latin texts have been significantly modified or sometimes even entirely retranslated.

Academica. Edited by H. Rackham. Cambridge: Harvard University Press, 1933.

Brutus. Edited by G. L. Hendrickson and H. M. Hubbell. Cambridge: Harvard University Press, 1939.

De amicitia. Edited by William Armistead Falconer. Cambridge: Harvard University Press, 1923.

De divinatione. Edited by William Armistead Falconer. Cambridge: Harvard University Press, 1923.

De fato. Edited by H. Rackham. Cambridge: Harvard University Press, 1942.

De finibus. Edited by H. Rackham. Cambridge: Harvard University Press, 1914.

De inventione. Edited by H. M. Hubbell. Cambridge: Harvard University Press, 1942.

De legibus. Edited by C. W. Keyes. Cambridge: Harvard University Press, 1928.

De natura deorum. Edited by H. Rackham. Cambridge: Harvard University Press, 1933.

De officiis. Edited by Walter Miller. Cambridge: Harvard University Press, 1913.

De oratore Books I–II. Edited by E. W. Sutton. Cambridge: Harvard University Press, 1942.

De oratore Book III. Edited by H. Rackham. Cambridge: Harvard University Press, 1942.

De re publica. Edited by C. W. Keyes. Cambridge: Harvard University Press, 1928.

De senectute. Edited by William Armistead Falconer. Cambridge: Harvard University Press, 1923.

Orator. Edited by G. L. Hendrickson and H. M. Hubbell. Cambridge: Harvard University Press, 1939.

Paradoxa Stoicorum. Edited by H. Rackham. Cambridge: Harvard University Press, 1942.

Topica. Edited by H. M. Hubbell. Cambridge: Harvard University Press, 1942.

Tusculanarum disputationum. Edited by J. E. King. Cambridge: Harvard University Press, 1927.

Introduction

Ciceronian Ideas in Early European
Social and Political Thought

The history of European political and social ideas from the twelfth century forward into the sixteenth (and indeed beyond) cannot be recounted
adequately without thorough familiarity with the myriad prior sources on
which their formulation relied. Greco-Roman antiquity provided a wealth
of material: the major classical philosophers (or at least those whose works
were known at the time) as well as historians, poets, and dramatists. The
Fathers of the Roman Church also played a significant role in shaping the
social and political thought of later times, not only by their own visions
of Christian politics but also—even if inadvertently—by transmitting the
doctrines of their pagan forebears. Not to be overlooked in this story are
postclassical authors dating from the sixth century into the early Middle
Ages, whose writings contained and disseminated much of the learning
of the Christian as well as pre-Christian past. It is reasonable to say that
understanding the intellectual background of the centuries before the year
1000—roughly the beginning of what the historian R. I. Moore has termed
"the First European Revolution"[1]—is absolutely necessary to grasp emerging theories of society and politics in early Europe.[2] No responsible intellectual historian who concentrates on the social and political thought of
the period in question can overlook the processes by means of which texts
from the previous millennium and a half were received and disseminated.[3]

The ancient thinker who has perhaps loomed largest in this regard
is Aristotle. Despite the fact that his major treatises related to social and
political issues, the *Nicomachean Ethics* and the *Politics*, were not translated
into Latin until the middle of the thirteenth century, there is substantial
evidence to suggest that some of his central teachings were available before

then by various indirect means.[4] At one time, the dominant line of scholarship treated the circulation of Aristotelian ideas in western Europe as the occasion of little less than a "revolution" in theoretical reflection on society and politics, driven in particular by Aristotle's postulation of man as a political creature, thereby rooting politics firmly in nature.[5] This reading has, however, been revised in more recent times on account of its simplistic and often inaccurate portrayal of social and political theory both before and after the availability of the complete texts of the *Ethics* and *Politics*.[6] Yet the almost exclusive foregrounding of Aristotle's contributions is still very much in evidence.[7] What informs all of these interpretations is the underlying assumption that the rapid appearance of Aristotle's writings in *some way* occasioned a profound shift in the discourse and doctrines central to medieval and early modern reflections on society and politics.

The purpose of the present book is, broadly stated, to generate a counternarrative that dislodges Aristotle from the pride of place accorded to him in the study of European social and political thought during its initial centuries. More specifically, concentration on Aristotelianism seems to me to mask the importance of a figure whose impact was far more pervasive yet remains profoundly underappreciated: the Roman orator, statesman, and philosopher Marcus Tullius Cicero. It is too often forgotten that many of Cicero's texts were known, read, and utilized throughout Christian times, commencing in antiquity with Lactantius, Saint Ambrose, and Saint Augustine, among many others.[8] Moreover, Cicero's ideas were a staple of early European thought, available and disseminated from at least the eleventh century onward. How extensive was this knowledge? The most broadly circulated, cited, and adapted of his genuine works were his early instructional manual on rhetoric, *De inventione*, and his last writing, *De officiis*, a treatise on moral and social philosophy addressed to his son and finished only slightly before his assassination in 43 B.C.E.[9] But a large number of Cicero's other texts were to some degree available, even if in many cases rare.[10] By the mid-twelfth century, William of Malmesbury enjoyed demonstrable access to and familiarity with at least nineteen works in the Ciceronian corpus, including most of the rhetorical and philosophical treatises.[11] And even in the case of texts by Cicero that had fallen out of circulation—such as his *De re publica*—there were intermediary authorities (Lactantius and Augustine being the best known) who reported his words that might otherwise have been lost to the ages.[12] Among the literate, Cicero was a household

name when Plato and Aristotle were mere ghosts of the ancient world. This
fact planted Cicero deeply in the medieval consciousness. In contrast to the
assertions of some scholars,[13] very little changed when Aristotle's political
and social works began to circulate during the course of the thirteenth century. Cicero remained an anchor, as we shall see.

A great deal of influential scholarly literature of the last century or so
located in Cicero's writings a turning point in the historiography of Western social and political theory. At the beginning of the twentieth century,
A. J. Carlyle, in the opening pages of volume 1 of the magisterial six-volume
A History of Mediæval Political Theory in the West, judged that "there is no
change in political theory so startling in its completeness as the change
from the theory of Aristotle to the later philosophical view represented
by Cicero. . . . We have ventured to suggest that the dividing line between
the ancient and the modern political theory must be sought, if anywhere,
in the period between Aristotle and Cicero."[14] Both Charles McIlwain and
George Sabine, two of the most influential historians of political thought
during the first half of the twentieth century, endorsed Carlyle's position—
indeed, quoted him directly.[15] Carlyle identified three reasons for placing
Cicero at the forefront of a fundamental reorientation in the way in which
political theorizing proceeded in the West, namely, his "three related conceptions of natural law, natural equality, and the natural society of men in
the State."[16] To be sure, while Carlyle's rationale for his historical claim was
not universally accepted, his conclusion that Cicero's thought represented
a break from the Greek past has nevertheless received endorsement by later
scholars. Thus Robert Denoon Cumming, while challenging Carlyle and
his supporters, nonetheless asserted that what "we are at the beginning of
in Cicero is reliance on a theory of human nature as a context for treating
social and political problems," even if "Cicero's treatment does not carry
any egalitarian or revolutionary implications."[17] More recently, Neal Wood,
referring to Carlyle's as well as Cumming's interpretations, observed that
"what can be accepted from both is that Cicero, for whatever reasons, represents a new direction for social and political thought. Perhaps 'transition
to modern political thought' is preferable to 'beginnings of modern political thought.'"[18] At the beginning of the present century, Siep Stuurman's
monumental cross-cultural survey, The Invention of Humanity, ascribes to
Cicero (especially, but not exclusively, in his Stoic mood) a key role in fur-
thering the cause of "a common humanity" within the Western tradition,

in contrast to the overwhelmingly parochial orientation of the classical Greeks.[19]

Yet, given this large measure of enthusiasm for the singular contribution of Cicero, there has been surprisingly little attention devoted by scholars to Cicero's reputation and status as a social and political thinker, especially during the post-1000 period in which Europe was emerging. Carlyle, for all of the praise he heaps upon the epoch-making character of Cicero's thought in the first volume of *A History of Mediæval Political Theory in the West*, barely mentions the Roman in the second and third volumes (and not at all in the final three). Similarly, McIlwain's book offers not another word about the role Cicero played subsequently, up to the close of the Middle Ages. Likewise Cumming and Wood. A study by Benjamin Straumann, purporting to trace the lineages of Roman constitutional thought (with a special emphasis on Cicero) into the 1700s, devotes a scant few pages to the Ciceronian impact from the twelfth through the mid-sixteenth century.[20] And another contribution to current scholarship, *Debating Medieval Natural Law*, refers only twice (!), and entirely in passing, to Cicero.[21] In spite of occasional forays into an examination of the roles Cicero played in the emergence of early European political and social thought,[22] there has been no concerted attempt to trace these lineages across a broad array of Latin texts from the 1100s onward.[23]

The present book seeks to fill in some missing pieces of this puzzle. It is necessary to state clearly and unambiguously several purposes that I do *not* aim to achieve here. First, I shall not endeavor to offer an interpretation of Cicero's thought on its own terms. There are many fine studies— indeed a body of academic literature that is presently burgeoning, even overflowing, after decades of stagnation—that carefully analyze his ideas and the intellectual contexts relevant to them. Rather, I focus on a set of key themes from his writings that resonated with authors from the early European era. My goal is not to assess which authors during the period under consideration (roughly the beginning of the twelfth century to the middle of the sixteenth) got Cicero "right" or "wrong," or to what extent they did so. I acknowledge that I am reading "backward." By this, I mean that my exposition of Cicero has been guided by concepts that interested and attracted authors in early Europe. Second, I make no claim to inclusivity. My goal is not to offer a comprehensive survey of the European authors and texts engaged with Cicero's ideas. Such a project would not only be enormous—if not impossible, and well beyond my capabilities—but also largely irrelevant to what I desire to accomplish in this book. Nor, strictly speaking, am I producing a transmissional history. Once again, there is excellent scholarship that conducts this enterprise. A mere historian of ideas thrives (parasitically?) on such research but makes no claim to contribute to its endeavor. Finally, no attempt will be made to address the fraught issues surrounding Italian, primarily Florentine, Renaissance "civic humanism" and its relationship with Cicero. The very term "civic humanism," coined by Hans Baron in the early twentieth century, has been a lightning rod for scholars, who variously endorse, reject, or revise its validity as a description of the dominant intellectual ethos and political agenda embraced by thinkers in *quattrocento* Italy.[24] Moreover, unlike the texts that I discuss, the tenor of Renaissance readings of Cicero sought to adopt—whether successfully or not—the standpoint of modern historiography, that is to say, an overarching concern with a historically accurate interpretation of his writings uncongenial to the figures addressed presently. In sum, the Italian *quattrocento* approach to Cicero, broadly speaking, requires a lengthy tome in itself—one that to my knowledge has not yet been (and should be) written—which would move in a direction very different than the one I pursue here.[25]

So, what are the *positive* aims that characterize this book? My primary purpose is to elucidate quite diverse, and sometimes intellectually competing, receptions and adaptations of Cicero. Indeed, I would claim that this is a more worthwhile inquiry than the study of medieval Aristotelianism addressed above, inasmuch as Cicero's teachings about society and politics exercised far wider and deeper impact in early European thought than did Aristotle's. I am interested in the vast range of ways in which elements of Cicero's project regarding human social and political relations were integrated into an array of conceptual perspectives. I contend that ideas "travel," but that they journey along numerous paths, many (if not all) of which afford us insight into the multiplicity of historical as well as philosophical lessons of a given "tradition." Thus I embrace an approach quite different from either of the two conventional ways in which scholars of medieval and early modern political theory treat the relationship between authors and their successors—that is, the problem of "influence." On the one hand, the so-called Cambridge School, associated in particular with Quentin Skinner, banishes altogether any historiographical methodology that permits the assignment of direct intellectual effects of a given text and/or writer upon later ones: "The attempt to trace influences must be irreducibly arbitrary," not least because any such effort yields conclusions that are either nearly always false or, if on rare occasions true, are trivial.[26] If not quite devoid of explanatory force, ascriptions of "influence," says Skinner, prove virtually impossible to validate at the practical level.[27] On the other hand, scholars such as Francis Oakley, returning to more traditional historiography but armed with new methodological weapons, reaffirm that "the fact of influence is, in a given instance, noteworthy, significant, possessed of a measure of explanatory power."[28] Oakley offers in support of this proposition a fine-grained analysis of how core conciliarist ideas of the early fifteenth century directly shaped the constitutionalist political theory of the sixteenth and seventeenth centuries.

I suspect that the methodological struggle over the validity of influence as a lens through which to study the history of political ideas may be intractable. But that does not greatly concern me, since my own approach to understanding early European Ciceronianism makes no pretense to track intellectual impact per se. Instead, my examination of Cicero's place in medieval and early modern social and political thought aligns with an emergent alternative form of inquiry termed "classical reception studies." Building on the insight of literary scholars who resist the imposition of any single, reified cultural "tradition," the receptionalist view rests upon two central tenets: first, that (Western) worlds of thought subsequent to Greco-Roman antiquity ineluctably bear some marks of the classical past, and second, that appropriations of that heritage always reflect "the manifold and complex cultural processes in which these ancient references are functioning."[29] Acceptance of these two principles leads one to conclude that the main job of the receptionalist study of classical texts is to comprehend the myriad ways in which they entered into and were transformed by their subsequent audiences. For the most part, as nearly as I can ascertain, most of the energy among advocates of classical reception studies has been directed toward illustrations of the multiple entrances of the images, literary expressions, and ideas into modern and contemporary culture.[30] As one of the founding figures in the field, Charles Martindale, noted, classical reception studies is of quite recent birth—the mid-1990s, an eyeblink in academics—but its potential application is broad and (I think) profound.[31] Thus readers should not be tempted to interpret my effort here as a study of the "influence" Cicero exercised on his inheritors. To suppose otherwise overlooks my explicit aim of discovering multiple forms of reception of Cicero's social and political writings and ideas in a manner unconcerned with how a specific doctrine or doctrines might have been "influential" per se. This is the sense in which Matthew Kempshall, speaking of the medieval reception of Ciceronian rhetoric, denies the existence of a single "classical tradition." There may be, he acknowledges, a "common language" and "shared assumptions" that "serve as a starting-point across the board," but these were "discussed and applied in different ways, and with different emphases, by different authors in different periods."[32]

A skeptical reader might discern the taint of relativism in the adoption of classical reception studies as my conceptual springboard. Do I mean that any medieval or early modern author or text invoking the name of Cicero or quoting from one of his works must be counted as advocating some version of Ciceronianism, tossed in with all the others? I do not. In line with my own previous work on Aristotelianism in medieval moral and political thought,[33] I strongly defend the view that it is both possible and necessary to differentiate between Ciceronianism and mere citation of one of Cicero's writings. Rather, Cicero's framework, in its manifold expressions, revolves around the notion that human beings are drawn together by a set of fundamental communal bonds that impose duties upon them—a notion of *societas* or fellowship that renders them responsible toward one another. The very character of Cicero's conception of multiple human engagements invites the sort of wide-ranging appropriations and adaptations that permit us, on the one hand, to identify a capacious Ciceronianism and, on the other, to establish conceptual limits to distinguish a Ciceronian thinker from one who merely refers to Cicero as an authority. Doing the latter successfully is a tricky proposition, a true challenge for the scholar, especially because specifying those who reside within the paradigm is not always simple.

In chapter 1, I open with a survey of the relevant parts of Cicero's social and political theory, beginning with his postulation that every human creature is endowed with an associative urge, but that this instinct, derived from a latent natural capacity for rational reflection conjoined to an inherent but inchoate power of language, must be drawn out. Reason, he repeatedly insists, is a gift from the gods and is what we share uniquely with the divine, but its manifestation and actualization depend purely on the collaborative efforts of human beings. Once realized, in turn, people employ their ability to reason in order to establish the terms of their cooperation, a function of discovering the requirements of justice grounded in natural law. The civilizing of humankind generates, in turn, a general recognition that we possess by nature a vast range of entanglements with our fellow human beings. To humanity as a whole, we owe a basic obligation to behave justly, conceived in the sense of equity without regard for distinctions of status, ethnicity, or any other divisions among peoples. With our families, we possess a closeness that marks a sort of instinctual particularity. Our friendships, if properly realized, are mirrors of our own virtues. And our country demands our readiness to sacrifice ourselves (whether our time and energy, our property, or even our lives) in the name of communal virtue. All of these duties are aligned with nature, yet none of them seems to be, on Cicero's account, entirely overweening. We are creatures positioned to make judgments about which obligations are most compelling according to our natural capability to reason. The different duties that pertain to us simultaneously shape our social and political relationships with one another and define our moral orientations. The Ciceronian framework thus presents a plethora of different building blocks from which to construct multiple intellectual edifices. The aim of the first chapter of this book is the explication of these dimensions of Cicero's thought.

During the course of the twelfth century, as examined in chapter 2, a wide array of central Ciceronian ideas appear and are adapted in many genres in order to address the diverse concerns endemic to theories of rhetoric, law, spirituality, history, and morality. None of these topics should be entirely surprising, given Cicero's career. He composed highly influential works on eloquence, most notably *De inventione* and *De oratore*.[34] He was a leading figure in the practice of law in the late Roman Republic, and many of his speeches from legal proceedings survive, providing insights into contemporaneous historical conditions. In addition, he made important contributions to the realm of so-called practical philosophy, ranging from his moral theory in *De officiis* to the political thought contained in *De re publica* and *De legibus*, as well as his reflections on religious matters in *De natura deorum*. (A complete census of Cicero's writings relevant to this project is provided at the beginning of chapter 2.) The specific texts from the 1100s that will be examined in the second chapter are Thierry of Chartres's commentary on *De inventione*, which enjoyed wide distribution during the Middle Ages; one of the earliest and most popular commentaries on Gratian's *Decretum*, the foundational work on church law, penned by Rufinus, a noted canon lawyer; the universal history *Chronica sive Historia de duabus civitatibus* of Otto of Freising; Aelred of Rievaulx's *De spirituali amicitia*, a dialogue about friendship among religious; and the anonymous *Moralium dogmate philosophorum*, once attributed to William of Conches, which collated moral lessons derived from classical Roman philosophers and historians and in turn provided an invaluable resource for later authors.

Chapter 3 concentrates on the only self-identified Ciceronian of the Latin Middle Ages (at least of whom I am aware): the English churchman and philosopher John of Salisbury. Throughout his major philosophical works, the *Policraticus* and the *Metalogicon* (both completed in 1159), John declares himself an adherent of the moderate skepticism of the so-called New Academy, precisely the school of philosophy that Cicero embraced. More significantly for present purposes, John's writings—including more "practical" works, such as his letters—repeatedly articulate key themes associated with Ciceronian thought in such a way that they generate the guiding precepts of his intellectual outlook. These include nature, reason, justice, social and political community, and friendship.

Chapter 4 moves into the thirteenth and fourteenth centuries and thus the realm of university-based scholasticism. It is conventionally supposed, with good reason, that the philosophy of the schoolmen was dominated by the works of Aristotle that had been translated into Latin and for the most part disseminated in the West after circa 1200. I argue, however, that the rise of scholastic Aristotelianism, especially in the field of social and political theory, did not result in the neglect—let alone replacement—of Cicero's ideas but rather, in many cases, supplemented and reinforced them. Thus Cicero remained a potent force in the universities, to the extent that Aristotle's philosophy was in many instances read through a Ciceronian lens. This becomes evident, for example, from consideration of Henry of Ghent's *quodlibets*, Ptolemy of Lucca's continuation of a treatise entitled *De regimine principum* (the composition of which is considered to have been begun by Thomas Aquinas), the *De regia potestate et papali* by John of Paris, and James of Viterbo's pro-papal tract *De regimine Christiano*. Each of these works was completed around 1300 and bears the distinctive marks of Aristotelian learning. Yet upon closer examination, each reveals a clear debt to Cicero.

Chapter 5 addresses the crucial role that Ciceronian ideas play in the *Defensor pacis* by Marsiglio (a.k.a. Marsilius) of Padua. Completed in 1324, the *Defensor* is ordinarily considered to be the archetype of medieval political Aristotelianism, so much so that one sixteenth-century critic famously called its author "a man more Aristotelian than Christian."[35] It is true that Marsiglio cites the *Politics* and many of Aristotle's other writings constantly, at least in the first section of his tract. But quotation is not equivalent to intellectual indebtedness. Underneath the Aristotelian veneer of the *Defensor*, one finds a steadfast commitment to Ciceronian principles that profoundly informs Marsiglio's theoretical and political project. Indeed, when one contrasts the Ciceronian and the Aristotelian elements of the *Defensor*, the former seem more foundational than the latter.

The study of early European political thought tends to focus mainly—even exclusively—on Latin-language texts. But this inclination obscures the story of the contributions made by authors who composed in the vernacular. Chapter 6 investigates how Cicero's thought informed the work of three extremely important but generally underappreciated French-language formulators of political ideas: Brunetto Latini (writing ca. 1265), Nicole Oresme (ca. 1370), and Christine de Pizan (ca. 1405). Latini was a Florentine civil servant driven into exile in France, where he composed not only his masterwork, *Li livres dou tresor*, but also a partial vernacular translation and commentary on Cicero's *De inventione*. The extensive moral and political sections of *Tresor* demonstrate an overwhelming reliance upon Ciceronian ideas. Oresme's French translations of and commentaries on Aristotle's *Politics* and *Ethics* (and also the pseudo-Aristotle *Economics*) often evince a decidedly Ciceronian perspective. And the royal courtier Christine de Pizan, among the most prolific political authors of the later Middle Ages, mines the range of Cicero's writings in her defense of women and her celebration of peace, both composed in French. Cicero's impact, in short, was not limited to Latin texts.

One might naturally associate Ciceronian thought with Italian Renaissance civic humanism and its republican orientation, as so many scholars have done (a topic that I will not address for reasons previously stated). Widespread concentration on the cities of Renaissance Italy has filtered out the ways in which Cicero's social and political ideas were also put to work for the very different purpose of promoting of imperial causes, as the seventh chapter contends. The fourteenth-century schoolman Engelbert of

Admont and the fifteenth-century humanist (and eventual pope) Aeneas Silvius Piccolomini, along with his contemporary Nicholas of Cusa, all found in Cicero's writings ample material to defend imperialism, and especially the value of the Roman Empire, as interpreted from a Christian perspective. These imperialist appropriations of Cicero form the focus of chapter 7.

But Ciceronian doctrines could equally be employed to attack and dismantle European aspirations to imperial domination. As the eighth chapter reveals, the sixteenth-century Spanish Dominican Bartolomé de Las Casas, who became bishop of Chiapas, produced numerous treatises against the European (mis)treatment of the indigenous peoples of the Americas and depended heavily on Ciceronian principles to counter Aristotelian-inflected justifications of imperial conquest. No less than proponents of empire, Las Casas found Ciceronian views regarding the universal characteristics of human nature to be congenial to supporting his position.

Permit me to emphasize once again that this book does not propose to identify any "true" or "essential" precept that defines Ciceronianism from the twelfth to the sixteenth century. My project here is instead to illuminate how elements of Cicero's social and political thought were transformed, recombined, and otherwise adapted in order to suit a vast range of intellectual pursuits. Cicero's ideas, perhaps even more than Aristotle's, were sufficiently capacious to allow for widely diversified applications and reconfigurations. Ciceronian doctrines could not be stretched infinitely, but they could prove useful in addressing problems arising from a broad array of contexts and concerns.

CHAPTER 1

Prelude to the Early European Cicero(s)

Both the originality and the coherence of Ciceronian contributions to Western philosophy—especially social and political philosophy—have often been doubted by his advocates little less than his detractors. Thus at the beginning of the twentieth century, A. J. Carlyle observed that Cicero lacked "any great power of mind, or any great power of political analysis. . . . He has no contribution of his own to make to philosophy."[1] Decades later, Neal Wood described him as "a mediocre philosopher, unoriginal and eclectic."[2] Luciano Perelli considers Cicero to be caught in a twofold trap, accused both of providing a derivative transmission of the wisdom of ancient Greece and of serving as little more than a shill or mouthpiece for the Roman republican aristocracy and its values.[3] Similar remarks could easily be multiplied many times over. And the judgments I have cited, it should be noted, come from scholars who sought to restore Cicero's reputation from "the long shadow" cast by Germanic intellectual historiography, especially as associated with Theodor Mommsen, a towering figure of nineteenth-century classics scholarship.[4] There are clear indications, however, that the dismissal of Cicero as a second-rate thinker has undergone significant reevaluation of late. In 1995, J. G. F. Powell, in his introduction to a collection of essays entitled *Cicero the Philosopher*, identified a "renewed scholarly interest in Cicero as a philosophical writer" during "the last ten or fifteen years."[5] This development has only blossomed in the intervening two decades or so.[6] Furthermore, beyond his historical standing, Cicero has become a darling of the contemporary philosophical movement know as "neo-Stoicism" or "neo-Romanism" that articulates and defends republican theory as an alternative to liberalism.[7] After so many years in the wilderness, the return of Cicero as a figure central not merely to Roman philosophy but also to the history of Western social and political philosophy is long overdue.[8]

As commendable as this revival may be, it has generally not affected the study of the later reception of Ciceronian social and political ideas in Europe prior to the Renaissance, with only a few exceptions. Marcia Colish's monumental two-volume study, *The Stoic Tradition from Antiquity to the Early Middle Ages*, takes the story of Cicero's transmission only up to the sixth century. The scholarship of John O. Ward and his collaborators traces in minute detail the adaptation of Ciceronian rhetoric from the twelfth through the fifteenth century, but it tackles issues of social and political thought only tangentially.[9] Frédérique Lachaud's masterly book *L'Éthique du pouvoir au Moyen Âge* examines important features of Cicero's impact on political thought from the mid-twelfth to the mid-fourteenth century, although she concentrates mainly on *De officiis* and limits her inquiry to England. Kempshall has produced an exhaustive but focused analysis of the dissemination of Cicero's key idea of the definition of the *res publica* during the medieval and early modern periods.[10] A special issue of the journal *Convenit Selecta* entitled "Cicero and the Middle Ages" contains many useful articles, but no particular concentration on political theory.[11] The essay collection *Cicero Refused to Die: Ciceronian Influence Through the Centuries*, edited by Nancy van Deusen, does not contain any chapters that specifically address Cicero's social and political ideas. None of these scholarly works, then, fully conveys how the writings of Cicero impacted European intellectual culture generally, and social and political thought specifically, from the twelfth to the sixteenth century. Yet few educated individuals of the period, regardless of intellectual orientation or spiritual commitment, escaped the reach of Ciceronian philosophy.

The present chapter offers an overview of Ciceronian themes concerning the theoretical foundations and implications of social and political order to which many authors after circa 1100 were especially attracted. My exegesis should be judged not as an effort to provide a full and comprehensive interpretation of the sum and substance of Cicero's social and political thought but rather as a synopsis of the key Ciceronian doctrines that were widely adapted in early European texts. In this cause, I examine mainly the writings from his philosophical and rhetorical corpus that can be genuinely attributed to him and that are relevant to the social and political theory of early Europe.[12] In order of composition (as proposed by recent scholarship), they are: *De inventione* (ca. 87–81 B.C.E.), *De oratore* (55–52), *De re publica* (54–57), *De legibus* (51–46), *Brutus* (46), *Paradoxa Stoicorum* (46), *Orator* (46), *De finibus* (45), *Tusculanarum disputationum* (45), *De natura deorum* (45), *De senectute* (45–44), *De divinatione* (44), *De fato* (44), *De amicitia* (a.k.a. *Laelius*) (44), *Topica* (44), and *De officiis* (44).[13] I do not mean to imply that every medieval and early modern author enjoyed access to each and every one of these texts. Indeed, some of Cicero's writings were known, at best, in incomplete or even highly fragmentary form. The scholarship on this topic has been subject to considerable dispute. Nor do I suggest that the differences that distinguish Cicero's various writings were generally recognized, although the potential inconsistency of many of his leading principles over time and context is worthy of note. To the extent that central themes of Ciceronian philosophy are evident from the beginning to the end of his life, and that these ideas were appropriated (at least in part) by early European thinkers, however, I feel satisfied that such a synthesis is both plausible and justifiable. Indeed, the only features of the Ciceronian oeuvre that I discuss below are those to which at least some writers considered in this book would have been exposed and upon which they relied. In line with the classical reception theory that I discuss in the introduction, I have neither the ambition nor the desire to engage in source hunting.

REASON, SPEECH, AND EQUALITY

Perhaps the most fundamental and distinctive feature of Cicero's thought for present purposes is his positing of the linguistic and rational foundations of human association. In *De inventione* and *De oratore*, he identifies persuasive speech, combined with reason, as the groundwork of human interaction, arguing that the realization of social intercourse requires the activity of an orator acting in concert with his fellow human beings. All human beings possess a potential for sociability implicit in their common linguistic and rational nature.[14] Yet their primordial existence was a scattered and brutish one, devoid of cities, laws, and the fruits of civil community. They would have been destined to remain permanently in this condition, Cicero believes, without the "existence of one from among the infinite multitude of mankind who, either alone or with a few others, could induce what is given to everyone by nature" (*De oratore* 1.31). Such a person was the first orator, who, by the application of eloquence and reason, inspired the establishment of communities, the foundation of cities, and the institution of laws and rights. As Cicero explains,

> At a certain time, a great and wise man discovered a natural property [of speech] contained within the souls of human beings and a great source of opportunity afforded thereby, if one could draw it out and render it better through education.... He transformed them from wild beasts and savages into tame and gentle creatures on account of heeding speech and reason more diligently. It does not seem to me, at least, that a wisdom either silent or lacking speech could have accomplished the sudden conversion of men from their habits and the conveyance of them into different modes of life. (*De inventione* 1.2–3)

Society could never have arisen without the primitive orator, who was both a persuasive speaker and a man of special insight and wisdom, capable of activating that latent power that existed within all men. But it is not only in his oratorical writings that Cicero proposes that reason and eloquent speech provide the origins of social order. In the *Tusculanarum disputationum* 1.62, he praises the capacity for language possessed by "the man who first united the scattered human units into a body and summoned them to the fellowship of social life," as a result of which all of the material and moral blessings of civilization were attained (also see 5.5). And in *De officiis* 1.12, he observes that "nature likewise by the power of reason associates man with man in the common bonds of speech and life." There would, in sum, be no organized systems of society and politics in the absence of the rational and linguistic faculties with which human beings are endowed.

Cicero refers sometimes to reason as the primary source of such human association, sometimes to language, and sometimes to both equally. Thus in *De finibus* 2.45 he announces, "Reason has inspired man with a relish for his kind, produced a natural uniformity of language and habit, and prompted the individual, starting from friendship and family affections to expand his interests in forming social ties first with fellow citizens and then with all mankind." By apparent contrast, Cicero proclaims in *De natura deorum* 2.148, "Take the gift of speech.... It is this that has united us in the bonds of justice, law and civil order, this that has separated us from savagery and barbarism." And in *Brutus* 59 he states, "as reason is the glory of man, so the lamp of reason is eloquence." Is there any inconsistency here? Arguably, Cicero simply elides reason and speech, or rather equates them. They are mutually complementary; both rationality without speech and the reverse are empty and worthless for him.[15] Thus one ought not to read too much into his apparent conflation of the two. This is not to imply, however, that there is no tension between rationality and language, eloquence and wisdom. Cicero realized the challenges presented by his characterization of persuasive speech as central to the foundation of social relations on account of the supposed conceptual incongruity of wisdom and rhetoric.[16] The wise man seeks to discover truths that are necessarily esoteric or inaccessible to the untutored masses; philosophy requires strict adherence to the principles of logic and rational argumentation. By contrast, because rhetoric teaches effectiveness in appealing to public opinion and commonly held belief, it might seem to be regulated by standards other than those of pure truth-seeking. Nothing could be further from the case.

Cicero charges the orator to discover what is truly good for his fellow creatures (in the manner of the philosopher) as well as to communicate it to them in the most forceful and convincing manner so that they may put it to use. His writings consistently ascribe to the successors of the primeval orator a special duty toward the maintenance and defense of the principles of communal life. In *De inventione* 1.5, he declares that "eloquence is to be studied ... all the more vigorously, lest evil men are the most powerful to the detriment of good men and the common disaster of everyone. ... For this [eloquence] attains the greatest advantage for the republic if wisdom, the director (*moderatrix*) of all matters, is present." Likewise, in *De oratore* 1.34, he proclaims: "The guidance (*moderatione*) and wisdom of the perfect orator preserves not only his own dignity, but also the well-being of most individuals and of the whole republic." It would seem to be precisely the combination of eloquence and wisdom characteristic of the orator that assures that he will speak on behalf of the interests of the entire community. By contrast, the philosopher may know the good but lacks the skill or training to convey it to the multitude. Inherent in the subject matter of oratory, then, is a regard for one's fellow human beings and especially fellow citizens, which imposes upon the orator an overarching duty to disseminate the dictates of reason in the service of public welfare.[17]

Throughout his works, Cicero clearly understood the inescapable implication of this attribution to humanity of the universal characteristics of reason and speech, namely, that human beings are fundamentally equal. In contrast with Aristotle (and the Greeks generally), the characteristics of ethnicity or place of origin were irrelevant to Cicero's evaluation of humanity as possessed of rational and linguistic competence and as capable of acting on the basis thereof. Indeed, he did not shy away from upholding this view as a central facet of his thought. "No single thing," he remarks in *De legibus* 1.29–30, "is so like another, so exactly its counterpart, as all of us are to one another. . . . No one would be so like his own self as all men would be like all others. . . . There is no difference in kind between man and man." It is from this precept that one of Cicero's most characteristic ideas emerges, namely, the existence of a union, a natural bond, that all humans share, rooted in their common possession of speech and reason. Time and again, he insists upon the principle that mankind is a whole, a unity, by its very nature. Typical of this position is his declaration in *De finibus* 5.65 that "there is nothing more glorious nor of wider range than the solidarity of mankind, that species of alliance and partnership of interests and that actual affection that exists between man and man." Likewise, Cicero asserts in *De officiis* that "it is our duty to respect, defend, and maintain the common bonds of union and fellowship subsisting between all the members of the human race" (1.149; see also 3.52–53). We have responsibilities toward other forms of human association (family, friends, country, as addressed below), but one of our deepest obligations is toward mankind in general. If all human beings are indeed equal, it follows for Cicero that they are united into a single fellowship.

REASON AND VIRTUE

Men are superior to other animals. Cicero recognizes that humans, like all other sentient creatures, are naturally driven by an instinct for self-preservation. "Every living creature," he says in *De finibus* 5.24, "loves itself and from the moment of birth strives to secure its own preservation; because the earliest impulse bestowed on it by nature for its life-long protection is the instinct for self-preservation and for the maintenance of itself." Cicero reaffirms this view in *De officiis* 1.11: "Nature has endowed every species of living creature with the instinct of self-preservation, of avoiding what seems likely to cause injury to life or limb and acquiring and providing everything needful for life." While animals are also often naturally gregarious—he cites the example of bees—human beings are so "to a much greater extent" (*De officiis* 1.157; see also *De amicitia* 51). By no means does he wish to deny an affinity between animals and men in this regard. Yet on the other hand, for Cicero, human beings are qualitatively more advanced than beasts, precisely on account of their possession of reason and speech, which yield the moral foundations of society. According to Cicero, reason promotes the persistence of the social bonds of the human species in three ways: through defense of self-interest arising from the instinct of self-preservation, instruction in virtue, and discovery of natural law. He acknowledges, first of all, that human beings congregate because reason reveals to them the advantages that stem from cooperation. Cicero explains at great length that, when rational creatures work together, discernible benefits abound: protection from the elements and the improvement of productive capacities, no less than the pleasures of social intercourse and the advantages of economic exchange. Reason teaches that persons can live a materially more satisfactory existence in a community than under the conditions of solitude (*De officiis* 2.12–15; *De legibus* 1.25–27). Yet Cicero also recognizes that rational self-interest is an insufficient basis for a stable and harmonious society. He remarks that "just as we obtain great utility from consent and cooperation among men, so there is no pestilence as detestable as that which men have wrought upon men" (*De officiis* 2.16). If self-interest alone were at the heart of social relations, then no community would endure, since men would cooperate only when it suited them, and they would always try to take advantage of, or even oppose, their fellows whenever personal gain so dictated.

Natural reason resolves this dilemma through the discovery and dissemination of the virtues, especially justice. Cicero maintains that society, and hence our very capacity to conceive of a common welfare, depends on the cultivation of virtue. He observes that "since, therefore, one may have no doubt how men may be both most helpful and most harmful to men, I state that virtue exists for this reason: To reconcile the minds of men and to bind them to each one's aid" (*De officiis* 2.17). Virtue constitutes an imperative of nature. In *De inventione* 1.159, he had defined virtue as "a habit of mind in harmony with reason and the order of nature," and he discusses in detail the parts thereof, namely, wisdom, justice, courage, and temperance—that is, the four classical cardinal virtues. Virtue is directly dependent upon the cultivation of the rational faculties: "Virtue is defined as the perfection of reason" (*De finibus* 5.38); "virtue is reason completely developed; and this certainly is natural" (*De legibus* 1.45). In turn, the mark of a harmonious communal setting is the presence of virtue as an ingrained feature of its organization. The derivation of virtue is strictly in accordance with nature, which has "bestowed an intellect capable of receiving every virtue, and implanted in it at birth and without instruction embryonic notions of the loftiest ideas.... But of virtue itself she merely gave the germ and no more" (*De finibus* 5.59; also 5.43). In this sense, "Man's nature is not perfect, yet virtue may be realized in man" (*De natura deorum* 2.39). Nature itself, however, is not entirely adequate to the task of rendering people virtuous. We have seen already that, according to Cicero, all human beings share in the capacities for reason and speech. But at the same time, all people do not employ their rational powers and therefore are not equally virtuous. This is explained, first of all, by the fact that reason must be drawn out and improved until the point that it demonstrates virtue, and many individuals lack the instruction to realize the potential lying within their faculty: "That faculty which is highest and most excellent in man she [nature] left lacking ... and thus, as it were, laid the foundations for education and instilled into those faculties which the mind already had what may be termed the rudiments of virtue.... It is our task ... to supplement those mere beginnings by searching out the further developments that were implicit in them, until what we seek is fully attained" (*De finibus* 5.59–60).

Only the "rudimentary beginnings of intelligence ... are imprinted on all minds alike" by nature, Cicero asserts (*De legibus* 1.30). Human beings still require guidance to develop this fundamental capacity. Reason is constantly subject to corrupting pressures that many (if not most) people find impossible to resist. He observes that "the corruption caused by bad habits is so great that the sparks of fire, so to speak, which Nature has kindled in us, are extinguished by this corruption" (*De legibus* 1.33). As Cicero underscores in *Tusculanarum disputationum* 5.78, "Never could custom conquer nature; for nature is always unconquered; but as for us, we have corrupted our souls, ... we have enervated and weakened them by false beliefs and evil habits." That equality possessed by human beings at birth is too often eradicated by differences of environment, so that virtue is ultimately achieved by a very few persons, and the multitude remains in a state of viciousness.

Moreover, the virtues for Cicero are not entirely on par. In *De officiis*, he ranks the four cardinal virtues according to the contributions they make to the maintenance of the bonds of human association. Wisdom, in its customary meaning as the pursuit of contemplative truth, does not directly enhance sociability: "Action (*actio*) is better than mere theoretical knowledge, for the study and knowledge of the universe would be lame and defective, were no practical results to follow" (*De officiis* 1.153). Properly conceived, wisdom must submit to the demands of justice, which, for Cicero, is the virtue that ultimately ensures that men remain united in their associations. The same, he believes, is true of courage and temperance (1.157–58). As a general rule, justice is preeminent among the virtues, because it imposes upon men the duties most crucial to (indeed, nearly coextensive with) the perpetuation of human association. Cicero declares that "there is nothing more illustrious nor of wider range than the bond between human beings and the sort of fellowship and useful intercommunication and love among human beings, which . . . is termed justice" (*De finibus* 5.65). In his view, "the society of humans amongst themselves and the quasi-communal life are maintained" solely on the basis of adherence to the requirements of justice (*De officiis* 1.20). In the absence of a universal measure of justice, social organization itself, which is for him the *sine qua non* of humanity, would be rendered impossible.

Cicero thus posits a close connection between the exercise of reason and justice. As he remarks in *De legibus* 1.33, "Those who have been given reason by nature have also been given right reason, and therefore law too, which is right reason in commands and prohibitions; and if they have been given law, then they have been given justice too." Justice is concerned "with preserving fellowship among men, with assigning to each his own, and with faithfulness to agreements one has made" (*De officiis* 1.15). Without justice, the preservation of the species would be endangered. The role of justice is "to procure and to conserve whatever is required for the activities of life, in order both to preserve the fellowship and bonding between men" and to acquire "benefits for oneself and those dear to one" (*De officiis* 1.17). In short, justice is the indispensable quality of human nature productive of social relations. But what obligations does justice impose upon us? Cicero proposes an account of what constitutes justice by reference to injustice: "Of injustice there are two types: men may inflict injury; or else, when it is being inflicted upon others, they may fail to deflect it, even though they could. Anyone who makes an unjust attack on another, whether driven by anger or by some other agitation, seems to be laying hands, so to speak, upon a fellow. But also, the man who does not defend someone, or obstruct the injustice when he can, is at fault just as if he had abandoned his own parents or friends or country" (*De officiis* 1.23). By extrapolation, justice involves two components: one negative and the other positive. One must refrain from injury while also protecting one's fellows if at all possible. As Cicero asserts elsewhere in *De officiis*, "All men should have this one object, that the benefit of each individual and the benefit of all together should be the same. If anyone arrogates it to himself, all human intercourse will be dissolved" (3.26). To do so, he continues, violates the rational foundations on which justice itself is premised (3.27).

The Ciceronian conception of justice, in turn, rests on his notion of nature and natural law. Cicero holds that nature imposes upon us a certain code or measure of conduct, arising in particular from the requirement to promote the ends and interests of human society. The commission of an injury (such as theft or fraud) constitutes a violation of natural law precisely because it "is necessarily disruptive of that which is most in accordance with nature, the generation of human society" (*De officiis* 3.21). In order to prevent the perpetual endangerment of the bonds of society, the law of nature is afforded prescriptive force. Cicero contends that recognition of the dictates of justice emerges "much more effectively from natural reason itself, which is law for human beings and divinity alike" (*De officiis* 3.23). "Injustice," he says, "is fatal to social life and fellowship between man and man." To prevent such a breakdown of public order, and hence to know what sorts of behavior are required by justice, one must reason about the common good. Because by "nature there are interests that all have in common," Cicero asserts that "we are all subject to one and the same natural law" and that "we are certainly forbidden to harm another person on the basis of natural law" (*De officiis* 3.27). Thus, in the acts of intercommunication among human beings that advance the good of all, mankind is bound together ever more tightly in myriad forms of association. One's duty on the basis of natural law is always to act for the general welfare when some sort of conflict exists between private benefit and the interests of society as a whole.

Cicero often illustrates this point by reference to the natural ordering of the human body and the maintenance of its health. He asserted throughout his writings that the human person was naturally composed of both flesh and intellect, and he held the latter to be superior to the former (*De finibus*

5.34). Yet nature has not neglected to organize man's physical being in such a manner that it is able to preserve itself. Every bodily part and organ has its appropriate function: "There is no part of our body that is not of less value than we are ourselves," that is, it is a whole greater than the sum of its parts, all of which are required to perform their proper role if the body is to survive (*De natura deorum* 2.32). "Nature," he says, "seems to have had a wonderful plan for the construction of our bodies" (*De officiis* 1.126). Cicero's main concern, however, is when man's corporal existence becomes diseased. As he comments in *De finibus* 5.35,

> It is necessary that these [human] organs should be healthy and vigorous and possessed of their natural motions and uses; no part must be lacking and no part must be diseased or enfeebled—this is a requirement of nature. Again, there is a certain form of bodily activity which keeps the motions and postures in harmony with nature; and any error in any of these . . . —for example, if a man were to walk on his hands, or backwards instead of forwards—would make a man alienated from himself, as if he had stripped off his proper humanity and hated his own nature.

Similar remarks may be found throughout the Ciceronian corpus (for example, *De finibus* 5.47; *Tusculanarum disputationum* 3.15, 4.28–29). Cicero, in turn, employs this organic conception of the body in his analysis of the commission of an injury. Should such an event occur, "those bonds of human society, which are most in accord with nature's laws, must of necessity be broken." He then proposes that "suppose, by way of comparison, that each one of our bodily members should conceive this idea and imagine that it could be strong and well if it should draw off to itself the health and strength of its neighboring member, the whole body would be enfeebled and die" (*De officiis* 2.121–22). This is precisely what happens when a tyrant governs. Cicero countenances the slaying of a tyrannical ruler, "whom it is morally right to kill" on the grounds that "as certain members are amputated, if they show signs themselves of being bloodless and virtually lifeless and thus jeopardize the health of the other parts of the body, so those fierce and savage monsters in human form should be cut off from what we may call the common bond of humanity" (*De officiis* 3.32). The stakes, then, could hardly be higher for Cicero's use of an organic analogy. It becomes not merely a model for the well-ordered polity but a justification for the violent elimination of a tyrant (in Cicero's case, Julius Caesar) who endangers the health of the political body. The moral reason embedded in nature places an obligation upon the defender of the bonds that pertain to human unity.

A DIVINE GIFT

The rational capabilities of man that constitute human nature and undergird justice are, in turn, understood by Cicero as gifts from the gods. That man shares in divine reason, in Ciceronian terms, is precisely what distinguishes human beings from other sentient creatures (*De legibus* 1.22): "Since there is nothing better than reason, and it is found both in humans and in god, reason forms the first bond between human and god. And those who share reason also share right reason; and since that is law, we humans must be considered to be closely allied to gods by law. Furthermore, those who share law also share the procedures of justice.... It is not possible for there to be a divine mind without reason, nor does divine reason lack this force in sanctioning right and wrong" (*De legibus* 1.23, 2.10). Humanity is inextricably linked to divinity, then, by the very rationality that generates justice. The gods are the ultimate guarantee of the universal standard and requirements of just action that pertain to mankind without exception. They insure, in other words, the properties inherent in human beings that render them capable of a fully social existence. The absence of recognition of divinity and thus of pious worship, Cicero says in *De natura deorum* 1.4, "will entail the disappearance of loyalty and social union as well, and of justice itself, the queen of all the virtues." But the gods are virtuous as a property of their very being, while man must make an effort to realize his virtue: "The surpassing virtue of the gods is the result of their nature, but the virtue of men is the result of hard work" (*Topica* 76). This reinforces Cicero's point that the "sparks" and "seeds" of the virtues implanted in humanity as a divine gift do not entail that people are virtuous at birth. Rather, human beings are by nature inclined to act in accordance with their natural reason (*Paradoxa Stoicorum* 14). But they must be trained to use their reason in order to realize and fulfill their divinely granted potential for virtue.

Cicero imputes to religious worship both practical and theoretical roles. He fully acknowledges that religion makes a direct contribution to the maintenance of the social bonds that unite humanity in its entirety as well as specific communities. In *De legibus* 2.16, he asks, "Who will deny that such beliefs are useful when he remembers how often oaths are used to confirm agreements, how important to our well-being is the sanctity of treaties, how many persons are deterred from crime by the fear of divine punishment, and how sacred an association of citizens becomes when the immortal gods are made members of it, either as judges or as witnesses?" Belief in divinity has a pragmatic dimension that nevertheless accords with, and indeed reinforces, the natural gifts of reason and social interaction.

This dual aspect of worship is evident also in Cicero's attitude toward what he regards to be superstition. He holds that it is necessary to excise superstitious elements from the worship of the gods to the greatest extent possible. His treatment of superstitious ideas—especially those concerning prognostication—in *De divinatione* 1.2 is very carefully constructed. On the one hand, he recognizes that there is a universality to the view that divination is authentic or legitimate: "Now I am aware of no people, however refined and learned or however savage or ignorant, which does not think that signs are given of future events, and that certain persons can recognize those signs and foretell events before they occur." Moreover, he fears that rejecting divination might readily be interpreted as undermining the civic dimension of religious cult that formed a crucial part of Roman tradition as well as challenging the wisdom of the forefathers, which is impious (*De divinatione* 2.148). Yet, on the other hand, Cicero's rationalism leads him to maintain that "just as it is a duty to extend the influence of true religion, which is closely associated with knowledge of nature, so it is a duty to weed out every root of superstition" (*De divinatione* 2.149). While in rare cases it may be possible to make predictions by the use of one's reason in accord with natural law, it is unbecoming of a philosopher to promote falsities or fabrications (*De divinatione* 1.111, 2.27, 2.150). In the end, Cicero adopts a pragmatic position consonant with the claim in *De divinatione* 2.70 that religion performs a valuable public function: "Out of respect for the opinion of the masses and because of the great service to the state, we maintain the augural practices, discipline, religious rites and laws, as well as the authority of the augural college" (of which he was a member).

A close corollary to Cicero's assertion of the universality of divination is that all men intuitively know and admit the existence of the gods, precisely on the grounds that reason is shared with them. "There is no race, no one in the world, we are told, so barbarous that its mind has no inkling of a belief in the gods," Cicero observes. "All men think that a divine power and a divine nature exist" (*Tusculanarum disputationum* 1.3).[18] This does not merely mean, however, that convention or consent is sufficient to demonstrate the existence of deities (*De natura deorum* 1.62 and *Tusculanarum disputationum* 1.30). Rather, the gods instill an instinct in human beings to believe in them, which is in turn reinforced by the application of reason by which means their natures come to be known (*Tusculanarum disputationum* 1.36). Once again, natural inclination comes to fruition by the employment of man's active intellect (*De natura deorum* 2.164). Hence, in light of Cicero's linkage of reason and divinity, those who decline to use their reason and who break fellowship with others by injuring them are thereby guilty of irreverence (*De officiis* 3.28). Rational human nature's affinity with divinity also has civilizing consequences. "Nothing at all that is done on earth," Cicero thinks, "is more pleasing to that supreme god than the assemblies and gatherings of men" (*De re publica* 6.13 [*Somnium Scipionus*]). The deities care not only for individuals but also for the communal life founded on reason and speech.

How, then, do human beings live in accordance with their fundamentally social natures, guided by the justice that arises from divinely instilled reason, along with its companion, speech? The answer, quite simply, is that these attributes prove to be nature's method of endowing the human species with the capacity to cooperate, which is necessary for its perpetuation (*De officiis* 1.11). Indeed, Cicero calls justice "the skill to treat with consideration and wisdom those with whom we are associated, in order that we may through their cooperation have our natural wants supplied in full and overwhelming measure" (*De officiis* 2.18). As has been previously noted, one main result of natural human sociability is the preservation and protection of the species. As a consequence, violence and force play no role in the process of social formation depicted by Cicero—indeed, coercion seems antithetical to his account. Society rests on rational agreement, not on intimidation and threats of injury. Otherwise, no social order could be just, since justice itself requires for Cicero the absence of harm, as we have seen (*De officiis* 1.20). Cicero underscores the incompatibility of violence and mature human civilization in *Pro Sestio*. He begins by repeating the familiar formula of social origination. After describing the transformation of human existence from disorder to order, Cicero concludes, "Now the chief distinguishing feature between that early crude existence and this later civilized life that I have described lies in the difference between the rule of law and that of force. If you will not have the one, you must have the other" (*Pro Sestio* 92). When people conduct themselves according to law, which is based upon natural reason, they are living in a manner most consistent with true human nature. When they live in a violent manner, beyond and outside the law, they are in effect living not as human beings but as beasts, in denial of their capacities for reason and speech, as well as all the benefits of peaceful association that flow therefrom. In sum, the use of physical force can never be a virtue, according to Cicero. If we realize most completely our natural humanity when we demur from physical force, then virtue itself (which Cicero defines as "reason perfected, which is certainly in accord with nature") may never be said to partake of that which is unnatural (*De legibus* 1.45). True peace—the sort that derives from uncoerced human fellowship—accords with nature and is thus coextensive with justice.

FROM SOCIETY TO GOVERNMENT

If all human beings lived such a purely rational "civilized" life, and hence a completely just and virtuous one, they could and would exist in total peace with one another, and the original condition of society would be perpetuated *ad infinitum*. Unfortunately, although men are naturally inclined toward virtue, they are also subject to the corrupting effects of their environment, as already discussed. As a consequence, a number of them (Cicero seems to suppose a majority) will ignore the duties imposed on them by their reason in preference to the fulfillment of their baser desires; they will instead begin to harm one another in violation of the principle of justice, thus ending the tranquility engendered by sociability. At that moment, the universal fellow feeling that previously united people disappears, and an alternate means must be found to reestablish a semblance of the order that reason alone once secured. Specifically, human beings are induced to authorize forms of political power to supplement natural law in order to prevent the injuries that they are capable of causing to one another. As Cicero explains in *De officiis* 2.41, one group is oppressed by another in the pursuit of self-interest. In order to remedy abuses to which they are now subjected, the oppressed turn to "men of high moral character [who] were made kings in order that the people might enjoy justice. For, as the masses in their helplessness were oppressed by the strong, they appealed for protection to some one man who was conspicuous for his virtue." Governance by men esteemed virtuous ensured for a time that equity and security would be guaranteed. Such kings could be trusted because they ruled on the basis of their virtuous knowledge of the law of nature, from which justice arose.

Yet Cicero recognizes that entrusting unlimited political power to kings is a precarious enterprise. Primitive kingship functioned effectively so long as "a just and good man" occupied the throne. When communities failed to generate such a ruler, however, "laws were invented which would speak to everyone at the same time with the same voice.... The reason for con- stitutional laws is the same as that for kings. For equitable right is always sought" (De officiis 2.41–42). A legal system substituted for personalized political rule, but the fundamental purpose of both was identical: to guar- antee justice and hence to safeguard the community. In this sense, statutory law, like the good ruler, must conform to natural law and the dictates of justice. The special character of civil law, as distinct from natural law, stems from its applicability to persons as citizens rather than as members of the human species. But civil law ought neither to violate the precepts of natural law nor to exempt citizens from their social duties. As Cicero says, "Civil law is not always the same as universal [that is, natural] law; still, universal law should be the same as civil law" (De officiis 3.69). The statutes of com- munities must embrace and cohere with the requirements of what Cicero describes as "true law" (veri iuris): civil law is not the product of arbitrary human determination (De legibus 1.42–45).

Given that civil law depends upon a rational origin in "what is true and just," its authorization can properly rest only with those who possess the virtues, especially justice; the statutes that are framed and approved by such people should alone be counted as valid. Law exists not merely when it is formally promulgated (De legibus 2.11–12). As De legibus 2.13 explains, "If ignorant and inexperienced people have prescribed deadly poisons in place of true medicines, these cannot be called the prescriptions of phy- sicians; so neither in a people can a statute of any sort be called a law even though the people have accepted it in spite of its being pernicious." No enactment of the multitude, regardless of how overwhelming the pop- ular support, deserves to be accorded respect and obedience unless it is consonant with natural law. Cicero remarks in De re publica 5.8 that the vir- tuous ruler "considers the welfare of the people rather than their wishes."[19] Even when positive law does not prohibit acts that are injurious, no one may engage in such conduct precisely because it is "still forbidden by natural law" (*De officiis* 3.69). In sum, since the purpose of human law is to bring social arrangements into line with the dictates of justice, civil statutes are both subordinate to natural law and lend support to it.

A noteworthy example of this point, found in *De officiis*, concerns the existence of private property. In the natural state of human association, any notion of property held in personal hands would have been meaningless, since all men there practice justice in their reason. "There is," Cicero says, "no such thing as private ownership established by nature.... Therefore, inasmuch as in each case some of the things which had been common property became the property of individuals, each one should retain possession of what has fallen to his lot" (1.21). The shift from affable sociability to the exercise of political power changes all of that. The intrusion of injustice constitutes precisely the reason that Cicero stipulates that government itself first came into existence: the establishment of some semblance of equity between the oppressed and their oppressors. Some people in mankind's natural condition, overwhelmed by base desires, no longer wish to share common possessions for the good of all. Claiming a monopoly over such goods, the oppressors break the natural bond of fellowship. The only way in which the ensuing conflict may be halted is the creation of civil statutes and of government to enforce them (1.51, 2.73). In other words, while private property is unnatural, its implementation becomes necessary for the sake of maintaining public peace: "It is the peculiar function of the state and the city to guarantee to every man the free and undisturbed control over his own particular property" (2.79). Although inconsistent with justice pure and simple, personal possession assures a modicum of equitable order and harmony in the face of departure from the path of reason.

STATESMANSHIP AND REPUBLICAN INSTITUTIONS

It seems, then, that the very existence of political power and civil law signals the incapacity of much of humankind to live according to the law of nature that sanctions justice. Yet this does not warrant the monopolization of power by the virtuous. In light of Cicero's account of the discursive foundations of public life, the role of the orator/statesman is tied to a clear notion of citizenship and civic intercourse. "The practice of eloquence," he says in *De oratore* 2.33, is the "governing force in every tranquil and free community." According to Cicero's viewpoint, indeed, statesmanship is not merely assimilated to oratory but is impossible without it (*De finibus* 4.61). The role of the man of public affairs is to persuade his fellow citizens to follow the wisest course of action in order to achieve the common good. Eloquent speech must, therefore, be cultivated alongside wisdom as a prized asset for political life; the statesman requires these qualities in order to appeal to and convince an audience (*De oratore* 3.142–43). Likewise, even though ordinary citizens may lack the talent and skill of the orator, they are deemed to be competent to judge between competing arguments within the public arena and to choose in accordance with the best and most persuasive (that is, the wisest and most just) case that they hear (*De officiis* 2.48). Thus citizenship ought to be construed in an active sense: statesmen seek the approval of citizens, who, by virtue of their inherently rational and linguistic faculties, are all qualified to discern the public good. Public life is a kind of recapitulation of the initial entry of human beings into the social and political order. Hence, Cicero's discursive approach has overtly participatory implications. It encourages political actors to conceive of their roles in terms of open, rational persuasion and debate leading toward the civic recognition of the public good.

The ability of the orator to employ persuasive speech assumes, in turn, an institutional context in which to do so. For Cicero, the activities proper to the eloquent statesman could only be fully realized under a mixed constitution, specifically, that of the Roman Republic. His *De re publica* (or at least what remains of it) offers a spirited defense of the superiority of the republican system of Rome as the best form of government possible.[20] In particular, Cicero regards the mixed constitution as ultimately the most effective and desirable way to resolve the dilemmas posed by the unequal exercise of humanity's natural reason (see *De legibus* 1.33). He invokes a principle of moderation that presupposes a more or less inescapable distinction between the virtuous sorts, who are qualified to rule, and the common run of citizens, who do not fully command and utilize their rational capacities. Employing a musical metaphor, Cicero asserts that "a city achieves the agreement of dissimilar [persons] when there is a reasonable modulating of the highest, the lowest, and the intervening middle orders, just like tones, and what musicians call harmony in song is called concord in the city, which is the strongest and best bond of security in the republic" (*De re publica* 2.69).[21] The mixed constitution in particular provides a buffer against the immoderate tendencies of popular government, by drawing the people voluntarily into the rule of the most qualified. As Cicero points out in *De legibus* 3.28, "If the senate is in charge of public deliberation, and everyone defends what it has decreed, and if the remaining orders are willing to have the commonwealth guided by the deliberation of the leading order, then it's possible through the blending of rights, since the people have power and the senate has authority, to maintain that harmonious order of the state." In the absence of such a mixed government in which both popular liberty and aristocratic preeminence are appropriately distributed, such as occurred (in Cicero's view) with the introduction of the office of the tribune, "the importance of the optimates was reduced, and the force of the mob was strengthened," a development that may only be tempered by means of "a moderate and wise blending" (*De legibus* 3.17).[22] The distinctive virtue of the Roman republican constitution is its ability to balance the conflicting interests between the few wise men and the many lacking in their ability to exercise their reason.

According to Cicero, the stable political order enjoyed by Rome can be traced specifically to a convergence on the part of the populace as a whole on a single principle of justice that all accept, since the "concord" of which Cicero speaks "can never exist without justice" (*De re publica* 2.69). In justice, we find the source of the harmony that Cicero believes is uniquely possible under a republican constitution. Under it, many individuals and groups coalesce into a single people, a populace that is greater than the sum of its parts. Indeed, he asks, "What is the state except an association in justice?" (*De re publica* 1.49).[23] As expressed in Cicero's standard formulation in *De re publica* 1.39—a passage widely known throughout later times on account of its dissection by Saint Augustine—"A people is not any collection of beings brought together in any sort of way, but an assemblage of people in large numbers associated in an agreement about justice and a partnership for the common good."[24] The republic depends upon the existence of a single *res publica*, literally a "public thing," but more loosely a "matter of public affairs" or a "common good." Regardless of translation, the *res publica* exists as a basis for communal unification because it rests upon a principle of justice shared freely by all citizens. The moderation typical of the Roman republican system eliminates discord and dissent without thereby also erasing the ultimate claim to authority of those possessing superior virtue. Justice itself rests on a fine balance between conferring what is appropriate to various men according to their *dignitas* ("rank" or "authority") and "preserving the common advantage" (*De inventione* 2.160). Cicero maintains that a republic will be governed according to the rule of law, based on the fundamental principles of natural law, which assures equitable treatment to each and all. "Those who share law also share the procedures of justice," he says, "and those who have these things in common must be considered members of the same civic body (*civitatis*). If indeed they obey the same commands and authorities, then all the more so" (*De legibus* 1.22). In this sense, a republican constitution intrinsically—and for Cicero, uniquely—meets the dual requirements of good governance as orderly and equitable (*De legibus* 1.41–42).

OTHER HUMAN BONDS: PATRIOTISM

Beyond the generalized duty, entailed by justice, that men have by nature toward their fellow creatures, Cicero recognizes the existence and importance of multiple other forms of human attachment that also obligate human beings: to family (parents, children, kinfolk), to friends, to country. This constitutes a persistent theme across the body of his writings. In *De inventione* 2.161, for instance, he insists that every man is required to render "kind offices and loving service to his kin and country." Similarly, in *De officiis* 1.22 he declares, "We are not born for ourselves alone, but our country claims a share of our being, and our friends a share . . . men, too, are born for the sake of men, that they may mutually be able to help one another." Cicero is unclear about the ordering of these varied obligations, however. In *De finibus* 5.65 he offers a developmental account of how myriad relationships emerge, starting with the love of parents toward children and family based on marriage and parenthood, then blood and marital relationships beyond the immediate household, "later friendships, afterwards by the bonds of neighborhood, then to fellow citizens and political allies and comrades, and lastly by embracing the whole of the human race." In *De officiis* 1.60 he proposes a different ranking: "In social relations themselves there are gradations of duty so well defined that it can easily be seen which takes precedence of [*sic*] any other: Our first duty is to the immortal gods; our second, to country; our third, to parents; and so on, in a descending scale to the rest." But earlier in the same book, he seemingly alters the priority: "Parents are dear; dear are children, relatives, friends; but our native land embraces all our loves" (1.57). And in the following paragraph, Cicero now gives pride of place to country and parents equally, then children and family, and finally kinsmen; immediately thereafter, he praises friendship (1.58).

The range of positions he articulates regarding the priority of social relationships certainly seems contradictory, if not incoherent. A plausible way in which to make some sense out of these apparently clashing rank orderings is to refer to Cicero's overt contextualism: "In the performance of all these duties we shall have to consider which is most needful in each individual case and what each person can and cannot procure without our help" (De officiis 1.59). He cites instances in which we might prefer to aid a neighbor rather than a kinsman, and others in which the prioritization might be reversed. He continues, "Such questions as these must be taken into account in every act of moral duty, in order to become good calculators of duty, able by adding and subtracting to strike a balance correctly and find out just how much is due to each individual" (1.59). There is no absolute judgment that fits all actions all of the time. Martha Nussbaum seems to me to be entirely correct in her observation that "Cicero proposes a flexible account that recognizes many criteria as pertinent to duties of aid," inasmuch as he "preserves a role for flexible judgment in adjudicating the claims when they might conflict. We have a great deal of latitude when considering the cases."[25] No permanent hierarchical ordering of duties may be justified.

Among the various forms of human obligation, however, Cicero most commonly emphasizes duty to one's country.[26] Patria, Cicero repeatedly holds, often trumps all other moral duties. In De amicitia 39–40, he insists that no one should ever ask a friend to act in a manner "inimical to the commonwealth. . . . Therefore let this law be established in friendship: Neither ask dishonorable things, nor do them, if asked. And dishonorable it is to plead in defense of sins in general and especially those against the state, that he committed them for the sake of a friend."[27] The same principle pertains in the case of one's father: "The claims of country [are] paramount to all other duties. . . . [I]f things point to the destruction of the state, he will sacrifice his father to the safety of the country," since "our patria is the author of more benefits, and is an earlier father than the father who begot us" (De officiis 3.90). Simply put, "there is no social relation more close, none dearer than that which links each one of us with our republic." Cicero reasons that, in comparison with other human attachments, "a country (patria) embraces all of the affections of all of us. What good man would hesitate to confront death for her, if it would render her a service?" (De officiis 1.57). He is emphatic that this demands sacrificing "not only money, but also life for the country," and indeed, the true patriot must even be prepared to surrender "personal glory and honor" in order to secure the advantage of the nation (*De officiis* 1.83–84). Similar expressions of patriotic fervor are to be found throughout Cicero's writings. In *De legibus* 2.5, for instance, he proclaims that "one [*patria*] must stand first in our affection in which the name of 'republic' signifies the common citizenship; for her it is our duty to die, to give ourselves entirely, to place upon her altar and almost consecrate all that we have." It is hardly an exaggeration to observe that Cicero regards his own political career as a testament to the depth of his patriotic belief in the Roman way of life.

Cicero's conception of patriotism falls directly in line with his idea of statesmanship. Although he regards one's readiness to sacrifice one's life as a feature of patriotism, Cicero does not conceive of "love of country" in an essentially militaristic fashion. Quite to the contrary, *De officiis* 1.74 denounces the view, held by "most people," that "the achievements of war are more important than those of peace." In his view, the glorification of armed conflict amounts to a denigration of characteristically human qualities in favor of a bestial nature: "There are two ways of settling a dispute: the one, by discussion, the other, by force; and since the former is proper to human beings, the latter to the brute, we may resort to force only when discussion is not possible" (*De officiis* 1.34). In other words, warfare is inconsistent with distinctively human nature; it reflects the animalistic side of our existence. As has already been noted, peace is the true natural condition of humanity, according to Cicero. If men draw upon their rational and linguistic capacities—those characteristics with which they are born and that they share in common with the gods—they will be able to settle all disputes and govern themselves without recourse to violence. "The only rationale for going to war, therefore, is that we may live in peace (*pax*) uninjured," he remarks (*De officiis* 1.35).

Cicero maintains that Rome, at least as long as it was under "temperate" rule, followed policies consonant with the principle that armed conflict should be pursued only as a last resort, when negotiations had proven ineffective at settling dispute, and vanquished enemies were not generally enslaved or slaughtered but were (like Cicero's own ancestors) extended Roman citizenship and afforded the protection of legal and political rights within the republic. The successful prosecution of war does not confer any special glory upon the republic, if the result is something less than the restoration of peace and the advancement of civilized order. Hence, patriotism cannot find its fullest and highest expression in militarism, since violence stands starkly opposed to the foundations of government necessary for the realization of peace and order in a manner consonant with the law of nature.

The comparison of statesmanship with military command comes in the midst of a discussion of the virtue of courage in *De officiis* 1.62, illustrating Cicero's challenge to the facile equivalence of fortitude with acts of physical bravery, especially on the field of battle. In the common mind, the greatness of spirit that gives rise to courageous acts is almost always associated with deeds of military valor. Cicero believes that such apparent virtue is in fact generally vicious, because it is not constrained by justice: "If the lofty spirit that is manifest in times of danger and toil is devoid of justice, if it fights not for the common welfare but for itself, it is a vice; for not only is it not a virtue, but it is rather a savagery that repels all things human." As stated previously, Cicero stipulates that justice requires both refraining from the commission of injuries and assuring that others are not injured. But military conflict often results in harm to combatants and even noncombatants, whether its occurrence is a calculated cruelty or it is committed accidentally in the heat of battle. Martial courage thus readily succumbs to vice, Cicero contends, in a way that what we might call "civic courage" does not.

The person of preeminent civic courage is the statesman: "Courageousness in domestic affairs is by no means inferior to military courage; indeed, the former demands even greater effort and exertion than the latter" (*De officiis* 1.78). True greatness of spirit expresses itself in the ability to refrain from the use of physical force except when entirely necessary. The really courageous person is one who is cautious and guided by reason, who seeks the public benefit and places peace above whatever glory can be achieved from warfare: "The civilians who are in charge of the republic are no less beneficial than those persons who conduct its wars. And thus by their counsels wars are often avoided or concluded. . . . We must therefore value the reason which makes decisions above the courage which makes battle; yet we must be careful to do that not for the sake of avoiding war but because we have reasoned about what is useful. War, then, should be undertaken in such a way that nothing else than peace is seen to be the aim" (1.79–80).

The courage of the patriot, for Cicero, stems from prudent judgment about the propriety of warfare and from a love of peace rather than from a desire for battle and conquest. "To charge rashly into battle and engage the enemy hand to hand is monstrous and beastlike," he declares (*De officiis* 1.81). Granted, Cicero is no pacifist. Every citizen of the republic must be prepared, if need be, to fight when no other option is available. But the courageous patriot resists the blandishments of those "who put war before civil affairs" and "to whom dangerous and hot-headed counsels appear greater and better than calm and thoughtful ones" (1.82). This amounts to a nearly complete rejection of received wisdom about courage as the archetypal martial virtue and underscores Cicero's insistence that the measure of patriotism is one's contribution to civic deliberation.

OTHER HUMAN BONDS: FRIENDSHIP

Cicero's patriotic fervor ought not to distract us from recognizing another form of social relationship central to his thought, namely, his idea of friendship. As with his defense of the primacy of one's duty to country, friendship formed a recurrent theme in his writings. Indeed, he even composed a separate book on the topic, *De amicitia*. But already in *De inventione* 2.167–68, he had begun to inquire into the nature of friendship, albeit without coming to any definite conclusions. Likewise, in later work, but prior to the composition of *De amicitia*, he ruminated over the qualities necessary for distinguishing between true and false friends, especially the various motivations that may be ascribed to their relationships.[28] But in *De amicitia* his conception of friendship crystallized. Cicero regarded friendship to constitute a unique and powerful type of connection between people within the pantheon of human associations: "In comparison with the infinite ties uniting the human race and fashioned by nature herself, this thing called friendship has been so narrowed that the bonds of affection always united two persons only, or, at most, a few" (20). Such relationships are indeed rare (22). This is true, first and foremost, because they depend primarily on virtue among those who may properly be termed friends: "Virtue is the parent and preserver of friendship and without virtue friendship cannot exist at all" (20). And virtue, as Cicero teaches elsewhere, is a relatively unusual quality among human beings, whose characters are so often corrupted by the pursuit of wealth, power, reputation, or sensual pleasure. Why is virtue so crucial to friendship? The reason, he says, is "because virtue cannot attain her highest aims unattended, but only in union and fellowship with another" (83). As a consequence, friends must stand on an equal footing.

"He who looks upon a true friend, looks, as it were, upon a sort of image of himself," Cicero asserts (23).

Cicero carefully distinguishes between this conception of genuine friendship and the attitude of people who "regard their friends as they do their cattle, valuing most highly those who give the hope of the largest gain" (*De amicitia* 79). Expediency, in other words, is antithetical to friendship. The false friend is one who seeks his own advantage under the guise of affection. By contrast, real "friendship springs rather from nature than need, and from an inclination of the soul joined with a feeling of love rather than from calculation of how much profit the friendship is likely to afford" (27). One of the surest signals of a faithless friend is a propensity toward flattery, whether to speak it or to be prone to accepting it. Men who lack in virtue, and who are thus incapable of friendship, "delight in flattery, and when a complimentary speech is fashioned to suit their fancy, they think that the empty phrase is proof of their merits. There is nothing, therefore, in a friendship in which one of the parties to it does not wish to hear the truth and the other is ready to lie" (98). Indeed, for Cicero truthfulness is the standard of an authentically friendly bond. The genuine friend is one who dares "to give true advice with all frankness; in friendship let the influence of friends who are wise counselors be paramount, and let that influence be employed to advising, not only with frankness, but, if the occasion demands, even with sternness, and let the advice be followed when given" (44). The litmus test for friendship, then, is reciprocity of honesty and openness: "It is characteristic of true friendship both to give and to receive advice and, on the one hand, to give it with all freedom of speech, but without harshness, and on the other hand, to receive it patiently but without resentment, so nothing is to be considered a greater bane of friendship than fawning, cajolery, or flattery; for give it as many names as you choose, it deserves to be branded as a vice peculiar to fickle and false-hearted men who say everything with a view to pleasure and nothing with a view to truth" (91).

Among real friends, each speaks sincerely, and even admonishes, for the advantage of the other; at the same time, each listens to and respects the advice and even rebuke offered by his fellow friend, assuming that the words are offered "in a spirit of goodwill" (88). Moreover, Cicero draws a political lesson from the distinction between friend and flatterer. The life of a tyrant, he suggests, is one "in which there can be no faith, no affection, no trust in the continuance of goodwill; where every act arouses suspicion and anxiety and where friendship has no place. . . . Yet tyrants are courted under a pretence of affection, but only for the time being" (52–53). The tyrant, according to Cicero, can never know real friendship because he listens solely to what he wishes to hear. Truth is thereby anathema to him, to the extent that the person who would deign to speak honestly in the tyrant's presence endangers himself. "We live one way with a tyrant," Cicero cautions, "and another with a friend" (89). Recognizing the differences between the two is of critical importance.

CONCLUSION

The entirety of the Ciceronian conception of society and politics ultimately rests upon his conviction that human beings owe many debts to many sorts of people on many different grounds. However, Cicero often—albeit not universally—posits that the best and most fulfilling life is one centered on activity in public affairs in the pursuit of the common good of the *patria*. Without denigrating the wisdom of philosophy, Cicero always regarded contemplation to be inferior to action. He acknowledged that "becoming an expounder of philosophy" was the only alternative available to him during times when political involvement was beyond his reach (as when Julius Caesar grasped power) (*De divinatione* 2.6; *De officiis* 2.2–6). The man who is first and foremost committed to the common good, although sometimes forced into leisure, will always forego his private concerns when called upon to act in order to preserve the bonds of humanity (*De officiis* 1.158). But the contemplative life was always second best: "Those duties are closer to nature which depend upon the social instinct than those which depend upon knowledge. . . . The duties prescribed by justice must be given precedence over the pursuit of knowledge and the duties imposed by it; for the former concern the welfare of our fellow-men; and nothing ought to be more sacred in men's eyes than that" (*De officiis* 1.153, 155). For Cicero, the very essence of virtue was to be located in the *vita activa*: "Those whom nature has endowed with the capacity for administering public affairs should put aside all hesitation, enter the race for public office, and take a hand in directing government" (*De officiis* 1.72). As should be evident, he did not divorce philosophy from politics. But his priorities are clear. Having "thought that I exchanged politics for philosophy, . . . I have come to be consulted again about public affairs . . . and only so much time can be given to philosophy as will not be needed in the discharge of my duty to the commonwealth" (*De divinatione* 2.7). Such remarks occur repeatedly in his writings, reflecting his profound conviction that the duties entailed by justice, while properly informed by wisdom, are ultimately the most compelling of all. The true statesman-cum-orator has a calling greater than that of any other person. More generally, though, a person's virtue is compromised should he decline any form of engagement with his fellow human beings in order to pursue contemplative occupations—a significant reversal of the viewpoint commonplace in most ancient philosophies. In turn, numerous elements of Ciceronian social and political thought—albeit none of them in its entirety—proved attractive to and worthy of appropriation by an unlikely array of early European thinkers from the twelfth century onward.

CHAPTER 2

Words and Deeds

Some Twelfth-Century Ciceros

Nearly a century ago, the esteemed historian Charles Homer Haskins posited the occurrence of a broad and fundamental shift in Western intellectual culture during the High Middle Ages, which he termed "the Renaissance of the Twelfth Century."[1] Specifically, Haskins associated this seismic shift in medieval thought with a revival of interest in the pagan Latin classics, and particularly the works of Cicero: "Of prose writers, Cicero naturally came first, revered, if for nothing else, as the 'king of eloquence' and the chief representative of one of the seven arts, rhetoric."[2] Beyond Cicero's fame as a master of the rhetorical arts, Haskins acknowledged the reception and impact of the Roman's philosophical dialogues and treatises.[3] Not surprisingly, the so-called Haskins thesis has met with a wide array of criticism, revision, adaptation, qualification, and outright rejection.[4] There is one feature, however, that unites the diverse body of literature generated in response to Haskins: an almost complete disregard for and disinterest in the role played by Cicero in the development of twelfth-century thought. Admittedly, Cicero is given some small credit for his contribution to technical rhetorical studies during the twelfth century. But virtually nothing is observed about the role of his writings in the emergence of the period's social and political ideas. This view seems widespread, even though a substantial number of Cicero's main philosophical works, in which his overall scheme of the nature and bases of human social interaction was articulated, as well as his rhetorical treatises containing related conceptual elements had been widely disseminated before 1200.

Just how vast was this knowledge of Ciceronian treatises? As suggested in the introduction, striking evidence of the extent to which Cicero's writings could be accessed during the 1100s may be gleaned from the work of the early twelfth-century English historian William of Malmesbury, in particular (but not only) from a manuscript, now held by the Cambridge University Library, that M. R. James first associated with him in 1931.[5] This text is noteworthy because it contains a startling amount of Ciceroniana (including twelve speeches), as well as brief introductions, penned by William, to many of these texts.[6] Although none of Cicero's rhetorical works are to be found there, we may ascertain William's knowledge of them (specifically, *De inventione*, the pseudo-Cicero *Ad Herennium*, and possibly *Orator*) from their use in his histories, or, in the case of *Partitiones oratoriae*, from the existence of his own copy (Oxford, Bodl. Libr. Rawl. G. 139).[7] Likewise, it is evident from William's historical writings that some of the philosophical texts that do not appear in the manuscript collection (for example, *De senectute*, *De officiis*, *De amicitia*, and *De legibus*) were nevertheless known, and cited or quoted, by him.[8] Although William's familiarity with Cicero's corpus was especially wide-ranging—one scholar calls him the "greatest Ciceronian of the twelfth century"[9]—it hints at just how many of the Roman's writings might have been available to authors by the middle of the twelfth century.

Thus, in spite of the relatively poor treatment Cicero has received at the hands of scholars of the twelfth century, many of his leading ideas about social and political order found expression in quite diverse writings of the 1100s. The present chapter will support this claim by examining Ciceronian themes in five twelfth-century texts of extremely different characters. First, I shall consider the commentary on *De inventione* composed by Thierry of Chartres sometime in the fourth decade of the twelfth century. While we might expect such a treatise to comment on the relevant sections of Cicero's work, we will find that Thierry extends his analysis beyond a simple repetition of the ideas concerning speech and the origins of society found in *De inventione*. Second, I will examine the adaptation of some of Cicero's teachings in the *Summa decretorum* composed by the eminent canonist Rufinus around the middle of the twelfth century (the dating varies). Rufinus's commentary on Gratian's monumental *Decretum*, traditionally known as the *Concordia discordantium canonum* or *Concordantia discordantium canonum*—the foundational text in the medieval attempt to systematize the entire body of church law—proved to be highly regarded and extremely influential. Third, Cicero makes at least a fleeting appearance in a "universal" history entitled *Chronica sive Historia de duabus civitatibus* (dubbed by its English translator *The Two Cities*) written by Otto of Freising, a mid-twelfth-century bishop who was the uncle of Emperor Frederick I (Barbarossa). Otto's text purports to offer a chronological account of humanity from its inception onward. Fourth, I will appraise the presence of Ciceronianism in Aelred of Rievaulx's *De spirituali amicitia*, a work that epitomizes the virtual mania of twelfth-century thinkers for friendship. Although heavily reliant upon Cicero's *De amicitia*, Aelred's treatise demonstrates a rather more substantial foundation in the Roman's social philosophy. Finally, I will investigate the appropriation and adaption of Ciceronian teachings in the *Moralium dogma philosophorum*, a compilation of primarily moral and social writings, once ascribed to William of Conches but now regarded to be of uncertain authorship. While the *Moralium* is commonly treated as simply a compendium of sayings intended to provide a resource for other writers, we shall see that its author extrapolated and extended in original ways numerous elements of Cicero's thought, especially from *De officiis*. The relative lack of attention paid to Cicero's contributions to the "Twelfth-Century Renaissance" in the realms of social and political thought, however construed, requires considerable reconsideration and revision. While each of the authors mentioned here reshapes Ciceronian ideas to suit his own needs, Cicero's oeuvre proved to be a highly useful resource for them all.

THIERRY OF CHARTRES

Among the earliest twelfth-century appreciations of Cicero's substantive social and political doctrines occur in commentaries on *De inventione*, glosses on which were widely produced during the late eleventh and twelfth centuries.[10] The influential commentary composed by Thierry of Chartres during the 1130s, for example, devotes a disproportionate amount of attention to the "prologue" of *De inventione*, in which Cicero introduces the orator and his role.[11] Thierry demonstrates an astute understanding of the background to the Ciceronian argument, rapidly confronting the potential problem implicit in the relationship between wisdom and eloquence. He carefully analyzes the terms of Cicero's statement at the beginning of *De inventione* about the dangers posed by either wisdom or eloquence when not associated with the other. Thierry also locates Cicero in his intellectual milieu. He emphasizes how the Roman sought to refute Plato and, especially, Aristotle, for whom the art of persuasion "opposed in many ways the truth, because it supplanted truth with falsity in human opinion" (*Commentarius*, 56).[12] In this regard, Thierry highlights Cicero's concern with demonstrating that the worthiness of the study of rhetoric depends upon pragmatic considerations. Eloquence is not "good" or "evil" in itself but should be judged according to its value for human beings (56–57).

Thierry recognizes that the appeal to utility raises two further questions. First, to whom should rhetoric be useful? Second, how does one ensure that it will be useful? The answers to these queries are connected. Thierry contends that when eloquence is joined with wisdom, the orator will necessarily serve the welfare of the *res publica*, a term that he construes to mean both the private good of individuals and that of the civic body (*Commentarius*, 57). In order to achieve this goal, the orator must study all of the departments of speculative and practical wisdom, "which we call philosophy," as well as rhetoric: "By means of the conjunction of wisdom with eloquence, one is fit to defend one's country" (59). In a later passage, Thierry even cites *De oratore*—the sole reference to that work in his commentary—in support of the assertion that the orator must, at minimum, enjoy a broad basis of learning in order to perform his functions adequately (72).

The civic orientation of Cicero's conception of the union of wisdom and eloquence is reaffirmed by Thierry in his gloss on the Ciceronian account of the origins of human society. As reconstructed by Thierry, Cicero is taken to say:

> There was a certain time at the start of the world, during which men were in their original state and lived according to the character of wild animals and not one of them engaged in the study of wisdom, but only exercised the strength of the body without any reason; at this time, some man of wisdom and eloquence—since these properties would seem to be included in man's divine and rational soul, for which reason it would be known that he was suited to be capable of being persuaded—then and on account of this impulse wisely started using eloquence and suppressed the original state and gathered men together to live according to laws and taught the correct laws to the congregated persons. In this manner, he shows both the unformed state of the exercise of eloquence and the cause for which eloquence began to be exercised, and the occurrence of

an order which was most advantageous and was useful. (*Commentarius*, 60–61)

This general summary by Thierry, which precedes a more detailed examination of the passage, elaborates upon Cicero's text in interesting ways. Most significantly, he describes the primitive orator as "sapiens et eloquens," whereas Cicero merely calls him "vir magnus et sapiens," a variation that directly suggests that the duties of modern oratory are prefigured by the founding of the earliest societies. And he stresses that the need for the orator to persuade human beings to assemble establishes the "usefulness" (and hence goodness) of the "learning of the art of rhetoric" (*Commentarius*, 60). Thierry's commentary thus demonstrates an appreciation of the broader significance of Cicero's presentation of the emergence of human association.

In connection with the civil bearing of rhetoric, Thierry also attempts to explain why the study of philosophy, and hence the acquisition of wisdom, constitutes an assurance of the public utility of eloquence. What distinguishes the orator from the man who merely "speaks well" is virtue. Thierry describes the "greatness" and "wisdom" of the primitive orator as a manifestation of his "virtue" and "discretion" (*Commentarius*, 62). Furthermore, he contraposes wisdom to "cleverness" (*calliditatis*). Real eloquence manifests a philosophical education, replete with the study of *ethica* (59), whereas empty persuasion relies on skills that have no basis in philosophy. Hence, Thierry declares, "A distinction is to be noted between wisdom and cleverness, for no one is wise without virtue, yet cleverness is obtained by many people lacking virtue" (64). He arrives at this conclusion on the basis of very slender evidence in Cicero's text itself. In *De inventione* 1.2.3, Cicero remarks only that the speaker of "talent dependent upon malice" exercised "a depraved imitation of virtue" which destroyed men and their communal association. By contrast, Thierry goes on to ascribe virtue to the orator as a direct result of his combination of eloquence with wisdom. This seems to be the ultimate reason why, for Thierry, "eloquence in conjunction with wisdom is highly advantageous for cities," whereas "eloquence without wisdom is of little advantage for the arrangement and rule of cities" (*Commentarius*, 62–63). The orator's virtue, embedded in his wisdom, impels him to serve the good of the civic body, while the lack of wisdom attributable to the clever speaker means that he will pursue his own aims without regard for the welfare of his fellow creatures. Early commentators on *De inventione*, typified by Thierry of Chartres, were in large measure responsible for drawing attention to and promoting the Ciceronian vision of the orator among educated clerics and schoolmen.[13]

RUFINUS

As one of the most eminent canon lawyers working in Gratian's wake, Rufinus established a reputation as an especially elegant expositor of the great *Decretum*, a work that was notably dense and in need of explication.[14] He was demonstrably trained not only as a decretist but also as a Roman (or civil) lawyer, as one historian of canon law has argued.[15] Beyond his presence at the University of Bologna in its heyday as the leading European school of law, virtually nothing is known of him. More important for present purposes, Rufinus clearly knew and drew upon Ciceronian doctrines. Commenting on the *Decretum* was no easy task. It opens with a set of dense and compressed definitions of law and its various divisions and types— divine, natural, customary, and civil. For the most part, Gratian simply refers to and repeats the text of Isidore of Seville's *Etymologies* with very little added comment. By contrast, Rufinus prefaces his commentary with a few remarks about the need for law in general, as well as a brief overview of the structure and main topics of the *Decretum*; in addition, he provides more extensive exposition of the typology of law than Gratian.

For our purposes, Rufinus's explanation of the necessity of legal systems is the first instance of his deployment and modification of one of Cicero's characteristic ideas. Prior to the Fall, Rufinus says, human beings possessed a "dignity" founded on justice and knowledge. Once humanity lapsed into sin, both justice and knowledge became occluded; that is to say, although the capacities associated with reason may be obstructed, men do not entirely lose their capability to be just as well as intelligent. In other words, Rufinus sides with many contemporary theologians in rejecting the late Augustinian view of postlapsarian mankind as utterly corrupted and degraded. Rather, in Rufinus's view, the "natural order" that continues to exist beyond the Fall serves as a "reminder" and permits men to restore some semblance of justice and knowledge.[16] He thereafter moves his reader into Ciceronian territory: "Thus since natural capacity was not completely extinguished in man, he began indeed to be concerned about how he stood apart from brute animals, as with the privilege of knowing and hence of living by law. And when man decided to gather with his neighbors and to take thought for things of mutual benefit, as if from within dead ashes, the sparks of justice produced honest and, to be sure, venerable precepts, which taught reduction of the savage and wild customs of men to graceful and honest ways, submission to covenants of concord, and establishment of secure pacts."[17] As a direct consequence, according to Rufinus, there arose the law of nations, the Decalogue, the commandment of the Gospels to love, and finally the canons of the church.[18] Rufinus thus brings Ciceronian themes, in a rather distorted way, to bear on the explanation for the necessity of human submission to law. Gone is the wise and eloquent primitive orator. The gathering together of humanity seems, rather, to be a somewhat spontaneous occurrence. Yet the view typical of Cicero concerning the application of human reason in the discovery of justice, and with it law, remains intact.

Nor is this the only instance in which Rufinus evidently depends upon Cicero. In his quite substantial remarks concerning the law of nature, a topic addressed at the beginning of the first part of the *Decretum*, a Ciceronian perspective resonates with Rufinus's elaboration on Gratian's treatment of the subject. He points out that natural law may, properly speaking, be construed as "what nature teaches to all living beings," but he then concedes that his concern in the present context is with the specific features of the law of nature as it pertains to humanity. He then defines natural law "as a kind of natural propulsion, implanted by nature in each human being, to do good and to avoid evil.... [N]atural law has to do with the essential natures, and shows no more than that one thing is essentially just and another essentially unjust."[19] Rufinus insists that natural law confers upon man merely a propensity toward shunning injury and promoting rectitude; it is still necessary for human beings to apply these fundamental precepts to particular circumstances by articulating a moral code that governs practice in a manner consonant with the law of nature.[20]

Returning to his argument in the preface, he asserts that "the streams of human decency flow back to the sea of natural law, which, when almost lost to the first man, was revealed in the Mosaic law, perfected in the Gospel, and elaborated in the moral code," and finally concretized in statutory human law and in custom. All of this leads him directly back to the opening chapters of the *Decretum*, which Gratian in turn derived primarily from

Isidore.[21] It may be that many of the Ciceronian echoes concerning natural law and related matters that one may detect in the *Summa* are mediated through the Roman legal texts with which Rufinus was familiar. But then, as Charles Norris Cochrane succinctly observed many decades ago, Cicero "was the medium for the propagation of those ideas that informed the law and institutions of the empire" that constituted the basis of the civil system of statute known to Rufinus.[22] And, at least in the case of his Christianized explanation of the origins of human society, he seems to have straightforwardly adapted Cicero's own account.

OTTO OF FREISING

Otto of Freising was a mid-twelfth-century churchman who, as the uncle of Emperor Frederick I (Barbarossa), forged a career at the highest levels of the central European ecclesiastical structure. But Otto was also a highly educated cleric who had studied in Paris, which was the intellectual center of twelfth-century Europe, and apparently continued to show interest in contemporary learning. He authored two important works of historical narrative, one an account of the deeds of his nephew, with whom he traveled extensively. His other major writing, which is of immediate significance, was the "universal" history *Chronica sive Historia de duabus civitatibus*, which offers a chronological account of the human race from its inception to contemporary times. Although this text has usually been ignored for its contributions to political thought, scholars have occasionally acknowledged, however briefly, its significance for the early development of medieval social and political ideas.[23] Otto primarily adopts the framework of Saint Augustine (and of the Saint's follower, Orosius) in recounting the historical evolution, guided by divine providence, from the Fall to the present day of the main moments of the human race. But his Augustinian proclivities do not prevent Otto from weaving elements of Cicero's thought into the *Chronica*.

Thus, for example, Otto's account of the origins of temporal power veers away from Augustine's account in the *De civitate Dei* and instead is highly and intriguingly eclectic. Specifically, in the *Chronica*, he ascribes to the Assyrian ruler Ninus the beginnings of an era in which human conflict and conquest prevailed. According to Otto, Ninus "inflicted upon the world the disquietude of wars and brought practically the entire East under his control" (130).[24] How was Ninus able to accomplish such a previously unseen feat? Otto claims that this achievement was the result of the fact that "men were as yet simple and rustic, neither protecting themselves by arms nor training by warfare; they were not yet equipped with knowledge of military matters because they had not yet united under any laws or regulations up to this time" (130).[25] In support of this observation, Otto proceeds to quote *De inventione* 1.2 (and a similar passage from Eusebius, which was almost certainly cribbed from Cicero) to the effect that, in their primitive state, human beings were weak and bestial, lacking the organization (social, legal, and political) to protect themselves or even to recognize their common humanity. But Otto then turns Cicero entirely on his head. The peaceful realization of common humanity by means of eloquent oratory that appeals to reason is substituted for the mechanism of coercion. It is human weakness, rather than merely sin (as in Augustine), that authorizes the coercive quality of government as realized through conquest. The only resolution to the oppressive character of political regimes that Otto appears to imagine is the standard medieval trope of the reconciliation of the power of rulers (the temporal sword) with the spiritual sword of the church, once it was founded (404).

Elsewhere in the *Chronica*, there are at least hints of Ciceronian thought in play. Where Augustine apparently regarded fallen man as cut off from God and from his own nature, there are at least two places in Otto's text in which he adopts the more Ciceronian position that reason can never be extinguished from mankind because it reflects God's permanent grant to humanity, one that may be diminished but never extinguished. Why? Because it reflects a property of our created nature that we share with divinity—a view that converges with that of Cicero. In the prologue to book 7, Otto states flatly, "Every man is capable of reason, to the end that he might acknowledge God as his creator, and not overlook his own deeds because his heart is blind or fails to hear because his ears are deaf" (402). Humanity's status as a special creature, designated as such by God, distinguishes mankind from other animals. Man alone recognizes and reveres the divine and is capable of performing good deeds as a result. Otto recognizes that not all people (indeed, not many) exercise their reason to such effect. On the one hand, "when the first man had been created and had fallen from the delights of paradise, a merciful God left him a guide for learning the truth." But, on the other hand, "the sons of men were constantly led away therefrom; though some few continued in the knowledge of the truth yet the majority went astray" (280). Otto claims that this was the cause of the great flood narrated in the Old Testament. "The human race was propagated anew," only for the same devolution from truth to ignorance, from reason to passion, to occur once again (280). God granted to human beings the unique rational capacity to know Him, even in postlapsarian times; all possess the capacity to employ their reason, but a relatively small number do so. The resemblance to Cicero's position, albeit in Christianized form, should not be overlooked.

AELRED OF RIEVAULX

In literary as well as political settings, friendship (*amicitia*) constituted one of the more prominent themes characteristic of the twelfth-century western European worldview. Indeed, Brian Patrick McGuire once described the period from circa 1120 to circa 1180 as "the age of friendship."[26] Theorists of *amicitia* were often simultaneously its practitioners, building strategic networks by means of voluminous correspondence while also devoting energy to reflection upon its significance.[27] Many powerful and influential churchmen—such as the monastic Peter of Celle and the secular clerics Peter of Blois and John of Salisbury (who will be discussed at great length in the next chapter)—composed writings that in one way or another valorized the relationship between friends. For Peter of Celle, this was captured in his letter collections;[28] for Peter of Blois, primarily in a treatise called *De amicitia Christiana et de dilectione Dei et proximi*;[29] and for John of Salisbury, in the third book of his *Policraticus* as well as his own epistolary compilations.[30] Among the most widely disseminated twelfth-century treatises on friendship was a relatively short tract composed in dialogue form by the British Cistercian Aelred of Rievaulx entitled *De spirituali amicitia*, dated to between 1164 and his death in 1167.[31] Aelred's varied life encompassed careers both as an active author of literature in numerous genres (spiritual, hagiographical, historical) and as the abbot of a major monastery in North Yorkshire. He was deeply involved in the ecclesio-political conflicts that roiled mid-twelfth-century England and the church as a whole.[32]

The figure looming behind the body of friendship-themed writings was Cicero, or more specifically his *De amicitia*, which enjoyed immense popularity during the 1100s. Cicero posed a particular quandary for Aelred.

In the autobiographical preface to *De spirituali amicitia*, he recounts his fraught experience with reading *De amicitia*. As a young student full of confusion about the nature of true friendship, he stumbled across Cicero's text and found in it an "invaluable" guide (*De spirituali amicitia* prologue.1–3).[33] He reports that, somewhat later, he discovered his monastic calling and delved into the careful "study of the sacred writings," which led him to reject his previous worldly learning. The ideas he once admired in *De amicitia* seemed valueless and even "insipid" to him (prologue.4). Yet, Aelred tells us, he nonetheless began to reflect on whether Cicero's teachings about friendship might somehow be reconciled with "the authority of the Scriptures" (prologue.5). Eventually, he determined that biblical doctrines, along with "the writings of the holy fathers," about friendship were not at all incompatible with Ciceronian musings on the topic (prologue.6). And that epiphany was the genesis of *De spirituali amicitia*. Written in three compact books, the dialogue, purporting to contain Aelred's conversations with several fellow monks concerning the nature of friendship, lives up to its promise. *De amicitia* is Aelred's single most quoted and cited source, but scriptural passages and patristic allusions play a large role in the overarching representation of what it means to befriend and to maintain friendly relations with another person. Cicero can thereby be usefully reframed in order to defend and promote a conception of friendship that captures the characteristics of Christian (primarily monastic) bonds among people.[34]

On the surface, Aelred simply engages in a literary convention dating back at least as far as Saint Ambrose's *De officiis ministrorum*, namely, the Christian rewriting of an eminent classical pagan text.[35] I thoroughly endorse the observation of Brian Patrick McGuire that "dependence on Cicero has led to the charge that Aelred merely provided a Christian façade for Cicero's thoughts."[36] Whereas McGuire proposes to distance Aelred from Cicero, I have a rather different approach in mind: examining how Aelred reconstructed and refurbished Cicero's dialogue by attributing to it elements that are in fact not present there but that do reflect concepts found elsewhere in the Roman's corpus. So far as I have been able to determine, no scholar has addressed directly (or even gestured toward) this dimension of *De spirituali amicitia*. Simply stated, I submit that Aelred's treatise, under the guise of rendering the Ciceronian theory of friendship palatable to a Christian audience, develops an independent reinterpretation of *De amicitia* in the spirit of its author by introducing ideas found in some of Cicero's other writings, especially *De officiis*.[37] This claim is not as implausible as it might first appear. Although knowledge of Aelred's education is scant, I find it difficult to believe that he knew *De amicitia* yet did not possess familiarity with a larger range of works in the Ciceronian corpus. Indeed, if there is some validity in the suggestion that the adaptation of Ciceronian thought in *De spirituali amicitia* is a good deal more complicated than expected, it may be possible to draw some inferences about the extent of his reading.

It may be most useful to commence by identifying the basic principles on which Cicero and Aelred unquestionably converge. The most obvious and central of these are: (1) friendship is founded on the natural human impulse to associate;[38] (2) true friendship may exist only between men of equal virtue, since in a friend one finds a likeness of one's self;[39] (3) those who claim friendship based on expediency or mutual usefulness are not really friends at all;[40] (4) friendship entails moral reciprocity, in the sense that each friend has a duty to correct his fellow and no friend acts dishonorably for the sake of another.[41] Yet, even acknowledging these confluences, very often Aelred's invocation of the concepts and language found in *De amicitia* either overtly or implicitly reflects a "creative" reformulation of Cicero's positions. A large number of passages in *De spirituali amicitia*, when compared directly with their alleged Ciceronian source, depart considerably from their "original." Generally speaking, these variances reflect the quite subtle ways in which Aelred adapts elements of Cicero's theory of friendship to the narration of Christian stories and lessons. Given what he says in the prologue, this is only to be expected. But he goes much further than the imposition of Christian pieties on the text of *De amicitia*, sometimes even calling on Cicero for no discernable reason related directly to Christianity. Initially, these modifications may seem odd, but they often prove to be applications or extensions of Ciceronian doctrines espoused in other of the Roman's writings. In effect, Aelred sometimes "out-Ciceros Cicero" in his appropriations of *De amicitia*, to express the matter colloquially.

De spirituali amicitia incorporates the sort of Christian dogmas that we might expect, such as the idea that the social nature of human beings is divinely ordained or that friendship is a conjunction of nature and grace (1.53, 3.91). There are, however, more surprising instances in which Aelred merges Cicero and Christianity. Perhaps the most fascinating example stems from his extended recitation of mankind's expulsion from the Garden of Eden framed with reference to key elements of *De amicitia*. According to

Aelred, from the Genesis account of God's creation of man and woman we may derive two lessons: first, that human motivation is grounded in friendship and charity, and second, so "that nature might teach that all are equal or, as it were, collateral, and that among human beings—and this is a property of friendship—there exists neither superior nor inferior" (*De spirituali amicita* 1.57).[42] Aelred seemingly appeals to a doctrine of natural equality that shares important features with Cicero's insistence that all human beings share the capability to reason. Nor does he view the Fall as an immediate and complete loss of such parity. Rather, by means of a gradual process, charity grew "lukewarm . . . cupidity crept in and let private gain supplant the common good, avarice and envy supplant the splendor of friendship and charity by introducing into the debased morals of mankind contentions, rivalries, hatreds and suspicions" (1.58).[43] This ultimate condition did not, however, apply to each and every fallen man, for some "righteous" people remained: "Therefore, friendship, which like charity was first observed among all and by all people, by *natural law* (*naturali lege*) lingered among the righteous . . . who bound themselves by a stricter bond of love and friendship. . . . [T]hey kept their peace in the grace of mutual charity" (1.59, emphasis added). Try as I might, I can find no trace of the term "natural law" anywhere in *De amicitia*, but it is, as we know, a quintessential Ciceronian concept.

Nor was friendship entirely extirpated among even the most vicious, since "reason, which could not be extinguished in them, retained the attachment of friendship and companionship," signified, for instance, by economic transactions, although a mere shadow of the friendly engagement among equals present in Eden (*De spirituali amicitia* 1.60). The difference between friendship among the few and among the many is that the former relate to one another in accordance with nature, while the latter require law in order to compel the terms of the debased form of friendship, such as the enforcement of contracts (1.61). Aelred even refers to the quintessential Stoic doctrine, sometimes employed by Cicero, of the distinction between the "fools" and the "wise" (1.62–63). He follows this discussion, however, with a remarkable statement: "Especially among the virtues, the lesser—though they are not equal in rank—are frequently linked with the greater, the good with the better, the weaker with the stronger. Although the virtues vary among themselves by a difference of degree, still by some similarity they approximate each other. . . . Great is the difference among these virtues, but some relationship remains from the fact that they are virtues"

(1.65). In other words, as I read this passage, to posit an unbridgeable chasm between the virtuous few and the vicious many fails to comprehend evident gradations. Aelred does not simply espouse the view of *De amiticia* 72 that those of higher rank pull up social inferiors when friendships occur between them—that is, friendship is a means for the condition of the lower to be improved by association with the higher. Rather, he seems to maintain a position closer to Cicero's remark in *De officiis* 1.46—and perhaps echoed in *De finibus* 5.69—that, while not every man will be "ideally wise," still those who display virtues that are a mere "semblance" are not to be utterly shunned and that, consequently, there is a sort of "sliding scale" of degree when it comes to possession of morally commendable characteristics.

Another feature worthy of note in Aelred's quasi-Ciceronian reconstruction of the Fall and its aftermath is his reference to reason, which, he evidently believes, is both a divinely endowed aspect of human nature and is inextinguishable. *Ratio* and its variants are rarely found in *De amicitia*; in the few instances in which they do appear, they never connote reason in the sense of natural human rationality meant in *De spirituali amicitia*. Elsewhere in Cicero's corpus, reason is necessary for the realization of man's primitive capacity for association; it grounds the human ability to know justice and natural law; it is the divine "spark" which mankind shares with the gods. *De legibus* and *De officiis*, among many other Ciceronian writings, are unambiguously clear about this. Reason shows up regularly throughout Aelred's text, often in connection with the concept of "affectus," a key Cistercian term that, while commonly translated as "affection," in most cases is better rendered as "attachment."[44] Aelred distinguishes clearly between attachment and friendship, although they are to a certain extent interrelated. "Affectus" denotes "when someone wins the love of another because of such physical qualities as beauty or strength of eloquence" (where "love" has in the same passage been defined by Aelred as "the source and origin of friendship") (3.2). At its core, unadulterated attachment implies corporeal passion or desire. And yet attachment may also form a legitimate bond between people as a necessary feature of love. According to *De spirituali amicitia*, the critical feature that directs attachment along a proper course is reason. Aelred defines "love" as "an attachment of the rational soul," on the apparent rationale that "attachment without reason is an animal instinct, prone to anything illicit" (1.19, 2.57). On the one hand, "affectus" must not be left to follow its natural inclination toward sensuality. On the other hand, "reason joined to attachment" ensures that "love may be chaste through reason and delightful through attachment," guiding affective attraction away from carnality (3.3, 2.57).

Why would Aelred wish a chaste or spiritual friendship to include a passionate element at all? It is precisely this subjective factor that differentiates friendship from charity, he says. The latter requires perfect love of *all* of our fellows, including those "many who are a burden and a bore to us," whereas friendship involves "joyful, secure, pleasant, and sweet" experiences alone, in sum, "affectus" (2.19). Friendship quite simply rests on attachment expressed within rational bounds, which in turn is understood to be consonant with virtue. Aelred even draws a connection between reason and "affectus" in nonhuman creatures: "Although in all other respects animals are proven to be irrational, surely in this respect alone they so imitate the human spirit that they are almost thought to be *moved by reason*. They so follow the leader, so frolic together, so express and display their attachment in actions, and so enjoy one another's company with eagerness and pleasure that they seem to relish nothing more than what resembles friendship" (1.55, emphasis added). This is an extraordinary statement. Setting aside its anthropomorphism, Aelred not only accepts, but celebrates, that humans and animals share some small semblance of commonality that goes beyond sentience. I have no doubt that Cicero would reject out of hand the idea of animals as quasi-rational beings capable of some measure of friendship, but that is of no matter. Aelred has managed to arrive at this conclusion on the basis of a Ciceronian conception of reason—one not present in De amicitia—as a necessary component of properly constituted spiritual friendship (2.59).

Reason as employed by Aelred leads us to another quandary that regularly received attention among Cicero's early European readership: how does one rank the duties stemming from friendship in relation to the other sorts of duties incumbent upon human beings, such as to parents, kin, country, and humanity? Recall that Cicero did not believe that one could (or should) posit a fixed hierarchical ordering among these; circumstance matters in making any determination about which took precedence. Perhaps strangely, Cicero does not address in detail this concern in De amicitia, since that work seems a natural setting in which to take up the question. He does make it clear that true friends do not ask their fellows to do anything dishonorable, in the case of which the friendship must be terminated

(*De amicitia* 76). By contrast, Aelred is all too happy to engage with the issue. He proposes what I term both "positive" and "negative" dimensions, which, in spite of what my wording might imply, are entirely compatible.

The "positive" answer draws us back to the connection between reason and attachment. In *De amicitia* 75, Cicero asserts that "intemperate good-will" ought not to prevent one from "impeding a friend's great advantage (*magnas utilitates amicorum*)" by an inordinate display of emotion, if such involves his absence, however temporary. The point is that no true friend stands in the way of the legitimate improvement of his comrade's position. Aelred aims Cicero's injunction in a somewhat different direction. What is that "great advantage" of which Cicero speaks? And how might one friend hold back his own wishes for the good of his fellow? "Well-ordered friendship is this," Aelred asserts, "that reason (*ratio*) should so rule attachment (*affectus*) that we attend not to what the sweetness of friends suggests but what the good of the many (*multorum utilitas*) demands" (*De spirituali amicitia* 3.118). Aelred specifies both what such "great advantage" might constitute and how the friend might rein in his impulses. On both counts, the responses are exactly aligned with his conception of the role played by human reason in friendship. The "*utilitas*" in question is not personal interest but instead an overriding contribution to the common welfare. The true friend thinks of the "larger picture" of community when considering his own, potentially selfish affection. Aelred echoes Ciceronian sentiments in *De amicitia* and elsewhere, yet develops them to a greater extent.

Aelred's promotion of public need over private desire is reinforced when he turns to the question of the line to be drawn at which friendship must be severed (the "negative" element). As already noted, *De amicitia* simply refers to one friend demanding a "dishonorable act" from another. Aelred's invocation of the priority of goods external to the relationship between friends offers a great deal more specificity—of the sort that one finds elsewhere in the Ciceronian corpus. Simply put, he forcefully locates friendship beneath a great many other duties. In general, a friendly relationship must be dissolved "if a friend harms those whom you should equally love" (*De spirituali amicitia* 3.46). On the basis of this principle, Aelred stipulates the following conditions: "If a friend forms a plot against his father or his country, one that demands sudden and speedy correction, friendship is not violated if that friend is declared a personal enemy and a public foe.... Love should not outweigh religion, loyalty, love of your fellow citizens, or the safety of the people.... If [a friend] proves to be a menace to his father, his country, his fellow citizens, dependents or friends, you must immediately sever the bond of familiarity and not prefer the love of one person to the love of the many" (3.41, 3.46, 3.58). He hardly offers a ringing endorsement of the primacy of friendship in relation to the other duties a human being must execute. There is never a hint throughout *De spirituali amicitia* of a situation in which friendship might claim precedence over the multiple forms of duty that one owes. Why might this be the case? My own best guess is that "affectus" has no place in any of them. The love that grounds friendship is unique; its very pleasurable character requires that it be set aside when other obligations that also exist by nature call one to act. Implicitly, at least, Aelred recognizes that affection for one's friends must always yield to other natural social demands. The implicit denigration of the "sweetness" of friendship renders the entire project of *De spirituali amicitia* in a certain sense ironic, which Aelred most likely did not realize and would probably deny.

Regardless of the validity of this inference, Aelred transforms basic elements of *De amicitia* in ways that do not merely Christianize the text in a trivial manner but that draw out of it insights that bring it into line with broader contours of Ciceronianism as it was transmitted to the twelfth century. It is not too great a speculation to say that, in the absence of familiarity with other works in Cicero's corpus—*De officiis* at a minimum—*De spirituali amicitia* would have been a very different text. Further investigation of Aelred's likely Ciceronian source(s) in the full body of his writings is called for, but it is tangential to the project at hand. What matters at present is recognition that even when Cicero was expressly received and adapted, there might be other unacknowledged elements of his thought that lurk beneath the surface.

MORALIUM DOGMA PHILOSOPHORUM

Perhaps no twelfth-century text concerning social and political philosophy enjoyed a larger readership, and a greater amount of plundering, in subsequent centuries than the *Moralium*, a collection containing snippets of wisdom derived mainly from Roman philosophers and poets as well as the Church Fathers (on occasion) and scripture (even less frequently). Far too little is known about the inception of the *Moralium*.[45] During the nineteenth and twentieth centuries, considerable debate raged over its authorship. The modern editor of the treatise, John Holmberg, ascribed the *Moralium* to the hand of the philosopher and theologian William of Conches on external evidence,[46] while other scholars found reason to attribute it to Walter of Châtillon, a rough contemporary of William's, who was known as both a theologian and a poet.[47] John Williams concluded that no definitive evidence existed to support either attribution.[48] Indeed, there has been some speculation that neither William nor Walter was the compiler. What is clear, however, is that the *Moralium* received wide attention from later medieval thinkers, especially, but not only, in the thirteenth century. Ninety-eight manuscripts, spread among libraries located throughout Europe, have thus far been identified, several of which are definitely of twelfth-century origin.[49] Its provenance seems to be French, but even the precise region remains a matter of dispute. For a work that exercised such impact, our ignorance about it is truly stunning.

Beyond the fraught question of authorship, the question of its independent value has been posed. Williams admitted that "though not entirely lacking in originality, the work is essentially a compilation of ethical maxims drawn from the *De officiis* of Cicero," as well as "the writings of a considerable number of other Latin authors."[50] More recently, Michael Lapidge concedes that the *Moralium* is "little more than a florilegium, for some seven-eighths of it consists of quotation. The work laid most heavily under contribution is Cicero's *De officiis*."[51] It is true that the author (I will use this term in preference to "compiler," a choice that I think will be justified by what follows) states in his prologue that he intends to present the views primarily of that most eloquent Latin writer Cicero (and secondarily of the "erudite and most elegant" moralist Seneca) (*Moralium*, 5). It is also the case, by Holmberg's count, that Cicero is cited in total 165 times, as contrasted with 92 references to Seneca.[52] Yet a simple numerical computation does not give the *Moralium* its due. It is true that the work contains many direct quotations from Cicero's writings—not only *De officiis* but also *De inventione*. A careful study of the *Moralium*, undertaken on the basis of comparison with the original texts of Cicero, reveals a far more sophisticated manner in which they were deployed. Specifically, four factors must be pointed out. First, the author significantly rearranged the textual order of his main Ciceronian sources so as to frame his own structure for the presentation of his source materials. Second, many of his references to Cicero were in fact paraphrases (most likely of his own creation) rather than direct quotations, a fact that suggests that he wished to render Cicero amenable to his agenda. Third, in other places, he greatly compressed the words of Cicero, again, in my view, to serve his needs. Finally, and most intriguingly, he sometimes moved well beyond the stated views of Cicero, by means both of judicious pruning and of quite striking elaboration on the texts he purportedly follows. Granting that the general structure of the *Moralium* resembles that of *De officiis*, there are nevertheless noteworthy points of divergence between the two texts.

Two significant observations flow from the differences just noted. First, the author regards certain elements of Cicero's thought as irrelevant or untenable. Second, he treats Cicero as an inspiration for ideas that were specific to the author of the *Moralium* himself. The former category, most noticeably, consists of the *Moralium's* disinterest in the key Ciceronian teaching about the linguistic origins of human sociability. Although the author was familiar with *De inventione*, no echo of its doctrine about the primeval orator occurs. Likewise, Cicero's repeated insistence in *De officiis* that reason without speech is of little worth makes no appearance in the *Moralium*. Rather, the sociable nature of humankind is taken as a given. Nor do we find much reference to nature and natural law, as compared with *De officiis*. The occasional nods to the Ciceronian position regarding the regulative status of nature in regard to moral matters seem tangential to the interests of the author.

In light of the absence of interest in these two key elements of Cicero's thought, the *Moralium* bypasses the opening sections of *De officiis*, which involved the human capacity of language conjoined with the employment of natural reason. The text instead commences with Cicero's definitions of the four cardinal virtues of wisdom, justice, temperance, and courage, as well as their various subdivisions. Judged in purely quantitative terms, the author devotes three pages (in the critical edition) to wisdom, ten to courage, and eleven to temperance, whereas justice (and its correlate, injustice) receives seventeen pages of attention. While, as I suggested above, firm conclusions ought not to be drawn from computation alone, these numbers suggest the extent to which the *Moralium* focuses on justice as the key moral duty required of the honorable man. This highlighting of justice was as central to the argument of *De officiis* as to the *Moralium*. As with Cicero, the author of the *Moralium* compared justice favorably to the other virtues, on the grounds that wisdom is passive and thus inferior to action, whereas temperance and courage involve only a limited range of duties, namely, toward oneself and one's familiars. Justice, by contrast, takes as its field of activity the entirety of human social relations, because it encompasses fellow feeling toward the complete range of those who are owed duties, including the gods, our country, our parents, our friends, and human society in general (53, 27).[53] Although the *Moralium* compresses Cicero's argument in this regard, it provides a clear summary of the reasons for the superiority of justice enunciated in *De officiis* (*Moralium*, 52–53).

What is justice for the author of the *Moralium*? It is noteworthy that he does not follow precisely the definitions of justice found in either *De officiis* (1.15 and 1.20) or *De inventione* (2.160), with which he would have been familiar. Rather, he adopts the standard generic Roman law maxim that "justice is the virtue bestowing upon each his right" (*Moralium*, 7). How might one explain this divergence from Cicero? I conjecture that it has something to do with the fact that the definitions of justice given in both of Cicero's treatises are grounded in an appeal to natural reason, speech, and natural law, the exact topics that the author of the *Moralium* seeks to avoid, as noted previously.[54] Thus the *Moralium* does not endorse a purely Ciceronian rationale for the connection between the duties entailed by the virtue of justice and the existence and sustenance of the bonds of human society. Rather, its author circumvents the central elements of Ciceronian naturalism by introducing an alternative version of the significance of justice. "Justice," he says, "is the virtue that unites human society and communal life." He proceeds: "Society, that is, the cohabitation (*cohabitationem*) of humans, thus requires justice; when humans cohabitate, the individual acquires fields and other kinds of possessions that others lack. For that reason, jealousy and dissension occurs, unless justice intervenes, which bestows on each his rights. The life of the community—that is, its business (*negotia*)—is thus guarded; by means of these ways of living, such as commerce and combat, many are secured, which would otherwise diminish the advantage of individuals; this would otherwise cause their envy, unless justice intervenes" (12). Holmberg, the modern editor of the *Moralium*, offers no source for this remarkable passage; neither can I locate one. Certainly, the term "cohabitation" is not to be found in relevant portions of Cicero's writings, so far as I have been able to determine.[55] The *Moralium* then immediately returns to a recounting of *De officiis*'s explication of the relation between justice and private property (12–13). But here, too, a revision occurs. The *Moralium* quotes Cicero's remark that the appropriation of private goods runs counter to the "laws (*ius*) of human society," but the author adds, "and from this every sort of sedition, which results from the transferring of my property to your use" (13). This is not particularly surprising, given the author's apparent postulation of a material/economic system of social order as the basis of justice. The function of justice, so it appears, is to ensure the good of all by protecting the well-being of each part of the community that contributes to the welfare of the whole.

Does this mean that the author of the *Moralium* evinces no interest whatsoever in Ciceronian references to nature as the foundation of human social relations? By no means. But he employs an approach different from elements of Cicero's naturalism previously discussed. While ignoring *ius naturale* and its related concepts, the *Moralium* posits that the communal order may be analogized to the structure of the human body. Reworking Cicero, the *Moralium* says that it is a duty of justice "to exterminate from the human community a pestilent group of men" (13). It then follows Cicero in advocating the amputation of members of the body when they endanger the well-being of the whole, this being the case both with human beings and with communal life. What is significant is the context in which each author employs the metaphor. In *De officiis*, Cicero is discussing the legitimacy of killing tyrants. By contrast, the author of the *Moralium* introduces the organic analogy in order to make the point that justice, because it demands the protection of social bonds, entails the extermination of those who violate the valid property rights of their fellows.

This is not, I think, an insignificant revision. Indeed, it is reinforced by the other passage in which the *Moralium* uses the body metaphor in a manner much closer to Cicero's own position, namely, concerning the supposed profit to be gained from the loss of another person.[56] Specifically, seeking one's personal advantage at the expense of others "is fatal to human fellowship (*convictum*)" (69). To be disposed to "despoil or violate the goods of another" means that "those bonds of human society that are according to nature must necessarily be broken" (69). This lesson is derived from the analogy to the proper ordering of the body: "If each of our bodily members imagined that it could live off the health of its neighboring member, the whole body would debilitate and die; so it is in human society" (69–70). The balance required by justice in order to sustain the life of the community, while admittedly acknowledging the self-interest appropriate to everyone, still demands that no one may properly aggrandize himself at the expense of another. The *Moralium* then knits together, rearranges, and compresses a number of different passages of *De officiis* in support of the claim that theft is incompatible with nature. To steal from one's fellow human beings is not merely dishonorable, but it also destroys the bonds of human society necessary for our safety and security.[57] This view is entirely consistent with the repurposing of the Ciceronian conception of justice found in the *Moralium*.

A final dimension of the *Moralium*'s adaptation of Cicero's standard of just conduct occurs at the close of the treatise. Whereas Cicero ends *De officiis* with the condemnation of pleasure associated with Epicureanism, the author of the *Moralium* concludes with a call to pay close attention to the activities of others as well as ourselves. The prescriptions contained in the book, in other words, are not merely theoretical constructs but are guides to living honorably. The final paragraph of the *Moralium* directly quotes from *De officiis* 1.60 about the centrality of both practice and experience as essential to the discharge of one's duties. In the mind of the author, Cicero clearly represents the pinnacle of the project he envisioned in producing the *Moralium*, namely, offering lessons that his reader may apply to his own life. In turn, this emphasis on practical morality may help explain why the *Moralium* largely steers clear of Ciceronian rationalism and its concomitant doctrine of natural law. The foregrounding of reason might readily be interpreted as a diminution of the importance of how we live our lives as contrasted with the intellectual underpinnings of morality. I readily admit the highly speculative character of this observation, but I do not think it implausible. Other thinkers for whom Cicero's ideas were crucial also prioritized the active life as a key feature of Ciceronian teachings.

CONCLUSION

Readers unfamiliar with the extent to which Cicero's works were widely available and appropriated during the Middle Ages may be astonished by their ubiquity in twelfth-century writings. As should be evident, different aspects of Ciceronian social and political philosophy were emphasized and others downplayed, depending on the needs of specific thinkers who received and adapted it. Strictly speaking, none of these later thinkers may be counted as systematic theorists of society and politics in the manner

of John of Salisbury, who will be discussed in the next chapter. Yet typical Ciceronian themes, such as his account of the origins of community,
his theories of natural law and justice, and his valorization of the virtues
associated with friendship and participation in political affairs, appear
recurrently throughout numerous genres of twelfth-century writing that
we have surveyed. Each of these cases suggests (contra the critics of the
Haskins thesis mentioned in the introduction to this chapter) an extensive
appreciation of Cicero's valued status as a social and political philosopher
in the 1100s. The sheer diversity of the uses to which Cicero's ideas were put
consequently illustrates the larger point that it is unwarranted to speak of
a unified and monolithic "Ciceronian tradition" to which twelfth-century
texts constituted "contributions." Taken together, these works offer an especially compelling illustration of why classical reception studies affords a
superior method for the examination of Ciceronianism in early Europe.

CHAPTER 3

John of Salisbury

Self-Proclaimed Ciceronian

It would be impossible to narrate the story of the early European reception of Cicero without discussing the contribution of the mid-twelfth-century English philosopher and churchman John of Salisbury. John was something of a polymath. He authored a major work of social and political thought, the *Policraticus*, as well as a shorter treatise containing important discussions of pedagogy and speculative philosophy, entitled the *Metalogicon*, and a long satirical and didactic poem about philosophers and courtiers called the *Entheticus de dogmate philosophorum*. These works all date from the period between 1154 and 1159, although they may have had origins in John's school days in Paris between 1135 and 1147. In addition to these writings, John composed works of history and hagiography and two substantial collections of correspondence. All the while, he was also deeply engaged in the ecclesio-political affairs of his time—in particular, in the service of successive archbishops of Canterbury between 1148 and 1170.[1]

The core of John's thought has often been described as "humanistic" in orientation,[2] since he valorized human dignity and the concomitant dignity of nature: knowledge of both may be accessed by human beings through the application of reason. Yet at the same time, no person possesses such abundant intelligence as to know the truth in all its dimensions. John recognized that impediments exist that constrain the attainment of full wisdom by human beings. In support of this position, John explicitly professed to follow the moderately skeptical methodology laid out by Cicero and the New Academy.[3] Thus, in the prologue to the *Metalogicon*, he proclaims himself to be "an Academic in matters which to the wise man are doubtful," which for him means "I do not swear that what I say is true but, be it true or false, I remain content with probability alone" (122).[4] Quoting Cicero's

Tusculanarum disputationum and *De officiis*, he praises the principle of probability and rejects the "dialecticians" who propose to have attained certain knowledge (*Metalogicon*, 206–7). In the *Policraticus*,[5] likewise, John observes that "Cicero himself witnesses that he was transformed into one of those who is in doubt about each matter about which wise men may pose questions" (76; Nederman 152). Indeed, he dedicates several chapters to demonstrating "why the Academic School is preferable to others for imitation," namely, because "in the examination of truth each person reserves to himself freedom of judgment and the authority of writers is to be considered useless when it is subdued by a better argument" (7.prologue; Nederman 148). Referring to one of his favorite themes of *modestia* or *moderatio*,[6] John contends that the Academy alone evades what he terms "the precipice of falsehood" occasioned by rash assertions of certitude (7.10; Nederman 149). Academic teachings coincided quite closely with the broader tenor of his intellectual sensibilities.

Beyond his devotion to the Ciceronian New Academy, John adopts for his own purposes other of Cicero's views, such as the utter condemnation of Epicureanism as a philosophical system.[7] Moreover, John's Latin prose has rightfully been praised for its fidelity to the sophisticated and fluid use of language characteristic of Cicero's own style.[8] But no element of John's work so thoroughly reflects the spirit as well as the substance of Ciceronian thought as his insistence upon the practicality of philosophy. Like Cicero, John did not embrace the traditional doctrine that contemplation is inherently superior to and more praiseworthy than action. Quite to the contrary, he adopts the position that the entire point of philosophical inquiry is to provide guidance in the conduct of one's affairs. John's principles of philosophical inquiry should thus be viewed in the context of his broadly humanistic project: the identification of the features conducive to human fulfillment. The *Metalogicon* is meant to be a practical guidebook to such contentment through a morally guided quest for knowledge, a goal that John regards as of far greater worth and far more befitting the philosopher than the technical pursuits too commonly found in the schools. Similarly, in proposing the political ideas of the *Policraticus*, he sought above all to illustrate the principle that philosophy provides invaluable aid in achieving the good life of both the individual and the entire community.

It consequently seems quite peculiar—if not somewhat perverse— to remark, as Rodney Thomson did in his 1987 book on William of

Malmesbury, that "William was the greatest Ciceronian of the twelfth century.... The stocks of John of Salisbury, his main rival in this sphere, continue to fall."[9] William may have been familiar with the greatest number of texts composed by Cicero during the 1100s, as discussed previously, but his own writings reveal relatively little dedication to the overarching and distinctive Ciceronian way of thinking.[10] I do not mean to suggest that John's Ciceronian proclivities rendered him an unalloyed adherent to every feature of Cicero's doctrines. As in the case of all of the figures and texts examined in this book, some elements of Ciceronian thought are brought to the forefront by John and are adapted to his intellectual needs, especially in a Christian context; others are pushed into the background when they do not suit John's purposes. The present chapter will highlight several Ciceronian concepts that were especially relevant and useful to John's own intellectual project. These include Cicero's account of the genesis and evolution of civilized humanity; his naturalistic model of justice and political order; his attack on tyrannical government; the necessity of the worship of God on account, among other reasons, of His gift to humankind of a rational soul; and his theory of friendship and its practice. Each of these features of Ciceronian thought appropriated by John is, quite naturally, translated and transposed into a Christian framework. For all of his pronouncements of devotion to Cicero, John could never have embraced "pure" Ciceronianism.

ORIGINS OF SOCIETY

A fundamental issue addressed by John of Salisbury is the role played by nature in the foundations of social and political order. This concern is evident across the range of John's works. That he adopts such a naturalistic framework in the *Policraticus* might seem sensible, but it appears also as a crucial feature of the *Metalogicon*. This is so because John develops there a key Ciceronian theme, namely, that humans are transformed from animalistic primordial beings into civic creatures as a consequence of the realization of the inhering human capacities of reason and language. Thus education forms a highly relevant element of his naturalism. Why did John appeal to a Ciceronian conception of the natural foundations of society in the *Metalogicon*? The answer lies with the large sections of the text in which he seeks to refute the doctrine, ascribed to the (likely fictional) character "Cornificius" and his followers, that the qualities and powers with which men are born constitute the limit of their knowledge and faculties.[11] This implies that human beings, endowed with fixed natures, ought not to seek to improve their lot or condition on earth, ought not to develop their minds and skills. Instead, they may only find redemption directly in the grace of God, shunning the material world and their own natures completely (*Metalogicon*, 141–42). In opposition to "Cornificius," John argues that the mundane and sinful character of human nature does not end the debate. Rather, God through nature has granted to mankind the capacity to improve its lot on earth by diligent application of the native faculties of reason and speech. Men may accomplish much by nature alone, contrary to the Cornifician teaching that no attempt can (or perhaps should) be made to develop the characteristics associated with their postlapsarian state (125–26).

A major pillar supporting John's case against the lessons of "Cornificius" is an adapted version of Cicero's depiction of the primitive development of human association. John deploys his Ciceronian source in order to demonstrate that social interaction among men is an important wellspring of true (albeit partial, because merely mortal) happiness or blessedness (*beatitudo*). The *Metalogicon* regards nature, "the most benign parent and governor of all things in order most due," to be imprinted with a divine plan (124). Thus, if nature has granted to man alone the powers of speech and reason, this is so he above all other creatures may "gain blessedness" (125). Such a plan is evident, in the first place, from the observation and investigation by reason of the structure of the universe: "The one and true God, in order to bind the parts of the universe in a firm alliance and to keep charity alive, ordered them in such a way that one thing needed the help of another, and one made good the deficiency of another, every single one being as it were a member of every other one. All things if separated from one another are thus only half complete, but are made perfect when allied to others, since all things are held together by mutual support" (125). This theme of reciprocity runs throughout John's corpus; it is employed in his correspondence and forms the basis for his organic metaphor for the polity, addressed below. But, in the *Metalogicon*, the model of the mutual intercommunication of members is seen to indicate the natural course that ought to guide human behavior. "It is not possible even to imagine a kind of blessedness which knows nothing of communion or exists outside society," John declares, since reason's knowledge of the world dictates that this is the essence of nature as designed by the divine will (125). Therefore, whosoever wishes to achieve supreme happiness is well advised to seek earthly happiness in accordance with nature—that is, in association with his fellow human beings. To imperil society by assailing man's capacity to improve his rational powers—an accusation that John levels against "Cornificius"—is thus to cut him off from the happiness that God has allotted to him in the present life, as well as to exclude the possibility of fulfilling the terms of divinely bestowed grace.

John's view, in effect, is that rational human nature demands of man a level of sociability unparalleled in the rest of nature. In Ciceronian fashion, however, the *Metalogicon* argues that reason's discovery of the naturalness of association is insufficient per se. The rational faculty is individual and personal in its impact, so that, left to itself, it could never actually generate the community that it knows to be natural to and beneficial for human existence. Rather, reason must be made manifest by speech (and eloquent speech at that) if the sociability implicit within human nature is to be widely awakened and invigorated (126). Such enlightened eloquence "gave birth to so many glorious cities, brought together and made allies of so many kingdoms, and united and bound so many peoples in the bonds of charity, that whoever strives to put asunder what God has joined together for the common benefit of all would rightly be accounted the common enemy of all" (126). Speech is the mechanism by which mute wisdom translates its insights into public proclamations and persuades men to follow their natural inclination by surrendering their private interests in favor of the common good. Should human beings be deprived of this faculty of discourse, even if they retain their rational abilities, they "will become brute beasts, and cities will seem like farmyards rather than gatherings of human beings in the bonds of society so that by taking their share of responsibility and paying back friendship with friendship they may live according to the same principles of justice" (126–27). John's vision of society is thus comparable to Cicero's in its quasi-voluntary quality. Human association is not simply a matter of several persons living in close geographic proximity; it is an agreement to share a common life in faith, morals, economic transactions, and all the other features that compose a community. Speech alone renders such an explicit agreement possible, and it must be an eloquent use of language indeed that can convince basically selfish men that by nature they prefer the common good to personal welfare.

By means of these Ciceronian arguments, John believes that he has exposed the real significance of the Cornifician position. It is evident to him that "Cornificius" is an opponent of "all cities simultaneously and the whole of civil life," since by claiming that men should not develop their capacities for reason and speech, any opportunity for man to associate is in the process denied (127). While the price paid by man for original sin was high, it did not extend to the eradication of any communal proclivity whatsoever in his nature. Indeed, for human beings to be rendered utterly incapable of association, it would have been necessary to mute them and strip them of their reason, which did not occur as a result of the Fall. The Cornifician error is to interpret the fixity of postlapsarian human nature as a permanent condition; if this were correct, society could never have been formed originally, let alone maintained. John recognizes that conscious effort is required on the part of men if they are to join together in a communal life. Human nature is incapable of impelling them to congregate apart from the diligent application of rational inquiry combined with eloquent persuasion. Without this activity on behalf of social unity, the sinful and egoistic side of man will prevail, and no common civil relations and institutions can emerge. The *Metalogicon*'s understanding of the genesis of society is thereby profoundly indebted to Cicero's notion that nature's endowment is only a point of departure, one that men must develop and shape if they are truly to live in accordance with their own natural inclinations.

John's commitment to naturalism is reinforced in the *Policraticus*, in which he repeatedly asserts that "nature is the best guide to living."[12] The *Policraticus* follows the teaching in the *Metalogicon* that nature provides the foundation for human capabilities, but that they are only potentialities that must be realized and completed by the activity of men. "The beginning of each thing is from nature," he observes, but people must develop their natural capacities by means of practice until they master their art, a principle that "obtains in liberal and mechanical occupations" alike (*Policraticus* 6.19; Nederman 125). Nature provides a baseline, an opportunity, upon which human beings may (and should) build in order to improve their own conditions. The operations of nature offer a model for human conduct and association. "The civil life should imitate nature," John insists. "Otherwise, life is duly called not merely uncivil, but rather bestial and brute." He admits that other "creatures devoid of reason," such as bees, may be gregarious (6.21; Nederman 127). But inasmuch as "man is superior to other animals in that he exercises reason and understanding," the natural scheme for living well may only be realized with cooperation among the people who partake in it, based on their rational faculties (7.2; Nederman 150). Living together in an organized society requires men to put their natural inclinations to work.

THE BODY POLITIC AND JUSTICE

Without doubt the most obvious indication of John's naturalistic orientation is his extensive analogy between the human organism and social and political order, in other words, the body politic. The deployment of this metaphor, which takes up about a quarter of the total length of the *Policraticus*, has been widely and properly celebrated as a watershed contribution to the tradition of thought that models political organization along organic lines.[13] In particular, the version of the organic metaphor articulated in the *Policraticus* is unprecedented in detail and scope. There has been some debate regarding the source of John's inspiration for his organic naturalism. John himself ascribes the analogy to a letter of instruction purportedly written by Plutarch to Emperor Trajan, which has long been recognized as a forgery; more recently, scholars have concluded that John himself created it.[14] As to the actual stimulus for John's use of the metaphor, scholarship has pointed to Livy, scripture (most notably, 1 Corinthians 12) and the Fathers, Seneca, Roman law, and medieval neo-Platonism.[15] Given the character of the naturalism found in the *Policraticus*, however, the most plausible source is Cicero, who, as seen previously, employed the organic analogy in order to connect the maintenance of bodily health to social and political order.

While John moves far beyond the relatively schematic description of the body proffered by Cicero, it is noteworthy that he retains many elements of the terminology associated with the Roman system of government.[16] John begins with the observation that the commonwealth (*res publica*) may be likened to a "body which is animated by the grant of divine reward and which is driven by the command of the highest equity and ruled by a sort of rational management" (5.2; Nederman 66). He then proposes that the differentiation of the offices (*officia*) of political society may be represented in a manner similar to the distinction of the parts of the human anatomy. Like all bodies, the properly arranged political system is animated by a soul, which guides its activities. John asserts that the place of the soul belongs to "those who are the prefects of religion" (5.2; Nederman 67). As shall be discussed below, no political body may subsist without the clerical function. Yet the clerical soul of the polity is not, strictly speaking, a "member of the commonwealth," just as the eternal soul of man is not coextensive with the mortal physical organism that it directs. From this perspective, the political creature is an essentially temporal entity, ruled by the prince, who "holds the place of the head" and who "rightly deserves to be preferred before others." At the heart of the commonwealth lies the senate, composed of the counselors whose wisdom the ruler consults. The senses correspond to the governors of the provinces (presumably the equivalent of English sheriffs and bailiffs) who exercise jurisdiction in the king's name. The financial officers constitute the stomach and intestines of the body, while the two hands are analogized to the tax collector and the soldier, respectively. Finally, John compares the feet to the artisans and peasants "who raise, sustain and move forward the weight of the entire body" (5.2; Nederman 67). Each of these parts of the organism, according to the *Policraticus*, has its own specific functions and tasks that are fixed by its location within the overall scheme of the body.

One should not suppose that the point of John's organic depiction of the community was merely to justify hierarchy and division within society. To the contrary, the body politic is invoked in the *Policraticus* as the expression of a principle of cooperative harmony through which otherwise disparate individuals and interests are reconciled and bound together. In the *Metalogicon*, John recurrently stresses "reciprocity" as the salient characteristic of natural and social systems. In the case of the *Policraticus*, John insists that "there can be no faithful and firm cohesion where there is not an enduring union of wills and as it were a cementing together of souls. If this is lacking, it is in vain that the works of men are in harmony, since hollow pretence will develop into open injury, unless the real spirit of helpfulness is present" (5.7; Nederman 77). All the parts of the body, in other words, must be truly dedicated to a shared welfare that supersedes the aggregate private goods within the polity. The ruler and magistrates are advised to attend "to the common utility of all" (6.24; Nederman 136), the lesser parts are counseled "in all things to observe constant reference to the public unity" (6.20; Nederman 126), and in general "all the members" are expected to "provide watchfully for the common advantage of all" (6.24; Nederman 135). John praises ancient Carthage for promoting a spirit of cooperation in which "all labored together in common, and none idled" (6.22; Nederman 130). He claims that the life of the body politic can only be established and maintained by means of a joint commitment to a public good that benefits every part without distinction, so that "each and all are as it were members of one another by a sort of reciprocity, and each regards his own interest as best served by that which he knows to be most advantageous for the others" (6.20; Nederman 126). John's political body is one in which, beyond all social differentiation, "mutual charity would reign everywhere" (6.29; Nederman 142), because all wills are attuned to the same precept of an enduring common purpose that encompasses the true interests of the whole. Unity follows from cooperation, and cooperation stems from the existence of a good shared by the entire community and each of its members. This theme contains echoes of Cicero's idea of the fundamental unity of humanity.

A question remains, however, about what constitutes the substance of the common good of the body politic. How is the public welfare to be realized? In the physical organism, the joint purpose is achieved by the maintenance of the health of the whole body. Analogously, John contends that the "health" of the body politic, the public welfare, is coextensive with the dissemination of justice throughout the organs and members. John's definition of the common good in terms of justice is simultaneously embedded in a recognition of a correlative obligation on the part of all members of the commonwealth: "So long as the duties (*officia*) of each individual are performed with an eye to the advantage of the whole, as long, that is, as justice is practiced, the sweetness of honey pervades the allotted sphere of all" (6.22; Nederman 131). This begins John's move into overtly Ciceronian territory. Every organ of the body must conduct itself according to the dictates of justice if the polity is to exist as a corporate unity. All other public goods flow from the presence of justice in the corporate totality.

The reason why John makes justice the touchstone of the political organism's common good has much to do with the very manner in which he defines justice. Following Cicero's formulation in *De officiis* 1.23, the *Policraticus* asserts, "It is agreed that justice consists chiefly of not doing harm and of prohibiting out of duty to humanity those who seek to do harm. When you do harm, you assent to injury. And when you do not impede those who seek to do harm, you then serve injustice" (4.12; Nederman 62). The essence of justice pertains to a responsibility toward others; this duty is not simply constituted by a negative obligation to refrain from the commission of injury, but entails a positive duty to protect others from harm as well. To behave in accordance with justice requires one both to ensure that one's own acts do not threaten the good of others and to attend to the injurious actions that other people may commit. Justice is thus inherently productive of social cooperation, whereas injustice necessarily tends toward human disharmony and social disintegration. Since the exercise of justice is the salient characteristic of a polity oriented toward the common good, justice must determine the manner in which each of the members of the body politic performs its assigned functions. This includes not only the king, whom John regards as the chief purveyor of justice (4.2; Nederman 30–31), but also the other offices within the political organism, which also play a significant role in the actualization and maintenance of a just polity. Magistrates, judges, counselors, soldiers—even farmers and artisans—are ultimately charged with guarding and protecting the common good and acting in a just manner so as to promote the well-being of his fellow human beings.[17]

TYRANNY AND TYRANNICIDE

It may be recalled that Cicero's most overtly political use of organic imagery occurs in the passage of *De officiis* in which he analyzes the predicament of the tyrant and defends the legitimacy of tyrannicide. John of Salisbury in many ways recapitulates the connection Cicero draws between the health of the (political) body and the defense against tyranny. John contends that cooperation between the parts of the body is achieved through the disposition of each member toward the practice of justice in the whole, so that the organs and limbs have an obligation to resist the disease of injustice when it threatens to infect the organism. John thereby argues that the tyrant—the foe of that justice constitutive of the health and good order of the political organism—is to be opposed directly by those other parts of the body that share responsibility for the advancement of justice. In turn, to decline to enforce justice against the tyrannical ruler is to implicate oneself in the commission of tyranny. This leads John to assert that the tyrant is rightfully to be slain; his justification of tyrannicide may be regarded as a direct consequence of his approach to the body politic. No one who is not himself beyond the bounds of virtue can properly decline responsibility for opposing the rule of the tyrant, by violent means if necessary.

The first intimation of a link between John's discussion of tyrannicide and his conception of the body politic appears in book 3 of the *Policraticus*. John's reference to the doctrine of tyrannicide occurs there within the context of his treatment of flattery. This may seem an odd place to assert the legitimacy of slaying the tyrant. John's immediate purpose in invoking the idea is to demonstrate that while flattery is ordinarily evil, it is not always so. John reasons that so long as some measure of justice is present at court, the good man has a duty to speak frankly and openly to the ruler, and even to criticize those royal actions that he regards as opposed to moral rectitude and orthodox faith. To flatter the king, rather than to counsel him honestly, is to place private gain before public welfare. John believes the reverse to be true in the case of the tyrant. To flatter a tyrant is to protect oneself and one's community from the wrath and vengefulness that might guide the tyrannical ruler's reaction to honest advice. If by flattery and dissimulation one may turn a tyrant away from an evil policy, or at least mitigate the effects of such evil, then one has a clear obligation to do so. After all, John regarded the tyrant to be evil incarnate, the *imago pravitatis*, to whom no respect or subservience is owed (8.17; Nederman 190–91). Hence, for the sake of the whole polity, one should employ those means to which one has access, including flattery, in order to deflect the debilitating and sinful consequences of tyrannical rule.[18]

As part of his "proof" for the validity of this claim, John cites tyrannicide. His argument is deceptively simple: "In the secular literature [that is, Cicero] there is a caution that one must live differently with a tyrant than with a friend. It is not lawful to flatter a friend, but it is permitted to flatter (*mulcare*) the ears of a tyrant. For it is lawful to flatter whomever it is lawful to kill. Furthermore, it is not only lawful but equitable and just to kill a tyrant" (3.15; Nederman 25). (John's thinking about friendship will be addressed below.) This passage is, in reality, a mash-up of two apparently unrelated Ciceronian teachings: one, derived from *De amiticia* 89, that flattery is unbecoming a virtuous man, except when a tyrant is involved, in which case flattering him is justifiable; the other, found in *De officiis* 3.32, that robbing a tyrant does not violate nature because it is morally right to kill a tyrant. John weaves these two together into a syllogism in which the principle of the propriety of tyrannicide is the minor premise (the major premise is that whoever may be slain may be flattered).[19] The conclusion of the syllogism is that one may flatter a tyrant—precisely what we might expect in the context of the section about flattery in which the argument appears. Note that, in this passage, tyrannicide is merely assumed for the sake of justifying the use of flattery upon the tyrant.

But we ought not to neglect the fact that John does attempt to give some foundation to the minor premise of his syllogism in the same chapter of book 3. He further explains that the tyrant whom one may flatter is the usurper, the servant not of God but of his own will (*Policraticus* 3.15; Nederman 25). At this point, John's Christian orientation comes into play. To be a usurper, in this sense, is not merely to ascend to the throne by illegitimate means; it is rather to exercise power in accordance with arbitrary will and caprice. This reflects John's emphasis, throughout the *Policraticus*, on the significance of the moral will of the tyrant (8.17; Nederman 191–92). Inasmuch as the tyrant is defined by his characteristic viciousness, he necessarily misuses whatever power he employs, since all authority is from God and is therefore good. In consequence, "respect for the right and the just is either not sufficiently present or else wholly wanting from the face of tyrants" (8.17; Nederman 191). The question thus arises: how might it be possible to impose justice upon the vicious ruler, whose very office requires him to proclaim and execute just judgment?

John evinces a clear awareness of the dimensions of this problem in the passage under discussion. He suggests that we might fruitfully reconceptualize tyranny on the order of the "crime of *majesté*," that is, treasonous behavior against a superior. Under the law pertaining to it, John remarks, "It is permissible for all to prosecute those charged with the crime of *majesté*" (3.15; Nederman 25). In stating this, John merely repeats the customary legal precept that anyone (even a woman or a serf) may lay and testify to the charge of treason (6.25; Nederman 137–39). But John imparts to this concept new force by adding the proviso that tyranny itself ought to be understood as the ultimate form of treason, a crime against the very body of justice (*corpus iustitiae*). When viewed from this perspective, John argues, "not only do tyrants commit a crime against the public, but, if it is possible, more than the public," by which he presumably means God. In other words, since justice is ultimately a divinely endowed or inspired gift to a political community (4.1; Nederman 28–29), to offend against justice itself (the crime of the tyrant) is an affront to God's will as well as an assault on the body politic. This imputes to everyone concerned with the performance of justice the authority to act against, to prosecute, the tyrant by the appropriate means. Fear of retribution cannot excuse hesitation: "Truly there will be no one to avenge a public enemy," since the tyrant is the friend of none, nor does he enjoy any just claim upon loyalty. In short, the tyrant must be opposed by all who can do so. Indeed, John describes the eradication of the tyrant in terms of a duty: "Whoever does not prosecute [the tyrant] sins against himself and against the whole body of the secular republic (*in totum rei publicae mundanae corpus*)" (3.15; Nederman 25). So he does not regard tyrannicide as a matter of choice for the individual; it is instead an obligation that is incumbent upon every member of the community. By referring to the corporate "body" of the republic, and by associating it with the *corpus iustitiae*, John alludes to the later books of the *Policraticus* wherein he presents the organic metaphor. The implication is clear: to understand why every person in the polity is obliged to oppose the tyrant, even to the point of slaying the oppressor, demands that we turn our attention to the organic conception of the secular community, just as in Cicero's view.

All of this leads to the more famous statements concerning tyranny and tyrannicide contained within seven chapters, the complexity of which is beyond the scope of the present inquiry.[20] Briefly stated, John acknowledges the centrality of God as the ultimate source of the punishment of tyrannous rule. Tyrants may be slain in battle, or be struck down by natural disaster, or even die at an old age in bed—but every tyrant can expect punishment of the most horrific sort administered in the afterlife (8.21; Nederman 210–11). John regards the killing of a tyrant by one of his subjects to number among several possible fates that may accord with the plan of God's justice. In turn, John intends for his audience to draw a connection between the organic metaphor and his theologically informed treatment of the bad ends of tyrants. At the beginning of his discussion of tyranny in book 8, he refers the reader to his previous survey of "the duties of the prince and of the different members of the commonwealth." Review of that passage, John contends, renders it "easier to make known here, and in fewer words, the opposite characteristics of the tyrant" (8.17; Nederman 190). John envisages the characteristics of the polity ruled by the tyrant to be the reverse of the qualities of the well-ordered body politic. Thus despite his introduction of a Christian-inflected justification of tyrannicide, he does not entirely reject or overlook the more naturalistic arguments in the *Policraticus* that rest upon demonstrably Ciceronian foundations.

RELIGION AND THE BODY POLITIC

Another signal feature of John's social and political thought pertains to the role played by religion in the maintenance of social and political order modeled on the physiology of the human body. As mentioned earlier, he analogizes the soul to the clergy, on the apparent grounds that the function of religion is qualitatively distinct from those duties that pertain to the members of the temporal body politic. It may also be recalled that John claims as his authority a non-Christian text, the "Instruction of Trajan," which was of his own invention. Such overt anachronism might seem merely quaint, until we consider that for John religion plays a central part in his organic scheme. "Plutarch" ascribes the quickening of the political body to supernatural inspiration, with the consequence that the priesthood enjoys a special position within the organism: "Those things which institute and mold the practice of religion in us and which transmit the worship of God (here I do not follow Plutarch, who says 'of the Gods') acquire the position of the soul in the body of the republic" (5.2; Nederman 66–67). Metaphorically, no body (earthly community) can exist without the animation provided by the soul (priesthood or church), and thus the governor of the natural organism must be guided by its supernatural superior.[21]

Since this lesson is derived from a supposedly pagan authority, John clearly means it to be applied universally: religion is a civil necessity for *any* well-ordered political entity. Just as a soulless body is inert, so a community lacking due worship of divinity is unsustainable and dead. This is as valid for a non-Christian republic as for one that embraces the true faith. Indeed, John purports to struggle with the adaptation of the pagan ideas of "Plutarch" to a Christian polity. At one point, John remarks, "Because much that he ['Plutarch'] has to say concerning ceremonies and the worship of the gods, wherein he taught that a religious prince should be deeply indoctrinated, is treated from the standpoint of superstition, I shall omit the things that pertain to the cult of idolatry" (5.2; Nederman 67–68). Elsewhere, he worries that his reliance on the letter to Trajan "might in part even reflect on the sincerity of my own faith. However, since the holy fathers and the laws of princes seem to follow along the same track, let me touch on his doctrine briefly and in catholic language, adding a part of his stratagems. His point of departure is from reverence for supernatural beings; ours is from God, who is to be loved by all men alike and worshipped with all their heart" (5.3; Nederman 68).[22] There is, in effect, a parallelism or congruence between the views of the pagans about the necessity of religion in the social and political life of human beings and the position adopted by Christian thinkers and texts, a congruence that licenses John's use of "Plutarch" as an authority.

In this vein, John lauds the accomplishments of Numa Pompilius, who "introduced among the Romans certain ceremonies and sacrifices, to the end that under the pretense of immortal gods he might easily induce them to cultivate piety, religion, good faith and the other things which he wished to make known to them" (5.3; Dickinson 68). Perhaps surprisingly for a Christian, John seems largely untroubled by the falsity of Roman religion, given its efficacy in instilling a sense of civic harmony within the populace. He acknowledges that Numa's overt intention was "to curb the barbarism of the people, restrain them from wrong-doing, and cause them to keep a holiday from arms, cultivate justice, and steadily train themselves in civic affection toward one another, and he did in fact so succeed in taming that fierce people that the empire which they had seized, as it is said, by violence and wrong, they governed happily by the laws of justice and piety (5.3; Dickinson 69). This passage appears to confirm strongly the hypothesis that John's political theory rests heavily on a conception of religion, regardless of its truth, as useful to the promotion of those qualities conducive to civil order, as some scholars have recently observed.[23] Infidels no less than believers in the true faith benefit in political affairs from the adoption of religious ceremonies and sacrifices that induce them to cooperate in a just scheme of association.

This is not simply a utilitarian position, however, but rather a metaphysical one. Cicero had maintained that belief in the divine was a universal feature of humanity and that the deities conferred reason upon human beings, which in turn constituted the source of the inclination toward goodness. For John, likewise, life itself, let alone civil life, was impossible in the absence of the soul, which was the seat of reason, itself a gift from God: "All virtue, whether angelic or human, is a vestige of divinity impressed to a certain degree upon rational creatures. The indwelling Holy Sprit imprints sanctity upon the soul, the rivulets of which disperse it to many places" (3.1; Nederman 15). The resonance with Cicero's conception of the gift of a rational soul that the gods conveyed to the human race is difficult to ignore. In turn, this claim lays the foundation for his account of the body politic, and especially of the role played in it by the soul. Human life has a dual composition: a rational soul and corruptible flesh. Of these two qualities, John insists, the soul is primary, inasmuch as corporeal humanity "derives its life from the soul, since from no other source can the body possess it, being always quiescent by virtue of its paralyzing inertia and moving only by virtue of the spiritual element. The soul as well has its own life, for God is its life" (3.1; Nederman 14). In consequence, human nature itself depends upon the grant by God—by means of created nature infused with divine grace—of the rational capacity of the soul to attain knowledge and thus virtue: "The mind, by the life-giving power of the spirit, [must] be illuminated for the acquisition of knowledge and be inspired with the love of honor and zeal for virtue" (3.1; Nederman 15). Humans possess, by the reason with which God endows them, a desire to know and to do the good.

This is the case for all human beings, Christians and unbelievers alike, which explains why even pagans and other infidels are able to obtain knowledge and to act virtuously. All people are ensouled in this way, even if they are unaware of their debt to the one true God:

> As, therefore, it is the nature of the body to be alive and active, to yield to the soul's impulses, and to obey it as by a sort of harmony with it, so the soul derives life from the fact that it possesses activities in its own realm, undoubtedly receives its impulses from God, obeys Him with complete devotion, and acquiesces in all things. In proportion as it fails to respond, it fails to live. The body too falls to the torpor of death in any of its parts that cease to be animated by the soul. As long therefore as the body is alive in all its parts, it is entirely subject to the soul, which is diffused not part to part but exists as a whole and functions in each and every part. (3.1; Nederman 14)

John clearly transfers this conception of the soul's governance over the body, by analogy, to his conception of the role played by the clergy in animating the body politic. The so-called prefects of religion, whether they teach submission to a divine pantheon or to the Christian deity, necessarily form the core of a properly constituted earthly polity. The function of "taming" the wild beasts of primitive humanity by inculcating in them civic affection and justice that John ascribes to Numa Pompilius must be performed by some priesthood if a political community is to subsist. For John of Salisbury as for Cicero, the worship of divinity is constitutive of a cohesive social and political order, in view of the orientation toward virtue that is infused in the soul of every man that directs him to cooperate with his fellows. Public affairs emptied of the clerical soul could not subsist, or even come into existence.

FRIENDSHIP AND FLATTERY

Perhaps there is no aspect of John's thought that reflects his Ciceronian temperament more than his embrace of the human relation of friendship. And as with Cicero, this is true in practice as well as in theory for John. Nowhere in John's writings do we more completely encounter his belief that philosophy is really valuable only when it guides action. This is especially evident when we turn to the third book of the *Policraticus*, the main aim of which, as previously discussed, is to disparage the efforts of flatterers to manipulate their superiors for their own gain. But book 3 also contains repeated and extensive references to friendship and, in particular, to Cicero's treatise on the topic. Why might friendship matter in this context? In John's view, flattery, which predominates among courtly modes of speech, detracts from good government by leading the ruler and his counselors and servants down the path to vice. John says that flattery is always "accompanied by deception and fraud and betrayal and the infamy of lying" (3.5; Pike 165). John's standard of speech consists in free and open debate, sincere in seeking after the honorable and the virtuous course of conduct. In his view, one should "prefer to be criticized by anyone whomsoever rather than be praised by one who ... flatters; for no critic need be feared by the lover of truth" (1.14; Pike 210). Flattery is inimical to the kind of rational discourse oriented toward truth that he believes must accompany any government whose goal is truly to seek the common good and promote justice for the governed. Such a view follows directly from John's conception of language, articulated in the *Metalogicon*, as the indispensable medium through which the welfare and happiness of humanity as a whole are realized by gaining access to truth.

Flattery, by contrast, is antithetical to friendship. Flattery is the courtly form of Cicero's false friendship based on "profit" and "lucrative results": the flatterer seeks his own good without reference to the good of others. John explains that "since men ... love not their friends but themselves in each instance, it is necessary to have the garb of pretense in order to be pleasing" (*Policraticus* 3.7; Pike 170). Such costumes—which John consistently compares to the masks and tricks of actors on the stage[24]—constitute the relationship built on flattery. Real friendship, however, may only flourish "if utility ceases" and "one cherishes friendship on account of its own virtues." John agrees with Cicero that such friendship for its own sake is "rare," commenting (perhaps somewhat hyperbolically) that it occurs among only "three or four pairs of friends" amid "the multitude and variety of persons"—a direct reference to *De amicitia* 15 (3.7; Pike 171). What forms the foundation of friendship? John declares that cultivation of "benevolence toward everyone . . . is the fount of friendship and the first step toward charity" (3.5; Pike 163). Such benevolence is entirely distinct from flattery because it proceeds by "untrammeled honor, observant duty, the path of virtue, the acceptance of service, and the sincerity of words. And it is aided by fidelity, namely, constancy of speech and deed, and by truth, which is the foundation of all duties and goods" (3.5; Pike 163). As to the question of whether "there can be friendship or love among bad men," John sides with Cicero (*De amicitia* 65): "It cannot exist except among good men." Whatever similarities seem to create a harmonious bond among evil men, he insists, are merely faint imitations of the true bond of friendship that arises between persons fully inculcated in virtue (3.12; Pike 192).

We may wonder why, for John, the possession of virtue among friends constitutes the chief characteristic of friendship. In the context of John's immediate concern with courtly flattery, virtue stands in close and irrevocable connection to truth. Since virtue requires knowledge of the good, which is grounded in truth, the bond of friendship must rest on the mutual commitment of friends to seek and respect the truth. As a general precept of his thought, John emphasizes that open and free debate and criticism form a crucial quality of the public spheres of the court (as well as the school). Individuals should be protected in their liberty to engage in conscientious, constructive reproval of the morals of others and to challenge ideas that do not stand up to rational evaluation. Likewise, people should be prepared to listen to and to consider seriously such honest criticism when it is rendered. This quality seems particularly necessary in the case of friendship, which is guided by truthfulness. "If a friend makes a mistake he is to be instructed," John insists. "If he should instruct, he is to be listened to" (*Policraticus* 3.14; Pike 210). "Truth is stern," but the virtuous man wishes to know when he has gone astray, and the true friend provides this knowledge unflinchingly: "Better the chastisement of a friend than the fraudulent kissing-up (*oscula*) of a flatterer" (3.6; Pike 167). It is in this sense that friendship is a bond of faith (*fides*), because friends can be trusted to shun pretense and to speak the truth in all matters for the sake of one another (3.6; Pike 167). John does diverge from Cicero in one regard, however. Unlike Cicero, for whom friendship was an intimate or private relationship, the model of friendly intercourse described in book 3 of the *Policraticus* is thoroughly public. John sketches a standard of conduct against which may be judged the activities of actual courtiers, to the detriment of the latter.

But how does one apply the standard that John establishes? Treatment of those whose friendship is uncertain, or who are likely to be foes, requires an entirely different set of behaviors from those whom one counts as friends. As a general principle, John cites the dictum, derived from *De amicitia* 59, that "one is to live among enemies as though among friends, and to live among friends as if in the midst of enemies" (*Policraticus* 3.14; Pike 196). Practically speaking, it is necessary to treat a person at court of whom one is distrustful with a veneer of affection until his true intentions can be established. One may be polite and cordial, but by no means should a stranger be admitted immediately into one's circle of friends. If he proves to measure up to the expectations of friendship, he can be admitted into one's circle of friends. Thereafter, he may be engaged with honestly and valued for his own sake, which may mean that he will be subjected to open critical scrutiny when his words and deeds are judged unseemly. This is an irony of friendship for John: one of the features of a truly friendly bond is the readiness on the part of both parties to apply unsparing criticism to the other when such is appropriate and necessary. One friend so loves another that he will not shrink from the moral duty of correction.

FRIENDSHIP IN ACTION

The specific aim of book 3 of the *Policraticus* represents John of Salisbury's attempt (within the overarching agenda of his treatise) to apply lessons derived from Cicero to the court rather than the cloister, as Aelred did. The difference of circumstance is extremely important. The exigencies of the court require both a rigid adherence to the moral code of friendship and a readiness to recognize the limitations of that code in practice. This should not, however, be taken as a mere exercise in philosophical reflection. Rather, a close examination of John's two volumes of correspondence shows that his conception of the public model of friendship stated in book 3 is put directly to use in his relations with his friends. Given John's commitment to the application of the lessons of philosophy to the conduct of life, one should hardly be surprised that his theory of friendship lurks behind his practice. It is striking how overtly the remarks contained in letters to John's "familiars" are shaped by his adaptation of Ciceronian themes elucidated in book 3. References to *De amicitia* crop up regularly in the correspondence.

Virtues, mostly notably justice, are prominently featured throughout both volumes of John's letters.[25] In the first collection, dating from the period when John is immersed in everyday business at Canterbury, his concern about justice mainly touches on administrative matters. In epistles addressed to social superiors (such as Pope Adrian IV[26]) as well as to his near equals, John pleads against injury and calls for justice in the handling of legal cases and other official affairs.[27] At the core of these letters, one finds the presumption that friends, who are trusted to share a sense of the requirements of virtue, should be ready to act to maintain just causes. In the later collection, the appeal to justice shifts to the larger stage of ecclesio-political affairs. John repeatedly rails against the injuries done to the church—both Canterbury specifically and the Roman Church in general—by evil rulers (mainly the English king Henry II and the German emperor Frederick Barbarossa) and their henchmen. He insists that just people will realize the valid claims that ecclesiastical officials enjoy to the exercise of their offices free from the interference of secular princes who would constrain or suppress the legitimate liberties of the church.[28] At the same time, John also asserts that he personally has performed no act contrary to the legitimate authority of temporal rulers and thus should be absolved from any charge of violating the precepts of justice.[29] Referring to De amicitia 44, John posits it "as a law among friends that only good and honorable requests are made, and dishonorable ones are not granted," letting it be known that he will not abuse his relationship with friends in order to seek his own advantage in preference to following what he regards to be the right path.[30] Nor will he be swayed from defending the Holy Church by those who would attempt to manipulate him by claims of personal intimacy. The latter are, presumably, no friends at all. Friendship, he insists in one letter, is incompatible with "gain" (quaestum).[31]

John clearly ties the appeal to virtue among friends to the larger principle of truthfulness, echoing the language of De amicitia at times (and occasionally citing Cicero's text directly) in support of his sincerity. To Peter of Celle, his lifelong intimate, he proclaims that the bond of friendship renders one friend trustworthy to another, so that each may assume the truth of the other's words.[32] Indeed, the love of truth in public dealings, he confides to Peter, is what caused John grief in his courtly career: "That I profess liberty and I defend the truth are my crimes."[33] Still, truth is to be preferred to deception. This principle holds even in the case of addressing one's superiors in status. To Pope Adrian, John evinces a reluctance to engage in flattery, preferring to state "what all know but few declare in your hearing."[34] John's letters demonstrate a readiness to practice what he preaches concerning the requirement that friends speak truthfully to one another.

In particular, John is fully prepared to condemn friends whom he does not think have lived up to the standards of virtue and truth. His early collection of letters offers us several examples of censure aimed at his intimates. In a missive to an unnamed "close friend," John advises that "judgment of the character of our friends should always be sacred and revered."[35] This entails that friends can and ought to upbraid their fellows for faults. Another correspondent is chided for his "negligence" and warned to ensure that "your previous defect (*culpa*) is not turned by its continuation into a crime."[36] In the same spirit, John advises yet another friend that, in dealing with jealous colleagues, "you should make yourself a better man and not merely pretend that you are one. If you displease them because they hate virtue, you would hardly find it worthwhile to seek to please them, unless by making virtue acceptable to them."[37] In other words, John cautions against the temptation to flatter vicious men and counsels adherence to the path of truth and virtue, even at times when this may not seem to be the most expedient course. In language reminiscent of *De amicitia*, he declares that "truth's friend hears the truth with gladness, and the man who prefers the allurements of deceitful flattery to harsh, but saving, truth is damned."[38] In accordance with the expectation that friends speak the truth to one another, regardless of whether it may be painful to hear or bear, John does not refrain from stating his views with frank honesty, even (perhaps especially) to those to whom he is most loyal.

John realizes, however, that the dictate of truthfulness as the foundation of friendship depends upon reciprocity—that is, the openness of each party to listen respectfully to one another and to accept censure. Consequently, John himself often claims that he anticipates (even asks for) criticism from his friends. Given the Ciceronian theory of friendship expounded in the *Policraticus*, and its application in the letters, John frames his willingness to be subjected to honest criticism in terms fully consonant with the ideal of friendship he sets out to practice. In an especially revealing letter, he thanks his interlocutor for an earlier missive "in which with the authority of your magisterial learning you impressed upon me the necessity of the virtues."[39] John proceeds to admit his own shortcomings of character, closing with a statement of gratitude that comports well with the Ciceronian conception of friendship: "It is in this above all things that I shall recognize the loyalty of true friendship (*verae amicitiae*), if this delivers me to myself, so that vices are not spared and, standing face-to-face with myself, I may avoid them more securely henceforth, lest I always give worse displeasure to others by that which I do not myself recognize to be displeasing."[40] The sentiment seems honest enough, and entirely in keeping with what John says elsewhere. He evinces particular concern about the one-sided requests and impositions he seems to be making upon his friends. Time and again he expresses gratitude for the kindnesses of his friends and sorrow that he is unable to reciprocate as he might wish.[41] Should this failing on John's part become a burden, he begs to be scolded: "I wish [the principle of honor] to be observed between us who avow friendship, and if I transgress against it, I prefer to be corrected rather than heeded. I desire to be reproached if I should be lax in fulfilling friendship's duties when the opportunity arises."[42] John realizes that he presumes much from his friends, so he asks that they, bound to truth and virtue, inform him when his requests exceed an honorable measure. In light of John's avowed principles, we should expect no less from him.

John self-consciously puts into practice the Ciceronian doctrine of friendship espoused in the *Policraticus*. In one letter, he speaks of that "true friendship, whose origins, progress, and end" may be found "faithfully in the presence of Cicero's *Laelius*." Yet theory alone is inadequate. Philosophy provides us with the knowledge of how to live rightly. But it remains up to men to transform philosophical teachings into a guide for everyday action. The Ciceronian principles stated in book 3 of the *Policraticus* represent only a starting-point for a life of true friendship. They must be applied through the hard work of holding one's self and one's fellows up to the high moral standards that ought to obtain among friends. This means learning as a matter of everyday conduct to speak and listen to the truth, even when it would be more convenient, or more pleasurable, to dissemble. The bar for real friendship is a high one, but to settle for anything less is, for John, to eschew the ultimate moral and spiritual reward that it confers upon those who achieve it.

CONCLUSION

John of Salisbury's writings as well as his career demand to be viewed holistically as the life of someone who was engaged in the principled and philosophically (as well as religiously) informed practice of politics. He certainly adapted and applied many elements of Cicero's social and political thought appropriate to his circumstances. In his selective use of Ciceronian teachings, John acted typically. Perhaps more significantly, however, John captured the Ciceronian spirit in the conduct of his life as well as in his compositions. Just as Cicero held that the true value of the contemplative life was to afford guidance to the statesman, so John demonstrated that philosophy and public affairs belonged together. The task of philosophical inquiry for John is as an aid in discerning the good from the evil, the true from the false, and so to illuminate the path for navigating the tricky byways of public life. The life of the mind and the life of action were of a piece for John of Salisbury. In this sense, too, we ought to take very seriously John's self-description as a follower in the footsteps of Cicero.

Cicero in the Universities

Less than a century following John of Salisbury's death, the character of social and political thought altered fundamentally in Europe. When the Latin version of Aristotle's *Politics* by William of Moerbeke was disseminated after circa 1260, it soon became an object of careful study by the schoolmen affiliated with the great European universities that had emerged over the course of the later twelfth and thirteenth centuries. In particular, Moerbeke's problematic rendering of the *Politics*—reflected, for instance, in his simple transliteration of Greek words and phrases that were unfamiliar to him[1]—resulted in a profusion of detailed literal commentaries, such as those by Albertus Magnus (Cologne, later Paris) and Thomas Aquinas / Peter of Auvergne (Paris) in the 1260s and 1270s and by Walter Burley (Oxford) in the 1330s.[2] The purpose of such commentaries was to aid students in attaining proficiency in the *Politics* as a part of their formal studies. Their teachers, the Masters of Arts, also composed *quodlibets* and *quaestiones* (statements and resolutions of debated topics arising primarily from close readings of The Philosopher's texts).[3] These writings served as the basis for formal disputations within the universities among both students and Masters, fostering a pedagogical mind-set and methodology that has come to be known as scholasticism.[4] Evaluation of the nature of the *Politics*'s impact on social and political thought has varied widely among scholars.[5] But there is no doubt that its dissemination profoundly altered the ways in which early European thinkers conceived of human relations and their foundations in a theory of human nature.

Not surprisingly, the intellectual reorientation wrought by the rapid introduction of the *Politics* into the West has often led to the conclusion that Cicero, as well as other classical Latin figures such as Seneca, who enjoyed wide popularity in the twelfth century, were swept aside in favor of the "new" learning on the grounds that the Ciceronian and scholastic/Aristotelian modes of thinking are separate and discordant.[6] Only occasionally has there been some acknowledgment that schoolmen remained familiar with and dependent upon Ciceronian treatises and ideas. Elements of Cicero's thought have, for example, been detected in studies of Thomas Aquinas, who is generally regarded to be the preeminent representative of high medieval scholasticism. Nearly seventy-five years ago, E. K. Rand identified a number of cases in which Aquinas relied upon his Roman predecessor in preference to Aristotle, especially in connection with moral concepts and language.[7] In more recent times, Aquinas's interpreters have debated the extent to which he owes a debt to Cicero, not to mention the nature of that debt. For some, the role of Cicero in Aquinas's thought is foundational.[8] Others contend that the importance of Ciceronian ideas for Aquinas is quite limited.[9] It is indisputable, however, that Aquinas was familiar with a large number of Cicero's writings—*De inventione* and *De officiis*, certainly, but also the *Tusculanarum disputationum*, *De divinatione*, *De amicitia*, *Paradoxa Stoicorum*, and *De natura deorum* as well as the fragments of *De re publica* cited by Saint Augustine.[10] Yet to characterize Aquinas's social and political theory as Ciceronian would be extremely misleading. As Mary Keyes observes, for instance, "Aquinas cites Aristotle's argument in *Politics* I as proof for natural sociability, in preference to Cicero's arguments, with which he was certainly familiar."[11] More generally, Aquinas's main freestanding treatise on social and political philosophy, the unfinished *De regno*, contains only two passing references to Cicero and no discernible trace of profound Ciceronian influence.[12] The absence of distinctively Ciceronian doctrines is also notable in his unfinished commentary on Aristotle's *Politics* and in the relevant sections of the *Summa theologiae*.

But on this subject, as with others, it distorts medieval intellectual history to treat Aquinas as the paradigmatic scholastic thinker. Thus the present chapter instead turns to several other schoolmen in whose writings may be detected a more systematic reliance on key doctrines derived from Cicero's social and political ideas. Specifically, among the authors who meet this standard are four schoolmen associated with the University of Paris who flourished during roughly Aquinas's lifetime and slightly thereafter: the late thirteenth-century philosopher and theologian Henry of Ghent and two associates (and likely students) of Aquinas, Ptolemy of

Lucca and John of Paris, both of whom produced significant political treatises circa 1300, as well as the Paris-educated Augustinian friar James of
Viterbo. Although their intellectual and political concerns, not to mention
their audiences, were highly diverse, each of them adapted central elements
of Ciceronian social and political thought in order to articulate their own
theories. My point is that some products of scholastic training and culture,
no matter how greatly they might have been steeped in Aristotle, still drew
substantially on teachings found in Cicero's writings.

HENRY OF GHENT

While Aquinas is generally viewed as the epitome of early Parisian scholasticism, his near contemporary, Henry of Ghent, was certainly not very
far behind in his reputation as a scholar.[13] Unlike Aquinas, however, Henry
did not produce any commentaries on Aristotle, nor did he compose a
stand-alone work of political theory. Rather, his extant writings are primarily in the form of *quodlibets* and *quaestiones* covering a wide array of topics
ranging from metaphysical problems to social and political issues. As was
only to be expected, his main non-Christian authority was Aristotle. Henry
copiously cites the *Politics* as well as the *Nicomachean Ethics*, which had
been translated into Latin in the mid-1140s. Yet he also integrates Ciceronian teachings into his discussions of political matters; indeed, as we shall
see, he sometimes overtly prefers the ideas of Cicero to those of Aristotle.[14]
Henry's direct knowledge of Cicero's texts is largely (but not exclusively)
concentrated on *De officiis* and *De amicitia*, although he certainly would
have been cognizant of other Ciceronian writings, if only via intermediary
sources such as Augustine's *De civitate Dei*.

In some cases, Henry simply conflated Cicero with Aristotle, using
their texts interchangeably. This is evident, for instance, in his treatment
of friendship in Quodlibet 10, Question 12. In that passage, he attempts
to answer the question of whether friendship is a virtue per se or rather
is dependent upon prior possession of one or more of the virtues. This is
a problem that arises from an ambiguity in Aristotle's own wording in the
Ethics (*Quodlibetal Questions*, 30).[15] Henry concludes, generally speaking,
that the latter of the two positions is the correct one. In support of this conclusion, he cites passages both from the *Ethics* and from *De amicitia*, as well
as one from *De officiis*, to the effect that friends must be equals in virtue in

order to qualify for "true" friendship, in contrast with relations based on utility or pleasure (*Quodlibetal Questions*, 34). Regardless of the accuracy of Henry's interpretation, he certainly believes that Aristotle and Cicero are of a piece. In other contexts, however, Henry recognizes a divergence between the opinions of the Greek and the Roman philosophers, respectively. The reason for this appears to be Henry's acknowledgment either that Cicero's view was superior on the issues at stake or that they simply were not salient for Aristotle.

An especially noteworthy example of such a disparity may be located in Henry's treatment of the question of whether philosophical reflection exempts human beings from defending—even dying for—their country. On the issue, Henry takes direct exception to the view he attributes to Aristotle regarding this matter, proclaiming that

> I believe that the Philosopher did not have the right idea about the happy contemplative. . . . For, although the Philosopher held many things in accord with right reason—those things that the Catholic faith holds concerning them—he, nonetheless, was mistaken concerning many points about ordering them to the end itself of human life. . . . If, nonetheless, he held . . . that the happy contemplative was so withdrawn from human society that he was not obligated in anything pertaining to the republic—for this is contrary to the law of nature . . . from which he could not be released. . . . The contemplative remains naturally obligated to the republic. (*Quodlibetal Questions*, 52, 54)

Note Henry's reference to "natural law" and emphasis on the incapacity of men to remove themselves from social relations as well as employment of the language of *patria* and *res publica*, each of which run throughout Question 13 of the twelfth Quodlibet. These themes are brought together near the end of the Question, where he remarks, "For, however much a solitary man is withdrawn from human society, he always needs its solace in some respect, and for this reason he always remains naturally under obligation to it" (55–56). The echoes of Cicero are quite unmistakable.[16] This is hardly surprising, however, given that Henry had previously quoted, contra Aristotle, the widely cited passage from *De officiis* to the effect that all men are born for one another and that their country as well as their friends have a claim on their duties (*Quodlibetal Questions*, 52–53). But Henry does not stop there. He then quotes from a spurious speech he assigns to Cicero (*Pridie quam in exsilium iret*) and two passages from the first and fourth orations against Catiline, all of which laud the sacrifices one must be prepared to make for one's country. In sum, Henry sides with Cicero over Aristotle concerning the ultimate superiority of action over contemplation.

In this Question and elsewhere, as Matthew Kempshall has persuasively argued, we may see Henry's proclivity for a conception of the common good that deviates in important ways from Aristotle in the direction of Cicero.[17] Henry adopts a quasi-organicist Ciceronian attitude toward the political community. Considering private in contrast with public good, he asserts that there are never grounds for preferring the former to the latter. All men of necessity are "members" of some civil body; as we have already seen, no man can ever be entirely cut off from social and political interaction. In evidence for this claim, Henry refers to a physiological metaphor: "Just as the members are related in the body, so different persons are related in the republic. . . . But a member ought to risk its life for the sake of the entire body. Therefore, any person ought to die for his country" (*Quodlibetal Questions*, 48). He castigates those who would claim that people who possess their "own intellect" (that is, those whose entire life is focused on philosophical reflection) may licitly exempt themselves from self-sacrifice for the common good.[18] This position presumes that the private good of such a person is wholly distinct from, and more worthy than, the good of some member of the community lacking in intelligence and thus "cannot have his own personal good separate from the good of the whole. But if a part or a member had his own personal intellect and also a good that he could obtain separately, just like the contemplative had, he would never choose to die" (54). In response to such objections, Henry responds pointedly: "These claims cannot stand" (54). The reason is that the most apparently asocial human being may not legitimately deny his membership in the civil body: "Even if he is not part of it with regard to the exercise of many actions that pertain to political life concerning the governance of the home and the family and the like, he still remains a part of it with respect to the exercise of an action necessary for the preservation of the safety of the republic" (56). Although Henry does not mention the famous story of Cincinnatus called from the plow to serve Rome, he thereafter insists that a country's need for a leader overrides any assertion of the priority of the contemplative life.

A final instance I will address in which a significant Ciceronian component may be identified also relates to the nature of patriotism in Henry's thought. In Quodlibet 15, Question 16, Henry inquires into the justification of warfare and its relation to virtue. His immediate context, he admits, is the slaughter of Christians by Saracens at the end of the siege of Acre. In particular, he asks how the Christian denizens of Acre (soldiers as well as unarmed inhabitants) should have responded to their defeat. By making a last, hopeless stand against the enemy? Or by doing all they could to escape their attackers (58–59)? Before offering his ultimate reply—which is, in effect, that the proper answer depends upon the circumstances—Henry suggests the utility of investigating the nature of combat more broadly: "By raising the question to a slightly higher level, let us examine the waging of wars a little more deeply than the question proposed" (58). To achieve this goal, he relies heavily on the writings of Cicero—primarily De officiis—while occasionally bolstering Ciceronian claims with additional citation of Christian authorities, such as scripture and Saint Augustine. Henry commences with the central premise of Cicero's treatment of war, namely, that words—the rational speech of the orator—are always preferable to force, since the former is characteristic of human nature, whereas the latter is typical of wild beasts. However, following Cicero, Henry acknowledges that occasionally war may be inevitable, if the enemy will not engage in reasonable discussion. By means of extensive quotation from De officiis 1.34–36, he underscores that the purpose of war must only be peace and that the manner in which battle is conducted must be strictly constrained by justice (Quodlibetal Questions, 58–59). While Augustine is commonly regarded as the founder of the doctrine of the "just war,"[19] his dependence (and, indeed, that of other Church Fathers) on Cicero is too pronounced to be overlooked.[20] Henry clearly recognizes this and hence affords pride of place to Cicero, relegating Augustine to a supporting role.

At the center of Henry's justification of warfare under only limited conditions is his Ciceronian orientation toward patriotism. He returns to precisely the same passages from Cicero (and pseudo-Cicero) that he employed in order to justify the civic duty of all men to sacrifice themselves for the sake of the common good of the republic (Quodlibetal Questions, 63, 64–65, 67). From this principle, Henry now derives some additional conclusions about the relation between patriotism and war. The first, entirely in step with Cicero, is that a distinction must be drawn concerning the motivations for the conduct of war. If war is undertaken for some form of personal interest—whether the acquisition of wealth or the attainment of one's own glory—it ipso facto can never be just. Only in the service of the common good of one's country may combat be undertaken. There are only two reasons for war that meet this standard: "Either to recover goods that were unjustly taken . . . or to repel an injustice by which enemies try through war to take away goods, such as life, the fatherland, freedom, laws, and other goods, or spiritual ones" (59). On the latter grounds, the Christian inhabitants of Acre were fully and justly authorized to repel the Saracen invaders.

A second lesson that Henry deduces from his Ciceronian sources is that a soldier must distinguish courage from rashness. That is to say, there is no virtue in throwing oneself headlong into combat without regard for circumstance, rather than making a strategic judgment to withdraw from the field of battle. The latter should never be confused with cowardice. Henry paraphrases Cicero on this point: "If our soldier, then, was not confident of the help of his fellow soldiers and did not think that they were ready to proceed to war along with him, but still rushed into the enemy alone, hurling himself forward, he exposed himself to death without any reasonable cause." And that, Henry states plainly, "is the act of a fool" (*Quodlibetal Questions*, 61). Since the conduct of warfare should properly occur only for the reasons he has stipulated, in defense of one's county and way of life (material and spiritual), a combatant who proceeds to fight in such a manner that he is bound to lose is in reality no hero, since his actions contradict the very purpose of war itself. Such a man may not be counted as a patriot by any measure. In Henry's discussion of warfare, then, as in his conception of civil community and the duties that it demands, a Ciceronian framework is very much in evidence, albeit adapted in order to conform to the methods of scholastic inquiry. But it is clear that, at least under certain conditions, he was prepared to set aside the Aristotelianism of the schools, preferring the teachings of Cicero precisely on account of their relevance to his own intellectual concerns.[21]

PTOLEMY OF LUCCA

The Thomist treatise *De regno* was, as mentioned previously, left incomplete at the time of Aquinas's death, comprising only the first book and a small fragment of the second. But this does not mean that it languished

unfinished. Rather, in the years following his demise, one of Aquinas's associates, Ptolemy of Lucca, undertook the project of producing a full version
of the work. It was ultimately composed of four books, completed circa 1300
and circulated under the title *De regimine principum*. For centuries thereafter,
the entirety of the treatise was attributed to the hand of Aquinas, despite the
very different orientations of its contents preceding and succeeding book 2,
chapter 4 (the location in the text at which the break between authors surely
occurred). Specifically, the section of *De regimine* thought to be written by
Thomas contains a spirited defense of the legitimacy of kingship as the ideal
form of government, deriving its arguments from the Bible and Christian
theology as well as from Aristotle. Once Ptolemy picks up the composition,
its focus changes dramatically. In the part of book 2 known to be authored
by Ptolemy (*De regimine* 2.5–16), he analyzes critically the different forms of
lordship (*dominium*) in order to establish that the so-called political (essentially, republican) type is preferable; in book 3, he justifies the position that
the system of political lordship embodied by the republican consitution of
Rome was of particular excellence, and in book 4, he purports to prove that
the Roman Republic accords most thoroughly with the natural foundations
of social and political community and governance.

Much of the scholarly attention directed toward *De regimine* has concentrated on the nature of Ptolemy's republican commitments in relation
to his sources, especially Aristotle.[22] This emphasis, however, obscures the
vast extent of his praise for Rome's heyday.[23] In the penultimate chapter of
book 4, for instance, Ptolemy proclaims, "When it comes to the parts of
a polity having to do with government, I must especially use the Romans
as exemplars, because the Roman Republic was very distinguished in its
order" (4.26.1).[24] Ptolemy certainly demonstrates impressive, indeed nearly
incomparable, knowledge of Roman political institutions, leading figures,
and history. In addition to standard Latin sources for the history of the
Republic, including Cicero as well as Sallust, Vegetius, and Valerius Max-
imus, Ptolemy mined authorities less commonly cited in his time, such as
Livy and Eutropius. Moreover, he understood how to read across religious
texts for the information they might yield about secular history. Thus he
mined the books of Maccabees as a treasure trove of historical knowledge
about the political, social, and physical characteristics of Rome, often
employing them side by side with pagan sources as a confirmation or supplement.[25] Judging from the preponderance of the citations in Ptolemy's

portion of *De regimine,* one might conclude that the Latin accounts of the organization of the Republic and the conduct of its leaders, instead of Aristotle's analysis of the mixed constitution in the *Politics,* formed the central reference point for his argument. The historical superiority of the Roman Republic posited by Ptolemy provided the salient basis for his deployment of ancient texts—sacred as well as profane, philosophical as well as historical, Cicero no less than others.

As a result, and notwithstanding its multitudinous quotations from and citations of Aristotle's writings, *De regimine* relies instead upon the most eminent political theorist of republican Rome—namely, Cicero—in order to lay the foundations for his theoretical framework. This may seem an exceedingly odd assertion, given that Ptolemy's text contains only nine direct references to the Ciceronian corpus: two to the *Tusculanarum disputationum,* two to *De officiis,* and one each to *Philippics, De legibus, De amicitia,* and an unknown source that Ptolemy ascribes to Cicero. But the attribution of a Ciceronian character to Ptolemy's thought is not as implausible as it sounds. Nor am I alone in positing a central role for Cicero in *De regimine.* Benjamin Straumann concedes that, in many important respects, Ptolemy's "views are indeed Ciceronian."[26] My position at present moves somewhat further down the path than Straumann's by positing the absolutely fundamental role played by Ciceronian principles in Ptolemy's defense of republicanism in general and of the Roman Republic in particular. This claim may be justified not merely on the basis of the direct references to Cicero's writings by Ptolemy, but also, and more significantly, by his appropriation of key Ciceronian doctrines from the intermediary source of Augustine's *De civitate Dei* by completely reversing the meaning of that text, a strategy that became increasingly common during the later Middle Ages, as we shall discover in subsequent chapters.[27]

Perhaps the most conspicuous instance of how Ptolemy reverses Augustine in order to uphold a characteristically Ciceronian precept arises from his treatment of justice and its relation to the Roman Republic. Augustine famously picked a fight with Cicero regarding this subject. In conceptualizing the nature of a *res publica,* Cicero insisted that it was first necessary to define what is meant by "a people" in possession of its own "thing" or "business" (*res*). In *De re publica* 1.39, Cicero defines a "people" as "an assemblage associated by a common acknowledgment of right (*ius*) and by a community of interests." Augustine challenged Cicero's definition on the grounds that right exists only among God's chosen, residing in the extra-terrestrial city, organized wholly according to divine justice. Thus, Augustine concludes, there has never been and never can be a true republic on earth. Since there is no "people" in a Ciceronian sense, there is no temporal "republic." Ptolemy, by contrast, quotes approvingly—albeit in slightly modified form—precisely the Ciceronian doctrine excoriated by Augustine: "A city, as Augustine says, 'is a multitude of human beings bound together by some chain of society, which is rendered blessed through true virtue'" (*De regimine* 4.23.1). Ptolemy then immediately asserts that this definition accords with Aristotle's definition of ideal government. In other words, in this instance he reads Aristotle through Cicero's conception of the grounds on which humanity is united by means of a natural duty toward one's fellows. The critical dimension of Augustine's discussion of the Ciceronian meaning of a "people" fades entirely. The effect of the passage is to "Ciceronianize" both Augustine *and* Aristotle.

Ptolemy's endorsement of Cicero's central conception of the basis of human society is only reinforced by his reference to the special properties that determine the best form of earthly government. He aims to demonstrate a convergence between the qualities of Roman character nourished in the Republic and the requirements of righteous governance. Specifically, he asserts that the Romans merited their lordship on three grounds: "One reason comes from love of their fatherland, another from their zeal for justice, and a third from the virtue of [civil] benevolence" (*De regimine* 3.4.1). From this he concludes, "Considering the merits of the virtues among the Romans, divine goodness itself seems to concur in their rule" (3.6.5). Nor is this merely an empirical observation without theoretical significance. Rather, the Roman Republic was for him distinctively suited to redressing the failings of the human condition in its natural state, namely, that human beings are a frail and always endangered race, lacking the natural resources that other creatures enjoy, so they must struggle to gain and retain earthly security and welfare (see 3.9.1–5). Ptolemy articulates the foundation of all systems of government succinctly: "The reason is at hand to show what one could demand for the good of the republic, for the defense of the kingdom, or for any other cause that rationally pertains to the common good of one's lordship. Since we have supposed that human society is natural . . . all things necessary for the preservation of human society are done by natural right" (3.11.7). This is, as we know, a typically Ciceronian doctrine, perhaps most famously stated in *De officiis*, with which Ptolemy was familiar. The primary "natural" duty of government is to ensure that those whose preservation is threatened are served and hence that the bonds of human society are maintained and strengthened (*De regimine* 3.11.8).

How does Ptolemy's characterization of the naturalness of human community relate to his defense of the special divine "calling" of the Roman Republic? In his view, the three main virtues embraced by the Republic naturally, and in the absence of revelation, were identical to the end for which "the rule of Christ" was initiated: to promote sacrifice for the good of all and love of one's fellows rather than to seek personal self-glorification or private advantage. Before the birth of Jesus, the Roman Republic was already performing God's work by fostering precisely those virtues of patriotism, civil benevolence, and justice that prefigure the rule of Christ. This position, too, runs directly counter to Augustine's scorning of the possibility that Rome could ever have fulfilled the requirements of true justice by means of the patriotic fervor of its citizens. Ptolemy quotes from both *De officiis* and *De re publica* to the effect that love of fatherland encompasses and realizes the Christian dictate to love one's fellow human beings. Christ's rule adds the ultimate good of salvation to the republican virtues, but it does not disparage or deny the value of the latter. The personal characteristics that Ptolemy lauds are focused on the goal of "living" or "sufficiency" (the preservation of society through an art of politics that redresses the infirmities of nature), rather than on the Aristotelian purpose of "living well" (the realization of the virtues in those [few] citizens capable of attaining them). He supports his position in *De regimine* by direct reference to Cicero's *Tusculanarum disputationum* 2.15.1 and 3.11.8, passages in which the relationship between nature and human "art" is identified in such a fashion that both should provide for the necessities to meet the needs on which the maintenance of human life depends. Virtue as the key quality of political governance, which Rome typified, is composed of the qualities conducive to the defense of the bonds of nature, understood in terms of the provision to the community of the activities requisite for material survival.

In light of Ptolemy's adoption of a characteristically Ciceronian account of the natural basis of human cooperation—a point he elsewhere reinforces with a quotation from *De amicitia* 23[28]—it should be no great surprise that he also embraces Cicero's organicism to depict the proper ordering of communal life. Although Ptolemy draws heavily on the account of the body politic found in John of Salisbury's *Policraticus*, he filters the organic meta-phor through the Ciceronian lens of social solidarity: "It is necessary in any congregation (and above all, that is what a city is) for there to be distinct ranks among the citizens with regard to homes and households and with regard to arts and offices; nevertheless, all are united by the chain of society, which is the love shared by its citizens" (*De regimine* 4.4.9). The diversity of social roles, and its implication for political organization, is captured by another metaphor that can be traced back to Cicero (through the interme-diary of Augustine), namely, the analogy to musical harmony. Following *De re publica* 2.24, Ptolemy remarks, "I conclude that ... the city displays a certain harmony and sense of spirit, as Augustine says, 'from the high-est orders, from the lowest, and from those in the middle'" (*De regimine* 4.3.10). He reiterates the same metaphor in a later chapter of book 4 (4.23.1). In sum, the *De regimine* draws upon a plethora of images as well as doctrines of Ciceronian provenance, whether consciously or not, that amount to a thoroughgoing embrace of many of Cicero's leading social and political ideas. The fact that Ptolemy appropriated some of these concepts from his reading of Augustine's writings is entirely beside the point, inasmuch as his reversal of the Augustinian interpretation of Cicero frequently returns him to Ciceronian ground. The very foundation of Ptolemy's defense of the Roman Republic rests upon terrain originally explored by Cicero.

JOHN OF PARIS

John of Paris's tract *De potestate regia et papali* (usually dated to 1301–2) seemingly possesses all of the appropriate qualities to credit its author as a prominent exponent of medieval Aristotelianism. A Dominican who may have been among the later students of Thomas Aquinas, John certainly was familiar with Thomist writings. His milieu was that of Aristotelian scholas-ticism, inasmuch as he served as a Master in the Theology Faculty at the University of Paris.[29] Among historians of scholastic philosophy and theol-ogy, John is known for his treatises and questions on matters of speculative inquiry.[30] By contrast, *De potestate* is generally read as a polemical defense of the rights of King Philip IV of France against the claims to absolute papal authority over all temporalities—political as well as corporeal—asserted by Pope Boniface VIII and his supporters.[31] This does not mean, however, that it lacks theoretical value, as seen especially in John's approach to the origin and nature of temporal government. Like Aquinas and a host of other Parisian Aristotelians,[32] he defends the superiority of kingship over other forms of rule. Like Aristotle, he asserts that "man is by nature a political and civil animal. . . . Man only must necessarily live in a multitude and in such a multitude as is sufficient for all the necessities of life" (77).[33] But immediately after espousing this orthodox Aristotelian doctrine, John raises an issue that is decidedly beyond the scope of Aristotle's concerns, namely, the proper relationship between the good of the individual and the welfare of the community. It is fair to say that for Aristotle the individual as individual could claim no special standing. The *Politics* is famous for its dismissal of the role of individual persons in their own right precisely on the grounds that human nature fulfills itself only within the civic totality (1253a).

The individual poses far greater difficulty for John of Paris. In spite of reference to the *Politics*, *De potestate* seems to regard man in traditional Christian terms as a self-seeking and egoistical being whose primary concern is personal welfare. John does not think that the individual's fixation upon his own private advantage can be eliminated even in a perfect and self-sufficient community. There exists an unbridgeable chasm between individual advantage and common welfare. "What is particular is not the same as what is common. For it differs as to what is particular whereas what is common joins together," John observes, "so it is necessary that there should be provision made for the promotion of the common good in addition to that moving each individual to seek his own good" (*De potestate*, 77–78). It is as a bridle upon the self-interested aspect of human individuality—a factor that corresponds to the sinfulness of postlapsarian men residing in the earthly city—that government is instituted. Since men as individuals cannot look after the common good, a guardian of the public utility must be appointed.

John foresees that "a society in which everyone seeks only his own advantage will disperse and disintegrate divisively unless it is ordered to the good of all by some one ruler who has charge of the common good" (77). As with so many French thinkers after him, John treats the king as the embodiment of a public welfare, performing from a lofty office the communal tasks that individuals are incapable of performing for themselves.[34] No invisible hand may be invoked to conjure the common good out of the many forms of egoistic behavior. Nor will the introduction of royal rule alter the selfish impulses of individuals. While for John the common good enforced by the king is superior to any private benefit, individuals cannot be expected to respect the public welfare of their own accord. Hence, the monarch must be endowed with a coercive capacity if he is to impose the common utility over the community, a doctrine that apparently differs little from that of Saint Augustine, who deemed coercion necessary in order for rulers to keep in check the wholly self-serving motivations of those who inhabit the *civitas terrena*. John's claims about the relationship between individual and community would consequently seem to be at odds with his earlier statement that humans are by nature civil and political creatures. Is it possible to reconcile these two sides of his thought? *De potestate* itself sought to resolve this dilemma in Ciceronian fashion by asserting that however much men are naturally suited by physical need, linguistic facility, and gregarious instinct for communal life, their actual assembly is not a foregone conclusion. Human beings require active prompting in order to be transformed according to the associative inclinations endemic to their nature. In the absence of such stimulation, people will adopt a style of life appropriate to their sinful and depraved (hence, unnatural) status. John reports that "before the time of . . . the first persons to exercise rulership, men lived against nature without rule, not living as men but in the manner of beasts" (79). As evidence for this bit of anthropological speculation, *De potestate* cites Cicero's *De inventione*, as well as Orosius and (somewhat less accurately) Aristotle.

John postulates that such primordial men "live a solitary life," saved only from assimilation to the lesser animals by the fact that they are able to employ reason instead of relying merely on "natural instinct" (76). This isolated situation is clearly regarded by John as typical of mankind after the Fall, when humans renounced the fraternity of paradise and turned to an existence oriented toward their own benefit alone. In such circumstances, John observes, it is not sufficient that these primitive asocial beings retained their inclination to congregate with their fellow creatures. So bound were they to the promotion of their individual advantage that "these men could not by the use of the speech common to all men bring themselves to live the common life natural to them and to abandon a state more fitting for beasts than men" (79). Thus, in John's view, nature does not impart its own inherent principle of motion. There is no assurance that postlapsarian men will always and necessarily assemble together just because it is a feature of their nature to do so. Rather, because human nature has been rendered defective by the Fall, men only enter into communities when "others, moved by the situation of these men in their error, and using their reason to better effect, tried to bring them by more persuasive arguments to an ordered life in common under one ruler, as Cicero says" (79). The source for John's position requires no speculation.

De potestate's adaptation of Cicero proves to be of considerable significance. It allows John to demonstrate that while sin has weakened men's common nature, causing them to be less benevolently disposed toward their fellow creatures, they nevertheless retain the capacity to constrain voluntarily the unlimited pursuit of individual aims through the authorization of a guardian of the common good. The activation of this capacity for acknowledging the need for rulership depends, however, upon the cogent presentation of the rationale for and benefits of allegiance to the principle of public utility and to its royal embodiment. It may be that men "learn from natural instinct, which comes from God, that they should live as citizens in society," but it is nevertheless the case that "they should as a result choose (*elegant*) the sort of rulers appropriate for the sort of community in question" (82). In no way, then, may the initial institution of government be regarded as the imposition of coercion over an unwilling populace. The rule of kings is only legitimate (viz., in accordance with nature) when established by a consensual process in which men agree, on the basis of rational persuasion, to be governed in light of the common good. Individuals are not bound to submit to the public welfare represented by monarchy if they have not first assented to subject themselves to it as a result of eloquent reason. This assertion follows directly from John's Ciceronian point of departure.

Ciceronian themes recur in *De potestate* when John articulates his well-known distinction between *dominium* (lordship) and jurisdiction.[35] John contends that the lordship that a private lay person enjoys over his goods is a purely individual concern: property "is acquired by individual people through their own skill, labor and diligence (*industria*) and individuals qua individuals have right, power and valid lordship over it" (103).[36] Such *dominium* is both logically and historically prior to all modes of jurisdiction—that is, the determination of what is just and unjust with regard to the uses of private goods. John stipulates that "goods are not mutually ordered or interconnected nor do they have any common head who might order or administer them, since each person arranges what is his according to his will" (103). By contrast, jurisdiction arises in order to redress grievances and provide for common needs (such as territorial defense) which would otherwise be overlooked when each person pursues his private goals in isolation from other *domini*. The "ruler has been appointed by the people to take charge in such situations" as require a neutral arbitrator whose primary aim is to promote the good of the whole community (103–4). Jurisdiction, in other words, derives ex post facto from the solitary circumstances of *dominium* and enforces a public welfare that is distinct from the amalgamation of individual utilities.

The Ciceronian argument that John had articulated in his explanation of the origins and nature of society forms the background for the differentiation of *dominium* from jurisdiction. John indicates that lordship is pre-civil, originating in those particular interests that characterized man prior to the awakening of his social and political nature. For all the efforts of some scholars to compare John's concept of lordship favorably with the Lockean theory of property,[37] one important difference stands out. *De potestate* never refers to the condition of man prior to government as "natural" or "according to natural instinct." On the contrary, it would appear that this primordial world of unbridled individual appropriation and consumption corresponds precisely to that state that John previously described as "against nature." What conforms to nature, rather, is a system in which individuals relinquish a large measure of their autonomy in order to live in a peaceable and law-abiding community under the direction and governance of a ruler assigned to protect the common good. But the same passage also stipulates that the actual formation of a monarchy or analogous government cannot be left to blind natural instinct. As is clear from *De potestate*'s emphasis upon the elective element of kingship, legitimate rulership can only be established where it has been explicitly authorized by the conscious choice of the individuals who are to submit to it (82, 124, 183). The jurisdiction of the king is ultimately validated by the fact that it was originally imposed by individuals upon themselves for their own collective benefit.

In sum, John's reliance upon Cicero's account of the origins of human association permits him to steer a via media—one of *De potestate*'s favorite concepts—between a polity founded completely on coercion and one whose unity depends upon untutored natural disposition (69–73). Entry into the community is for John an affirmation of the citizen's natural inclination to assemble. Yet at the same time, political society cannot offer any ultimate remedy for human sin and must therefore be vigilant lest man's iniquity incapacitate his sociability. What makes it possible to coerce the individual in the name of the common good, within the context of a belief in the natural human propensity to associate, is the fact that each and every member of the community has confirmed his nature by originally choosing to unite with his fellows.

JAMES OF VITERBO

In contrast with John of Paris's project of reining in claims about absolute papal authority, James of Viterbo employed many of the same Ciceronian materials to argue the opposite case. James flourished during the second half of the thirteenth century as a student, and then teacher, at Paris, probably as a protégé of the Augustinian friar Giles of Rome, who himself studied under Thomas Aquinas. Ultimately, James received preferment to the archbishoprics of Benevento and Naples.[38] His sole contribution to political thought, *De regimine Christiano*, was composed in essentially the same context as John of Paris's *De potestate*, namely, the conflict between Pope Boniface VIII and King Philip IV of France regarding the nature and extent of papal power.[39] Unlike the *De potestate ecclesiastica* by his master, Giles, James's treatise has received relatively little attention within recent scholarly literature on medieval political thought.[40] The *Cambridge History of Medieval Political Thought* contains only three passing references to it, while Jürgen Miethke's *De potestate papae* affords it no extended discussion.[41] The only scholar of late to address *De regimine* at any great length, so far as I can discern, is Joseph Canning.[42]

De regimine is divided into two main sections. The first posits a careful analogy between the ordering of the Christian church and that of a kingdom. The second part, of far greater length, focuses of the character of power within the church as well as the relationship between spiritual and secular spheres. Current scholarship on James's text maintains that the first section, at least, owes a substantial debt to Aristotle directly as well as to The Philosopher's most eminent medieval interpreter, Thomas Aquinas.[43] It is true that at the beginning of part 1, James appeals to the classification of the basic forms of human association as families, cities, and kingdoms, in an evident extrapolation from the first book of the *Politics* (*De regimine*, 6–9).[44] But he does not then draw the Aristotelian conclusion that man is a political animal. Rather, his account of the human inclination to come together is decidedly Ciceronian: "For man is by nature a social animal (*animal*

sociale), and lives in multitudes, because this arises from the natural necessity, inasmuch as one man cannot live adequately by himself, but needs to
be helped by another. Hence also man has the gift of speech, through which
he can explain his thoughts to another man and, by this means, communicate and live together more advantageously with others. . . . It is natural for
men to live in societies. . . . The fellowship (societas) of the human race is
founded on speech" (8–9, 32–33). Such insistence upon mankind as essentially social in nature, along with a connection between human association
and the capacity for speech, is reflected in Cicero's thought. As occurred
often after the recovery of Aristotle's Ethics and Politics, mention of those
works did not preclude authors from imposing a Ciceronian interpretation
upon Aristotelian doctrine.

In order to grasp why James would have found Ciceronian, rather than
Aristotelian, philosophy more congenial to his own purposes in De regimine,
we must have some sense of his overarching approach to the defense of
papalism. On the one hand, James recurrently proposes parallels between
the proper organization of earthly and spiritual forms of government. In
particular, he maintains that both kings and popes rule over multitudes
of persons, who nevertheless collectively constitute communities, whether
designated by the word "kingdom" or "church" (12–17). On the other hand,
James insists upon an important disanalogy between the two, inasmuch
as royal authority rests purely upon nature, whereas papal power derives
from grace. "The church," he says, "is not a community of nature, however,
but of grace, . . . having been called and brought together by God through
grace" (12–13). One consequence of this bifurcation is that some aspects
of temporal social and political life are entirely unique to it, while other
dimensions pertain to the church and its system of government. In each
respect, Ciceronian ideas manifestly helped James shape his accounts both
of ecclesiastical and of secular realms of politics.

As medieval thinkers recognized, nature is ultimately God's creation.
But James consistently treats the human, natural world according to two
standards: one by the direct divine authorization instantiated by the church,
and the other by the efforts of man, reflecting his sociable nature, the maintenance of which constitutes the reason that government is instituted.
He concludes that "among men, therefore, to whom it is more natural to
live in society than any animal, is there a natural inclination toward the
institution of government; and government of this kind is said to exist by
human law, which arises from nature" (130–31). Government for James thus

"perfects the inclination of nature; and so it is called a human and natural power" (130–31). Several elements of this view need to be highlighted. Consistent with the point discussed above, organized political life is not natural per se. Rather, earthly government is authorized in order to preserve the social disposition embedded within human beings. "In the human multitude also there should be something by which the multitude may be ruled, especially because man is naturally a social and communal animal. For society and community would not be preserved but scattered if there were not someone having the care of the common good of the multitude and of the society" (314–15). This does not reflect the Aristotelian claim that man is by nature political. Rather, government depends upon the conscious "cooperation of natural inclination and institution; for it was introduced among men by human law, which arises from nature" (304–5). So James envisions the foundation of government to be human in origin, yet consonant with the natural orientation inherent in mankind to live socially.

If men are at their core social beings, however, why would political rule become necessary at all? The answer to this question offered in *De regimine* has distinctly Ciceronian overtones. Every human being, James says, possesses reason and intellect, by means of which he is capable of accessing natural law and acting in accordance with it: "That which is natural is common to all who have a share in nature," gentiles and Jews no less than Christians (130–31). Unfortunately, however, men's application of their rational capacities does not occur evenly. Rather, many (perhaps most) men are frail; they refrain from employing their reason and are instead overwhelmed by their passions: "Because of the ignorance that is in human nature, reason alone is not sufficient for the government of man; and hence it is expedient that the society of men (*hominum societas*), as being in many respects not sufficient to govern themselves, should be ruled and directed by some person or persons more vigorous than others in intellectual prudence. Moreover, because of human malice, men do evil deeds and injure one another, and so it is expedient for some to be the rulers of others, by whom men may be restrained from wickedness" (314–15). James's argument may be broken down as follows: first, human beings possess the power of reason, which in principle permits them to live socially in the absence of government; second, men are, however, impeded in the full utilization of their latent rational powers because they succumb to self-love and desire for personal (material) advantage; third, political authority is brought into existence in order to support and reinforce the sociability that is intrinsic to mankind but threatened by the failure to apply reason. The logic here overlaps with the position associated with Cicero. Politics is not natural in and of itself. At the same time, the emergence of government is wholly consistent with human nature.

Since James's essentially non-Aristotelian version of naturalism upholds the principle that temporal political authority is "instituted" by men, rather than conferred directly by God, he arrives at the conclusion that a ruler's position must be assigned by means of the active assent of those over whom he exercises power. In his view, "Someone achieves rulership rightly when he is appointed by the agreement and common consent of the multitude" (316–17). This position runs throughout *De regimine*. When temporal political authority is conferred upon some person in a "natural" manner, this occurs solely as the result of the voluntary determination made by the human beings who will obey him (134–35, 144–45). James expressly condemns as illegitimate the government of anyone "who, out of a desire for mastery, or by force or deceit or by some other unworthy means, usurps ruling power to himself" (316–17). When speaking of royal power in a purely naturalistic sense, consequently, it is irrelevant to James whether the king is Christian or pagan (although the former is preferable to him). In turn, the attribution of the foundation of earthly rulership to human choice converges with the very purpose of communal life for James, namely, the maintenance of the corporeal welfare of those in its charge. "The good which is sought in each community is sufficient provision for this life. Every community is instituted for the sake of this good, because one man cannot by himself provide himself with a commodious way of life without the help of other men. . . . For the greater the extent to which many men are united with one another, the more able they are to provide for themselves the means of life by mutual aid" (10–11). The primary role of the king in the promotion of moral virtue and/or spiritual salvation—a claim that was a hallmark of many medieval adherents to Aristotle—is unequivocally dismissed by James. At best, he admits that inasmuch as "external goods serve the virtuous life as instruments, it pertains to the king to procure and provide for the people a sufficiency of such goods as are necessary to this life" (150–51). As a consequence, *De regimine* posits a strict division between the goals of temporal government and those of the church, in such a manner that the most the former can contribute to the latter is the prevention of physical and material injury and the preservation of peace as an aid to the clergy's performance of its holy duties (152–53). For this very reason, the authorization of the rulership of the "natural" social order may and should be left to the multitude who willingly submit to it.

In turn, religion forms the bridge between the natural and supernatural realms, in the sense that belief in God is both inherent in men and completed by means of grace. Prior to the emergence of the faiths of the Law and then of the Gospel, James says, practices associated with religious belief nonetheless were formulated by man and flourished as a result of indirect divine inspiration, beginning "at the very foundation of the human race" (124–25). As a consequence, a priesthood existed to oversee its rites. The latter "comes from God through the mediation of nature, because the natural law says that God is to be worshipped and that sacrifices and offerings are to be made to Him; and to make these sacrifices and offerings pertains to priesthood. Hence, from the promptings of the law of nature, either spontaneously or by human institution, certain persons performed the priestly office by making sacrifices and offerings to God.... Priesthood of this kind ... arises from a general inclination placed within men by God" (126–27). James clearly recasts Cicero's conception of the universality of human religiosity in Christian terms. Indeed, he links recognition of divinity to "the virtues that exist according to nature as aptitudes" and in particular to "a certain virtue called religion, to which it pertains to exhibit due worship to God, and which is called a species of justice," a statement containing distinct Ciceronian echoes (126–27). Because it was derived from the God-given human disposition to pay cult to a deity, the pagan form of devotion to which Cicero subscribed is not utterly illegitimate but merely a partial expression of the ultimate realization which is found in Christianity. James concludes that "the priesthood of nature is therefore not destroyed by that of the gospel, but perfected and formed, because grace does not abolish nature, but forms and perfects it" (128–29; see also 210–11). Moreover, in one sense at least, natural priesthood directly parallels royal power, which also derives from nature. James extrapolates from this that the "priesthood which is called natural and which arises from human institution was communicated to certain persons according to the will of men themselves," in contrast to the priests of the Law and the Gospel, who are selected by "divine precept" (132–35).

As the apex of religion, Christianity is the fulfillment of the orientation of mankind toward religion, although not now purely by nature, but by revelation. Yet nature still plays a significant role in the realization of the Christian faith. For God's direct disclosure of Himself by means of scripture is granted not to all of creation, but only to rational beings. On the one hand, religions founded entirely on "human institution by the prompting of natural reason" are "imperfect and as it were unformed" (126–27). On the other hand, since men alone are endowed with reason, they and only they enjoy access to divine grace and the consequent potential for salvation. God's gift presumes "a nature that is capable of grace, of which kind is rational or intellectual nature" (34–37). According to James, divine forgiveness inheres solely in "the kind of government that belongs to rational creatures, and especially men, who are properly called rational creatures," namely, "the governing power that has been communicated to the church by Christ or through Christ" (114–15). And this sort of rule is "called a commonwealth (*res publica*), for a commonwealth is the property of a people," and "a people is a multitude associated by common agreement about what is right (*iuris*) and beneficial," as is clear from the definition of Cicero that Augustine often cites. According to this definition, indeed, no community is more truly called a commonwealth than the church, for only in her is there true justice and true benefit and true communion (60–61).

The positive evaluation of the Ciceronian conception of a republic has already been encountered elsewhere in the present chapter as the basis for Ptolemy of Lucca's positing the superiority of republican government. Thus the application of Cicero's definition of a commonwealth in a fashion that wholly negates the reason for Augustine's reference to it is by no means unprecedented. But perhaps James's ascription of the Ciceronian definition to the church, in a work intended to defend the absolute authority of the pope, is somewhat more striking. It exercised an impact among later generations of authors, such as Alvarus Pelagius.[45] Augustine's quarrel with Cicero's theory of the *res publica*, as discussed previously, pertained to the distinction between the "loves" of the earthly city, namely, corporeal fulfillment, and the "love" of the denizens of the divine city, in which true justice resides. James's understanding of the church as a commonwealth, by contrast, is on par with the other revaluations of the Augustinian critique of Cicero that have been examined, inasmuch as they all pertain to the defense of earthbound institutions, whether secular or ecclesiastical.

CONCLUSION

It should be evident that the eclectic character of scholasticism in general, and of many of its social and political thinkers in particular, permitted some

of the main features of Ciceronian theory to flourish despite the introduction of Aristotle's *Nicomachean Ethics* and *Politics* into Latin-speaking
Europe in the mid-thirteenth century. Indeed, a plausible argument can be
made that elements of Ciceronian thought paved the way for the relatively
rapid reception of Aristotelian social and political philosophy, inasmuch
as there might seem to be overlap between their respective appeals, for
example, to nature as the basis for human association. Nevertheless, the
unique qualities of Ciceronianism—even when they appeared under an
Aristotelian veneer—were sufficiently present that it is reasonable to conclude that they constituted an approach to social and political theory clearly
distinct from that afforded by Aristotle's writings.[46] This position becomes
especially convincing when we turn to the author who has usually been
regarded as the paragon of scholastic Aristotelianism: Marsiglio of Padua.

CHAPTER 5

Ciceronian Impulses
in Marsiglio of Padua

There are few political thinkers of the Middle Ages who have engendered as much controversy as the early fourteenth-century author Marsiglio (a.k.a. Marsilius, the Latin version of his name) of Padua.[1] In his own day, he was a notorious heretic, condemned on account of his blistering anti-papal polemic, the *Defensor pacis* (completed in 1324). In more recent centuries, he has become the object of intensive scholarly scrutiny. No problem has received greater latter-day attention than the identification of the source materials, Christian and pagan alike, upon which Marsiglio constructed his theories of both earthly and ecclesiastical politics. In his magisterial study of the *Defensor*, Alan Gewirth identified three primary "philosophic sources" for the secular portion of the work's doctrines: Augustinianism, Averroism, and, most of all, Aristotelianism.[2] According to Gewirth, a full and proper understanding of the *Defensor* requires that we acknowledge Marsiglio's debt to these three intellectual systems.[3] The scholarly literature generally agrees with Gewirth; attempts to trace the sources of the *Defensor*'s arguments about temporal politics have been confined, almost without exception, to locating its Aristotelian, Augustinian, and Averroistic strands of thought.[4]

Yet careful examination of the *Defensor* suggests that one would be remiss to exclude Cicero from any list of sources or authorities whose use ought to be investigated. Prima facie evidence indicates that Cicero looms large in Marsiglio's thought: *De officiis* is among the most frequently cited pagan texts in the *Defensor*.[5] More importantly, Marsiglio's explicit references to Cicero, when read in conjunction with other passages of the *Defensor*, point to a Ciceronian derivation for many of the basic features of the Marsiglian conception of the foundations of human society and the organization of political life. Nevertheless, most surveys of Marsiglio's text and ideas barely mention Cicero's name as a possible source of his political thought.[6] Certain recent commentators indeed have gone so far as to dismiss explicitly Cicero's significance for grasping the theoretical framework of the *Defensor* in contrast to, say, Aristotle.[7] A few scholars do acknowledge Marsiglio's admiration for Cicero but regard it as a historical rather than a philosophical phenomenon, in the sense that the Paduan looks to his Roman predecessor's political career for practical inspiration instead of to his writings for theoretical insights.[8] Even in highly unusual cases of scholarship that do admit the presence of significant Ciceronian dimensions to the *Defensor*, one does not find detailed investigation into the ways in which Cicero's political teachings provide raw material for Marsiglio.[9] On only the very rarest occasions has a reader of the *Defensor* afforded some substantial weight to the Ciceronian component of the text.[10]

The present chapter demonstrates how Cicero's doctrines lie at the heart of Marsiglio's crucial claim that membership in human society necessarily entails duties toward other men, inasmuch as no community whatsoever is possible where a regard for one's fellows is lacking. Social cohesion requires, in particular, a natural duty to be just in one's conduct toward others. The very precondition for a communal existence is the recognition of a fixed principle of justice. These assertions not only have a demonstrably Ciceronian provenance but also play an important role in Marsiglian political theory. The overarching project of the *Defensor* was, to be sure, polemical, namely, to rally opposition to the temporal pretensions of the papacy. In order to achieve this goal, however, it was necessary for Marsiglio to construct normative proposals for the arrangement of the secular political community. Recognition of the Ciceronian background to Marsiglio's argument connects the philosophical premises of the *Defensor*'s challenge to papal government with some of the main aspects of its account of the secular community. The duty generated by the polity's dependence upon justice both defines the manner in which humans live a social existence and promotes a firm response to forces (like the papacy) that attempt to disturb the peaceful enjoyment of a communal life.

CICERO AND ANTI-PAPALISM

As a prelude to appreciating the full significance of the Ciceronian contribution to the *Defensor pacis*, we may begin with an overview of the text itself.[11] The *Defensor* is composed of three discourses. Dictio 1 discusses the origins and nature of earthly political authority; the second dictio, nearly quadruple the length of the first, critically surveys and then demolishes a variety of claims made on behalf of the rights of the church and, particularly, the papacy; a brief third discourse summarizes those conclusions derived from the preceding discussions that Marsiglio regards to be especially useful or worthy of emphasis.[12] The disjunction between the two main discourses of the *Defensor* is particularly striking. Yet one must resist the impression that the *Defensor* is composed of two separable, self-subsistent, and internally coherent treatises. Instead, it is possible to identify a single central theme that binds together the tract as a whole: the danger posed to human happiness (as experienced in the peaceful and self-sufficient community) by the interference of papal government in secular life. Marsiglio expressly proclaims that the "purpose" of the *Defensor* is "to expose the singular cause of strife" that currently infects parts of Europe (specifically, northern Italy, the so-called Regnum Italicum),[13] "so that it may henceforth be readily excluded from all kingdoms and cities, and informed rulers and subjects can live more securely and tranquilly" (1.1.7). At the end of Dictio 1, Marsiglio renews his contention that "there has occurred the separation of citizens and finally the degeneration of the Italian cities or polities," and he fears that "this pernicious pestilence, which is completely opposed to all human quietude and happiness, could readily infect other kingdoms of faithful Christians throughout the world with the same corrupt root of vice" (1.19.12, 13). And in the third discourse, he declares that "in the preceding, we have assigned the singular cause by means of which civil discord or intranquility now exists in certain kingdoms and communities, and will exist in all the remaining ones (unless prohibited) in the future" (3.1). The whole force of the *Defensor*'s argument is directed toward demonstrating the disruptive effects of the papacy's attempts to regulate temporal affairs. Approached from this perspective, Dictio 1 stipulates the arrangements necessary to bolster the stability and unity of secular communities so as to repulse papal interference, while Dictio 2 substitutes the principles of papal monarchy with those of a conciliar ecclesiology.[14]

Marsiglio resolves at the outset of the *Defensor* to demonstrate why rulers and communities—especially those in locales where the papacy's threat had not yet penetrated—ought to wager their salvation and temporal safety against the renunciation of the pope's right to intercede in earthly affairs.

Marsiglio insists that a dual obligation to aid one's fellows by opposing the papal regime overrides all considerations of self-interest or personal safety: "We ought to wish for peace, to seek it if we do not already have it, to conserve it once it is attained, and to repel with all our strength the strife opposed to it. To this end individual brethren, and in even greater degree groups and communities, are obliged to help one another, both from the feeling of heavenly love and from the bond or right of human society" (1.1.4). Marsiglio argues that our duty to act derives from both a spiritual and a temporal source. What God requires and what our secular situation demands converge. In each case, we are expected to do all we can to maintain the peace throughout Christendom as well as in our own locales. And our temporal obligation proves to be grounded in the distinctly Ciceronian theme of the responsibility to mankind as a whole on account of natural justice. Recall that Cicero closely associates peace with justice. In order to defend the duty to reject papal infringement upon earthly jurisdiction, then, Marsiglio invokes basic precepts of Cicero's conception of society. In the introductory remarks to the first discourse, the *Defensor* quotes at length from *De officiis* 1.2 to the effect that human beings exist, according to their natures, in order to serve their fellows rather than merely to satisfy themselves. Nature instills in man the duty to act for the public benefit above all else: "Whoever desires to and is capable of discerning the common utility is obliged to give ... his vigilant care and diligent efforts" to whatever threatens "harm to all states and communities" (1.1.4). Human sociability forms a universal bond, not confined to one's own community but extending beyond fixed political units to all civilized peoples.

This doctrine of natural duty is developed to a far greater degree in the conclusion to Dictio 1. Marsiglio again employs Cicero to authorize a broadly based, purely temporal obligation on the part of men to oppose interference with human "peace and happiness." The resistance advocated by the *Defensor* is of two sorts. First, one must repel enemies of earthly tranquility by revealing their identities to all who will listen. Instruction can be a powerful tool in the war against those who seek to disturb the social order. But, second, one must move beyond education to direct action: whoever takes up the banner of discord and temporal misery must be halted by any means available to knowledgeable antagonists. Marsiglio insists that "every man is obligated to do this for another by a certain quasi-natural law (*ius quasi-naturale*), the duty of friendship and human society" (1.19.3). Man is subject to the requirement to seek the good of his fellows without regard for his personal welfare. Marsiglio indicates that any other mode of conduct would be unjust, a position for which he cites explicitly Ciceronian grounds:

> To these [namely, the tasks of identifying and fighting the enemies of human happiness] all are obligated who have the knowledge and ability to take action; and those who neglect or omit them on whatever grounds are unjust, as Tully testified in *De officiis*, Book I, Chapter V, when he said, "There are two kinds of injustice: One, of those men who inflict it; the other, of those who do not drive away the injury from those upon whom it is inflicted, if they can." See, then, according to this notable statement of Tully, that not only those are unjust who inflict injury on others, but also those who have the knowledge and ability to prevent injury being inflicted on others, yet do not prevent it. (1.19.3)

Marsiglio maintains that a necessary corollary of the natural bond of human association is a duty to perform justice in both its aspects: not only to refrain from doing injury, but also to protect others from harm when it is imminent. The clear implication is that society itself is impossible without the acknowledgment of this obligation arising from the Ciceronian principle of justice.

Marsiglio consequently appeals to Cicero to affirm the existence of rigorous standards of responsibility binding on all persons and communities claiming to be included within the civilized fraternity. If one knows of any injury in the process of commission and yet declines to repulse it, one is culpable just as surely as if one were the source of the harm. According to Marsiglio's interpretation of this principle, those who live in polities untouched by civil strife are not thereby absolved of regard for the occurrence of intranquility in other places. Rather, should one be aware of some cause of human misery while failing to stem it as much as one can, one is equally at fault and blameworthy for the unhappiness that occurs. By inference, Marsiglio's Ciceronianism seems to commit him to the maintenance of several other philosophical claims that form the basis for his notion of a universal duty. On purely logical grounds, Marsiglio would have to subscribe to the following propositions in order to uphold this doctrine: (1) society is most essentially composed of a universal and naturally ordained fellowship of human beings; (2) the foundation of association among members of this fellowship is justice; and (3) knowledge of justice and the performance of just deeds is ultimately unconstrained by any set of legal or political institutions. As shall be illustrated, Marsiglio expressly embraced these three claims as the foundation for accepting the position that whenever a human being is aware of a violation of justice, regardless of the location (or jurisdiction) of its occurrence, that person is duty-bound to do whatever is within his power to prevent or halt injury.

ORIGINS OF SOCIETY

The first proposition stated above is supported by an account of the origins of human society that relies heavily on the Ciceronian version of primordial events. Scholars have noted that Marsiglio did not adopt the Aristotelian definition of man as a political creature. Normally, this has been explained by reference to his Augustinian or Averroistic propensities.[15] But Marsiglio's understanding of the emergence of society is couched in terms of the stimulation of man's inherently associative tendencies by means of wise oration. Marsiglio reports that the human faculties of reason and speech were stirred and energized "by the persuasion or exhortation of prudent and able men. The latter, exceptionally endowed by nature with an inclination for this task, later through their own efforts made progress in their various pursuits and guided others either successively or simultaneously to the formation of a perfected community, to which men are naturally inclined so that they readily complied with this persuasion" (2.22.15). The natural disposition to associate is an implicit feature of human nature, requiring reasoned persuasion to stimulate and direct it toward realization. Marsiglio believes that the success or failure of this process of socialization is largely dependent upon the presence of one or a few men who are particularly well endowed with the rational and rhetorical faculties necessary to convince the mass of human beings to assemble as a community. The basic human properties of speech and reason render people prone to accept the arguments of primitive orators and to join together into a communal life.

Because they are susceptible to rational persuasion, human beings incline to social conduct. Hence, at that time "when men originally came together to establish the civil community and law, with the weightier part of them agreeing on matters pertaining to the sufficient life" (2.22.15), their ability to reach such a fixed agreement must inescapably have been premised on reasoned discussion guided by those who were exceptionally wise and eloquent. Marsiglio suggests that "what was necessary for living and living well was brought to completion by human reason and experience, and the perfect community was instituted" (2.3.5). Reason is universally implicit in human nature; it requires education and training of the sort provided by the especially talented person to bring it to fruition. In this fashion, Marsiglio's account of the natural bonds that unite men coincides with the position of Cicero. Society rests not on compulsion or coercion but on those rational and linguistic qualities that distinguish human beings from other living creatures.

We should not neglect, however, to acknowledge another motivation for the unification of mankind under the banner of society. Marsiglio quotes *De officiis* 1.11 approvingly to the effect that people share certain a fundamental characteristic with other sentient beings, that is, the goal of self-preservation (1.4.2, 3). But they are unique in the way in which they successfully achieve this aim: by means of satisfying the diverse functions that contribute to the physical needs of human creatures, which can only be fulfilled in the context of fixed communal relations. No part of the community can survive without the cooperation of the other parts in addressing common physical needs of mankind: "Since diverse things, which cannot be procured by men of one order or office, are necessary to those who desire to live sufficiently, there needed to be diverse human orders or offices within this association, exercising or procuring such diverse things which humans require for sufficient life" (1.4.5). So, the rational and linguistic capacities of men converge with their biological needs to form a community that expresses the full complement of their natures. In this fashion, the core of Marsiglio's case for the origins of human society rests upon overtly Ciceronian concepts.

JUSTICE AND THE GROWTH OF COMMUNITY

One consequence of Marsiglio's conception of the foundations of social intercourse is his emphasis on the necessity of justice as a prerequisite for the community. This is evident from his account of the stages through which communal life develops, which has generally been taken as simply a recapitulation of Aristotle's narrative in book 1 of the *Politics*.[16] But as shall become evident, the Aristotelian position is modified in significant ways. Marsiglio draws a careful distinction between the pre-civil and the post-civil condition of human existence. The pre-civil life is that of the "combination" of human beings in the family and household (*domus*) (1.3.3). The *Defensor* insists that the *domus* is not a community, since its governance is based completely on arbitrary discretion: "The head of a single household would have been allowed to pardon or punish domestic injuries according to his own will and pleasure" (1.3.4). In other words, within the family there is no operative principle of justice. Should he so desire, the male head of the household in the time prior to civil society could even have forgiven the crime of murder or mitigated the capital penalty, according to Marsiglio. The criteria employed in the rule of the primitive *domus* were completely discretionary.

Once the unit of the village (*vicus*) emerged, however, the situation changed profoundly. Marsiglio calls the *vicus* "the first community," in clear contrast to the noncommunal *domus* (1.3.3).[17] What distinguishes the village from the household, in particular, is the replacement of the arbitrary rule of the lord with the governance of an elder who avenges and equalizes injuries according to a rudimentary principle of justice. Marsiglio explains that in the village, "the elder had to dispose matters of justice and benefit by means of some reasonable ordinance or quasi-natural law (*lege quasi naturale*), because thus it seemed good for all to live on the basis of equity, although without great investigation but only by dictate of common reason and a certain duty of human society" (1.3.4). The system of justice endemic to the village, primitive though it may be, devolves from the basic obligations implicit in man's associative nature. No true social arrangement can be ruled in the manner of the family (that is, arbitrarily). Rather, unless the tenuous bonds of communal life are to be broken, and human beings revert to the disarray of individual households, justice must determine the conduct of relationships between persons. The Ciceronian features of this claim are palpable. The "duty of human society" from which the "quasi-natural law" of justice arises is precisely the duty that Marsiglio elsewhere in the *Defensor* upholds on the authority of Cicero (1.19.13).

Insofar as Marsiglio discerns the division between civility and pre-civility in the transition from household to village, the appearance of larger units of association like cities and kingdoms involves less a qualitative than a quantitative change in the arrangement of the community. Consequently, the transformation of the village into a fully formed ("perfected") political society is described by Marsiglio not so much as a function of the failings of the elder's rule than as a result of growing complexity within the society's component parts and activities (1.3.4–5, 1.4.3). If members of the community were to continue to live together in relative harmony and order, it became necessary for a separate and distinct system of justice to be introduced. Marsiglio explains that "because between men so congregated there occur contentions and quarrels which, if not regulated by the norm of justice, would cause fights and the separation of men and so at length the decay of the city, it is required in this relationship that a standard of justice be established and custodians or makers [of it]" (1.4.4). Indeed, the embodiment of this standard of justice in the law constitutes the salient achievement of the "perfected community," the *regnum* or *civitas* (1.10.4–5, 1.11.1). No community is complete without "standards of civil justice and benefit established by human authority, such as customs, statutes, plebiscites, decretals, and similar rules" (1.10.6). The formal justice of the *regnum* or of the *civitas* provides a surer and more accessible measure for human conduct as well as a more incorruptible foundation for judgment than does the village elder.

Permeating the *Defensor*, then, is the insistence that membership in human society is necessarily and inescapably coextensive with submission to the conditions imposed by justice. Marsiglio is resolutely committed to the view that even simple social relationships are impossible without some administration of justice: "On account of the absence of justice there would occur among men scandal and contention, and thence fighting and separation and the insufficiency of worldly life which virtually all avoid according to nature" (1.9.12). In consequence, the primary responsibility of the public authority or "ruling part" (*pars principans*) must be to guard the common interest by compelling obedience to the standard of justice and correcting those persons who damage the social fabric by the commission of harmful acts. The Marsiglian ruler is assigned, most essentially, to regulate the duties arising from justice—the nonperformance of which would be detrimental to the continuation of human association. The *defensor pacis* is a *defensor iustitia*. On the one hand, this means that injurious acts done by citizens must be punished by the ruler (1.5.4, 7). But, on the other hand, it also suggests that the *pars principans* is expected to concern itself with those matters that individuals might otherwise neglect out of inattention or self-interest.[18]

JUSTICE AND THE LAW

Marsiglio was for a long time considered to be a proponent of legal positivism, according to which the content and force of law depend only on social facts and not on its intrinsic merits.[19] Such a doctrine differs radically from a Ciceronian conception of justice, rooted in natural law, as the basis for positive law. It is true that Marsiglio believes that human law is not enforceable until it has been promulgated according to the appropriate procedure and has thereby acquired the status of a coercive sanction (1.10.4, 1.12.3). But this does not entail that every statute that has been so promulgated is valid and binding simply as a consequence of its authorization.[20] Rather, the *Defensor* stipulates that the content of legislation must be directed strictly to the promotion of "civil justice and benefit" (1.12.2). This means, first of all, that each statute must lack the quality of partiality: it cannot favor the interests of a few at the expense of others, but must serve the common welfare alone. Indeed, if it fails to live up to this standard, Marsiglio called it a "bad law" (*legem pravam*) (1.12.8). He thus seems perfectly able to form a judgment about legislation independently of procedural considerations.

As a result, the *Defensor* must reject the view that bad laws are still meaningfully laws so long as they contain the requisite coercive component. Inasmuch as its "principal end is civil justice and the common benefit" (1.11.1), Marsiglio contends that law itself is properly defined as "the science or doctrine or universal judgment about matters of civil justice and benefit and their opposites" (1.10.3). This forms the ultimate standard of law: it demonstrates "what is just or unjust, beneficial or harmful, and as such is called the science or doctrine of right" (1.10.4). The *Defensor* explicitly establishes the independence and preeminence of a universal standard of justice by making reference to "true cognitions of matters of civil justice and benefit." In particular, Marsiglio asserts that while such cognitions should not be regarded as law until they have been given coercive authorization, still, "true cognition is necessarily required for a perfect law" (1.10.5). What legislative approval adds to "true cognition" is civil enforceability; conversely, no statute is enforceable that lacks a basis in knowledge of what is just. Hence, an enactment that fails to direct citizens toward modes of conduct consistent with justice and utility is not fully nomological, since at least part of what it is to be a law stems from congruence with factors independent of the legislative process. Marsiglio views laws as the embodiment of the justice that unites the community. He must maintain that "unjust laws" are not binding because they are destructive of social organization and command acts that are contrary to the communal duties arising from man's associative nature.

Marsiglio does not at this juncture identify the source of the absolute justice to which he expects law to conform, nor does he explain whence "true cognitions of justice" arise. But we may recall that Marsiglio described the standard of justice to which the village elder appealed as "lege quasi naturale" (1.3.4), and he spoke in the conclusion to Dictio 1 of the same natural law as the basis for the obligation to do justice (1.19.13). Therefore, we may plausibly turn to the *Defensor's* articulation of natural law for a clarification of the origins of justice and of our knowledge of it. Marsiglio distinguishes between two senses of natural law. The first, which closely resembles what Cicero terms *ius gentium*, is regarded by Marsiglio as purely figurative. Such law is deemed to be "natural" because it has been widely enacted in the civilized world and would therefore seem to be common to all peoples. Yet Marsiglio stresses that this law is not, strictly speaking, natural at all, since it still depends upon human promulgation for its efficacy (2.12.7). By contrast, the second sense of natural law is "the dictate of right reason in practical matters, classified under divine law: thus every act according with divine law is intrinsically licit, as is not the case with every act that accords with human laws, since in some ways they fall short of right reason" (2.12.8).[21] The source of "true cognitions" of justice can be regarded as the application of right reason to the discovery of the requirements of natural law (which are, in turn, divinely guaranteed). On this account, natural law is the ultimate standard against which all human legislation may be measured and judged by means of rational inquiry, a position that echoes Cicero's viewpoint.

Marsiglio thereby concludes that, when confronted with divergences between positive law and the knowledge of justice, "what is intrinsically licit and illicit should be considered with reference to divine law rather than human law, in those instances in which their commands, prohibitions and permissions differ" (2.12.9). Valid human statute is not arbitrary in the sense that anything willed by the legislator automatically qualifies as law. Instead, the dictates of justice, founded on natural law as a subcategory of divine law, supply the absolute criteria for distinguishing genuine from bogus, and thus binding from noncompulsory, decrees. Natural law constitutes a universally applicable source for the principles of absolute justice. In this way, Marsiglio demonstrates throughout the *Defensor* a conviction that the legitimacy of temporal legal institutions is conditional upon their congruence with a standard of just conduct that is both independent of human will and accessible through the application of human intellect. It is difficult to ignore the extent to which this doctrine correlates with Cicero's teachings about natural law. Like Cicero, Marsiglio refers the whole system of temporal legislation back to the basic precepts of justice that make human society possible.

RELIGIOUS FUNCTIONALISM

Marsiglio evinces a great deal of antipathy toward the Roman Church as it existed in his own day, on account of the agenda of the pope and his minions, who claim legitimate power in the temporal realm on the grounds of their spiritual authority. But, in spite of this implacable opposition to the church in its contemporary institutional form, Marsiglio was by no means a critic of religion per se. On the contrary, he regarded religion as a necessary feature of all developed human communities. The function performed by priests was, in his view, among those tasks whose exercise constitutes one of the key elements that keeps society unified. Marsiglio observed that "all nations . . . agreed that it was appropriate to establish the priesthood for the worship and honoring of God, and for the benefit resulting therefrom for the status of the present or the future world," stemming from the belief "that in the future world God will distribute rewards to those who do good and punishment to doers of evil" (1.5.10). In other words, religious belief had a twofold aspect. On the one hand, it was an innate feature of mankind as a whole. On the other hand, it served as the adhesive that bonded social relationships by its practical effects. In particular, he says, the ancient philosophers recognized that religion was especially "necessary for the status of this world. This was to ensure the goodness of human acts both individual and civil, on which depend almost completely the quiet or tranquility of communities and finally the sufficient life in the present world" (1.5.11). Thus pagan thinkers, regardless of whether they believed in the immortality of the soul or in physical resurrection, "feigned and persuaded others" that the "pleasures and pains" of eternal existence "are in accordance with the qualities of human deeds in this mortal life, in order that they might thereby induce in men reverence and fear of God, and a desire to flee the vices and to inculcate the virtues" (1.5.11). Marsiglio recognized the usefulness of religion in promoting adherence to moral precepts that in turn guided action—a position congenial to that upheld by Cicero.

In terms of the purely functional elements of religion discussed in the *Defensor*, Marsiglio was apparently indifferent to the character of the confession per se. Surveying some pagan views of the afterlife, Marsiglio concludes that "from fear of these, men eschewed wrongdoing, were instigated to perform virtuous works of piety and mercy, and were well disposed both in themselves and toward others. As a consequence, many disputes and injuries ceased in communities" (1.5.11). Instruction in divine law and worship had the effect of "taming" members of the community and rendering them suitable for the cooperation necessary for their survival and flourishing. For this reason, the priests of the ancient cults were carefully culled from among "virtuous and esteemed citizens" who were "removed from their passions and in whose words greater credence was placed because of their age and moral dignity" (1.5.13). The role played by the priesthood must therefore be congruent with the communal ends that rendered such religions "civil." But inasmuch as such political ends arose from and accorded with human nature for Marsiglio, pagan belief systems were necessitated by his very commitment to the peaceful unity of mankind.

Nor does Marsiglio imagine that the situation fundamentally changed with the advent of the "one true faith," anticipated by Mosaic law and confirmed by orthodoxy. He acknowledged that "correct views concerning God were not held by the gentile laws or religions ... and, in general, by all those doctrines which are outside the tradition of what is contained in the sacred canon called the Bible" (1.5.14). But the arrival of "the true priesthood, that of the Christians" by no means alters for Marsiglio "the necessity for the priestly part in the community" (1.5.14). He asserts that God inspired human beings to enter into communal arrangements to obtain a "sufficient" physical existence. He posits, however, that such divine guidance was indirect and distant in its causal efficacy. In the context of his discussion of the "causes" of civil regimes, he asserts that humanity adopted a "method of establishing governments which proceeds immediately from the human mind, although perhaps remotely from God as remote cause, who grants all earthly rulership" (1.9.2). In other words, particular forms of government arise from the exercise of human intellect and thus are susceptible to rational evaluation along naturalistic lines. Marsiglio certainly accepts the ultimately divine ordination of political institutions and authority. Although all political dominion ultimately derives from God, earthly political affairs immediately result from human reason. And regardless of whether communities are populated by Christians or infidels, the value of religion is an attribute of any developed social system.

This position, in turn, leads Marsiglio to identify continuity between the false pagan religions of antiquity and the true faith of Christianity in their respective functional contributions to the sustenance of temporal community. Certainly, the priests of the Christian church have the task of instructing "men in those things which, according to the evangelical law, it is necessary to believe, do, and omit in order to attain eternal salvation and avoid misery" (1.6.8). But the truth of the Christian confession by no means erases the need for it to reinforce, in addition, the moral qualities requisite for a tranquil and sufficient secular communal life. The priestly calling entails the promotion of "moderate human acts both immanent and transient [that is, self-regarding and other-regarding] arising from desire and knowledge, and which make men well disposed in soul for the status of both the present and the future world" (1.6.9; see also 2.8.4).[22] Thus, just as with all other functions necessary for the emergence and maintenance of the "perfected" community, the Christian priesthood must be conceived as twofold in character. The nature of the priestly part arises from one of the inclinations of the "human body or mind," specifically, the aims to achieve temporal as well as eternal happiness. But insofar as this function must be coordinated and reconciled with the public welfare shared with other segments of the community, priests also occupy one of the civil offices. In this sense, the priest is no different from the soldier or the housebuilder: "According as they are offices determined and established in the state, their final causes are the benefits and sufficiencies which perfect human actions and passions, and which are forthcoming from the functions of the aforesaid habits, or which cannot be had without them" (1.6.10). No less than any other part of the community, Marsiglio concludes, the natural habit designated by the term "priesthood" must be regulated to support and enhance the needs of the common good.[23] As with Cicero, no community can persist—perhaps even exist in the first place—in the absence of a religious practice that all its members embrace jointly inasmuch as it reinforces social solidarity and the bond of human affection.

CONCLUSION

Scholars have often been perplexed by what they perceive as a tension in the *Defensor pacis* between the philosophical and the polemical aspects of

Marsiglio's thought. Most often these commentators have diminished or dismissed one side of the *Defensor*'s argument in preference to the other. Thus Marsiglio either is associated with various "respectable" schools or traditions of political philosophy or is treated as a "mere" polemicist for whom philosophical discourse is purely derivative.[24] Once we acknowledge a Ciceronian background to the *Defensor*, however, we may begin to bridge the alleged gap between Marsiglio's political theory and his polemical cause. From the foundation yielded by Cicero, the *Defensor* asserts the existence of a universal, secular obligation on the part of all human beings and political communities who know of a threat to the welfare of their fellows to provide aid and prevent injury. In turn, this duty has immediate practical application. It presents the theoretical basis for a concerted program of trans-European opposition to the papacy's interference with the affairs of the Italian cities. For Marsiglio there is no distinction to be drawn between the theoretical and the polemical elements of his treatise. Philosophy exists to inform and guide political activity; public affairs are only conducted correctly when they accord with the duties specified by philosophical inquiry.

That Marsiglio treats theory and practice as directly interdependent reflects, I think, the profound influence of the Ciceronian conception of binding duties grounded in the nature of man and society. For within Cicero's theoretical framework, the consequence of the failure to perform one's duties to others is the disintegration of the community and the disappearance of all the advantages that social intercourse confers upon the individual. So Marsiglio's practical goal of establishing and maintaining temporal peace within Christendom is a necessary and inescapable outcome of acting upon obligations entailed by justice. Any person who knows his duty will do it not only because it is right, but also because it is advantageous. Thus the polemical end of the *Defensor pacis*—to stimulate action against the papacy—is effectively indistinguishable from the theoretical point of the text, which is to demonstrate the duty-laden foundations of human society.

CHAPTER 6

Cicero Speaks French

Standard surveys of Western medieval social and political thought have a pronounced tendency to write vernacular texts out of their narratives. Among English-language scholars, none of the major works of secondary literature—even those published quite recently—allude to non-Latin languages, except in the cases of Attic Greek, Hebrew, and Arabic, and only then to explain the genesis of Latin translations and reception of the ancient classic authors, particularly Aristotle.[1] It seems to be assumed that Latinate culture thoroughly dominated the propagation of social and political ideas until, perhaps, the Italian Renaissance and the German Reformation. There may have been a few counterinstances, but these are presumably marginal figures. This story is, however, in need of serious revision. Cicero's social and political writings afford a particularly vivid illustration of scholarly neglect of the non-Latin reception and adaptation of classical thought. French perhaps provides the best example of a European vernacular in which the presence of Cicero was felt.

The present chapter examines the integration of Ciceronian social and political theory into texts composed in French between the mid-thirteenth and the early fifteenth centuries, specifically by Brunetto Latini (ca. 1265), Nicole Oresme (ca. 1370), and Christine de Pizan (ca. 1405–14). Latini and Oresme both knew an array of Cicero's writings in their original language, while the evidence amassed by recent scholarship suggests that Christine possessed at least some competence in Latin letters.[2] Each of these authors was informed by central features of Ciceronian thought and, in turn, transformed them in distinctive and interesting ways in order to address his or her own particular concerns and circumstances. Indeed, there is no little irony that Oresme, in the prologues to his French-language commentaries on both Aristotle's *Ethics* and *Politics*, cited Cicero's *Academica* as justification for his own use of the vernacular. Just as Cicero commended writing about philosophical matters in his native Latin, rather than in Greek, so Oresme likewise defends his preference for composing in French on the grounds that it was more agreeable to address weighty matters in a language readily accessible to all.[3] As in the case of the other thinkers thus far examined, none of these figures writing in French was slavishly devoted to Cicero. My point here is to demonstrate that in the development of social and political theory in early Europe, Ciceronian voices spoke in vernacular "languages,"[4] in this case French, as well as in Latin.

BRUNETTO LATINI

The most notable early benchmark in the diffusion of Ciceronian thought in French is Brunetto Latini's *Li livres dou tresor*, a philosophical encyclopedia compiled and composed in the early 1260s.[5] As his name suggests, Latini was not himself of French heritage, but a Florentine who was trained as a professional rhetorician and mainly worked as a civil servant in his native city, serving as chancellor of its populist government during the 1250s. When the regime was overthrown in 1260 and an "elite" faction grabbed power, he was forced into exile for more than half a decade and took employment as a notary in several cities in France.[6] During this period, Latini produced a partial translation into the Italian language, together with an exposition, of Cicero's *De inventione* (under the title *La rettorica*), as well as Italian versions of several Ciceronian orations (*Orazioni*).[7] While in France, Latini also wrote *Tresor*, which is the treatise most germane to the present analysis of Ciceronian social and political thought in the French vernacular. *Tresor* is not a work of political theory per se. Rather, it takes the form of a survey of all human knowledge. It is divided into three books: the first treats the fields of theology, history, geography, and natural philosophy; the second examines ethics; and the third addresses *de bone parleure*, under which heading Latini includes rhetoric and politics.

As befits an author with Latini's education and career, his central focus on Ciceronian thought is directed toward the latter section, namely, the discussion of rhetoric and its association with public affairs. Throughout *Tresor*, Latini treats rhetoric as the defining feature of what is best and noblest about humanity. This is most evident in book 3. With *De inventione* 1.6 apparently in mind, Latini commences the book with the claim that "Tully says that the highest science of governing the city is rhetoric, that is to say, the science of speaking; for without speaking, there were not and would not have been either cities or the institution of justice or human companionship" (*Tresor* 3.1.2). Although the chapters immediately following this statement read like a brief commentary on *De inventione*, Latini's purpose is to introduce the study of rhetoric as a subject that a prospective city administrator must master. After examining the elements of rhetoric, he immediately moves on to discuss the duties connected with civic government. And among the primary requirements elucidated by Latini for appointment to public office is that one must be "a very good speaker" as well as knowledgeable in "everything concerning matters of truth" (*Tresor* 3.75.5, 8). These attributes indicate that a necessary precondition for competence as a governor is the attainment of the qualifications of the Ciceronian orator.

Tresor signals recognition that there are potential problems associated the Ciceronian conception of rhetoric as central to public affairs and governance. In particular, as Latini admits, a potential danger to the community arises when persuasive speech is not accompanied by a well-formed intellect. Adopting a view aligned with Cicero's, he remarks that "just as it is the case that speech is given to all men, ... wisdom (*sapience*) is given to a few" (3.1.2). Latini then enumerates four different types of relationship that are possible between eloquence and wisdom: when reason and good speech are present together, "it is the flower of the world"; when neither are present, it is a "great disaster"; when one speaks well but lacks reason, there is "very great peril"; and when one possesses reason, yet eloquence is absent, instruction and aid are required (3.1.2). Latini says nothing more about the second and fourth categories. Instead, he concentrates on promoting the union of wisdom and eloquence—and hence on averting the disaster that arises from their disjunction. In this regard, Latini adopts the Ciceronian position that oratory as the union of wisdom and eloquence is of the greatest benefit to the entire community: "And when wisdom is joined to speech, who will say that it cannot give rise to goodness?" (3.1.6). His evidence for the usefulness of oratory rests, in turn, on Cicero's claim that society itself would be impossible in the absence of speech:

> Tully says that, in the beginning, men lived according to the law of beasts, without their own houses and without knowledge of God,

in the forests and in rural retreats, without regard for marriage or cognizance of parents or children. Then there appeared a wise and well spoken man, who counseled the others and pointed out the greatness of the soul and the dignity of reason and of discretion, so that he recalled them from their savagery and urged them to come together as one and to protect reason and justice. And by the use of good speech which was accompanied by reason, this man was almost like a second God, who created the world for the sake of the arrangement of human companionship. (3.1.7)

Latini's appreciation of the contribution of the primitive orator, and especially his comparison of the activity of the wise and eloquent speaker to the creative power of God, is striking in its force. The orator is placed in *Tresor* at the very center of the communal affairs of his city. His words are the fount of civic life.

That Latini regards this oratorical role as a continuing feature of the community is made clear by the idea of "counsel" which runs throughout the third part of *Tresor*. At times, he seems to mean by "counsel" or "giving counsel" simply one of the three technical divisions of rhetoric (namely, *deliberativa*) enumerated by Cicero in *De inventione*.[8] But in the suggestion that the primitive orator "counseled," and that the man who merely speaks well does not "give counsel," there is an indication that the discipline of rhetoric teaches counsel in a normative sense. "Counsel" seems to connote wise speech for the purpose of public welfare or rectitude. This impression is reinforced by Latini when he turns directly to the governance of the city: citizens should seek "wise counsel" when deciding whom to appoint as their ruler (*Tresor* 3.75.1); they are charged with giving their governor "counsel and aid for maintaining his office" (3.74.4); and one of the primary duties of rulers is to assemble the chief and wise men of the city in order to request and consider their "counsel" regarding important matters, such as the conduct of diplomatic affairs (3.87–89 and 3.95). Oratory appears to form the basis for such counseling functions. The properly trained orator may be taken to speak on behalf of the interests of the community because his eloquence is coupled with the wisdom to recognize the public good. Thus not only the ruler, but the body of the citizens (or at least its leading segments), ought to be trained in the field of rhetoric.

When he addresses ethical questions in the second book of *Tresor*, Latini also closely follows Cicero (albeit with a Christian tinge), in particular, concerning the preeminent role played by justice in both the formation and the maintenance of social and political bonds and thus its precedence over all of the other virtues. Just as Latini upholds the Ciceronian view that speech was necessary to assemble men into community, he likewise asserts that "at the beginning of the world, when there was no king or emperor on the earth, people lived according to the law of beasts, some in one cave and others in another, without law and without communities" (2.91.1). But life in this primitive condition resulted in conflict and danger. In order to remedy the situation, Latini says, "A few good sensible men gathered together and ordained the people to live together and to keep human company, and they established justice and law, from which it is clearly evident that justice is the virtue that watches over human company and communal life, for when men live together and one has arable land and the other possessions he needs, another one might be moved by envy and discord if there were no justice" (2.91.1). Justice, according to Latini, has a dual source. On the one hand, it "is joined to nature and exists for the good and maintenance of many people.... Nature calls us to the works of justice.... [A]lmost everything that pertains to justice is written on our hearts as if by nature" (2.91.4, 8). Justice is a dictate of natural law. "It is more against the law of nature," he says, to take "away the common life of men," a position that he illustrates with an analogy derived straight from *De officiis*: "If one limb thought that it would be worth more by drawing off for itself the health of the next limb, the whole body would necessarily weaken and die" (*Tresor* 2.122.4). But Latini's Ciceronian naturalism is supplemented by a Christian dimension inasmuch as he introduces a divine element into the foundation of justice: "It is the law of God and the bond of human company" (2.91.4). By no means are these claims contradictory, given the widely propounded formula *natura, id est, Deus*.[9] Even prior to the appearance of Christianity, all human beings, by following the dictates of nature, were in a sense submitting to divinely ordained law and thus to God's justice.

In this vein, Latini also conflates Ciceronian and Christian conceptions of the specific duties required by justice. In a clear allusion to *De officiis* 1.23, which offers Cicero's classic definition of justice as both refraining from committing injury and shielding others from harm, Latini remarks, "If you want to be just, it is not enough to do no harm to others; you must oppose those who want to cause them harm, for not harming another is not justice" in its fullest sense (*Tresor* 2.91.6). Enforcing this principle of justice rigorously, in the view of Latini (following Cicero), is entirely necessary for the perpetuation of the bonds that tie human social and political communities together. But Latini also believes that the Ciceronian position precisely parallels the Christian one. "If you truly want to follow justice," he says, "love and fear the Lord Our God so that you will be loved by him; and this is the way you can love him: do good to every person and harm no one, and then they will call you just" (2.91.5). As with the dual bases of justice in natural and divine law, so the substance of the actions required of the just man arises from and depends upon both natural and divine sources, either in combination or separately. It is through nature as well as revelation that God commands humans to be just if they are to live peaceably and fruitfully together. Slightly modifying the teachings of *De officiis* 1.22 and *De inventione* 2.161, Latini remarks that we are bound to "love and serve diligently our relatives and our country, for first of all we are born for God and then for our parents and our country" (*Tresor* 2.99.1). God takes priority in the ensemble of human duties, but not totally at the expense of natural responsibilities to our fellow creatures.

Finally, Latini draws considerably from the Ciceronian concept of friendship propounded in *De amicitia*. It must be noted that there are two distinct discussions of friendship in *Tresor*. The first stems from Aristotle's *Nicomachean Ethics*, a French paraphrase of which constitutes the initial fifty chapters of book 2. Thereafter, Aristotle recedes from view, and a second, and far more extensive, survey of friendship emerges, premised instead on Cicero's principles. Latini joins Cicero in rejecting unconditionally those forms of friendship that rest on either profit or pleasure. Such relationships are of necessity fleeting and unreliable, whereas true friendship is enduring (*Tresor* 2.105–6). The reason this is so is because genuine friendship is founded on virtue, or more specifically, it occurs only among virtuous men, a position that Latini explicitly attributes to Cicero (2.102.1). Indeed, Latini insists, again following Cicero, "friendship must be put before all things. About this Cicero also says that friendship is worth much more than kinship, for love can perish with relatives and the name of relative always remains, but if love perishes between friends, the name of friendship perishes with it" (2.104.11). Friends, Latini observes, must be loyal to one another as well as value virtue and goodness, among other qualifications (2.102.1–2). Friends are so intertwined in their bonds that an injury to one is an injury to the other (2.103.5). Latini departs from the Ciceronian ideal of friendship in only one major regard, which depends on divine commandment, namely, that love for any of one's true friends cannot be greater than one's love for God. Friendship should transcend any concerns about earthly goods, but it may never violate the divine injunction to love God as oneself (2.103.4). This caveat aside, Latini's account of friendship otherwise aligns closely with that proposed by Cicero in *De amicitia*.

NICOLE ORESME

As noted at the beginning of chapter 4, the Latin translations of Aristotle's *Nicomachean Ethics* and *Politics* in the middle of the thirteenth century occasioned a profusion of literal commentaries, *quaestiones*, and *quodlibets* designed to aid students in mastering these texts as a part of their Arts curriculum as well as affording to their Masters an outlet for articulating their own positions. By contrast, Nicole Oresme produced French vernacular translations of and commentaries on both the *Ethics* and the *Politics* (and also the pseudo-Aristotle *Economics*), dating to the early 1370s, which fused scholastic learning with the world of the royal court.[10] As with so many other important thinkers of his era, Oresme moved seamlessly between academic, courtly, and ecclesiastical institutions (he died in 1382 while serving as bishop of Lisieux). Commissioned by King Charles V, his commentaries represented an early, and highly successful, effort to make available to a non-Latinate readership ideas otherwise accessible only in the lecture rooms of the universities.[11] (As Oresme's modern editor, Albert Menut, points out, however, Oresme was not the first to attempt a French translation of the *Politics*. In the first decade of the fourteenth century, a shadowy figure named Pierre de Paris produced a version of the work that is now lost.[12]) Unlike the Latin commentators, Oresme often moved well beyond the text of the *Politics* (and also of the *Ethics*) and developed Aristotelian themes creatively and in a manner more directly pertinent to his courtly audience. Oresme demonstrates an eclectic spirit that liberates his commentary from the constraints imposed by the purely scholarly circumstances of his predecessors, who were guided first and foremost by intellectual expectations.

One measure of this eclecticism is the use that Oresme regularly made of Cicero's writings as a way of elaborating and refining elements of Aristotle's thought. While it may stretch credibility to say that Oresme read the *Politics* and *Ethics* through a Ciceronian lens, there is sufficient evidence to say that Cicero constituted an important source for his interpretation of Aristotle's social and political philosophy. For example, to a far greater extent than Latini, Oresme expresses the sort of trepidation about the dangers posed by eloquent speech in the absence of wisdom that Cicero had acknowledged in *De inventione* and elsewhere. Commenting on how eloquence may result in demagoguery, Oresme points out that "Tully recounts at the beginning of *De inventione* concerning this question that the 'public affair' (*chose publique*) of Rome was greatly damaged and undermined by eloquence and that many great cities have suffered longstanding miseries and calamities as a result of men who were very talented in speaking and of great fluidity" (*Politiques* 176c). Oresme's reference to the *chose publique* (*res publica* in Cicero's Latin) is telling. He strongly implies that the goal of language is (or ought to be) the promotion of the common good necessary for a well-ordered community. It was a failure of eloquent speech to be put to its proper use that led to the breakdown of public order in Rome and elsewhere. This extrapolation is confirmed by Oresme's recognition of the importance of linguistic facility to the formation of human associations. In a fashion somewhat different from Cicero's, he invokes the necessity of eloquence for the creation of civil community with reference to Aristotle's conception of "voluntary kingship." What distinguishes this sort of governance from other types of rule is that subjects willingly submit to the king, whose authority is not merely just but also constitutive of the communal order. Such kings, in particular, "assemble the scattered and primitive folk and then teach them the patterns of civil life and political society as Cicero touches on at the beginning of *De inventione*" (107c). Interestingly, he immediately follows this assertion with a reference to relatively recent events in Europe: among examples of voluntary kings taming a wild and uncivilized people, he cites the conquests by the first rulers or kings of France and by Duke William of Normandy, who successfully invaded and subdued England. These may seem like odd choices on Oresme's part, but they apparently reflect his view that the inhabitants of the conquered territories were primitive prior to being civilized by their new overlords. Oresme may have been less sanguine than Latini about the capacities of human beings to assemble purely as the result of eloquent speech, but he captured a dimension of the Ciceronian position that social and political community depended on a persuasive leader to bring them together.

Oresme also expresses dissatisfaction, on largely Ciceronian grounds, with Aristotle's classification of constitutions. He mentions the basic

Aristotelian sixfold division and quite naturally upholds kingship as the best system of government (87c). (Interestingly, he also attacks the idea of world monarchy, proposed by Dante among others, on the grounds that "it is neither reasonable nor possible" [87d].) But he points out numerous occasions where Aristotle diverges from other sources or even appears in the *Politics* to contradict what he says in *Nicomachean Ethics*. Thus Oresme notes that Cicero (in a passage from *De re publica* quoted by Augustine in *De civitates Dei* 2.21) seems to have a different way of categorizing constitutions, inasmuch as he speaks of kingship, tyranny, and faction—the latter, as Oresme understands it, being identical to oligarchy. Oresme additionally ascribes to Cicero the claim that democracy is "a tyranny." Oresme goes on to translate the distinction between perfect and defective regimes into Ciceronian terms: what unites imperfect constitutions is the absence of the *chose publique*, the common good necessary for a well-ordered community.[13] Oresme stresses that "the *chose publique*" in such bad regimes "is not vicious ... but is simply and entirely non-existent" (88b). Thus imperfect regimes lack a core or a unity—an agreement among their constituent membership about the common good, to express the matter in Ciceronian terms. Yet Oresme also acknowledges that, bad though they may be, "nevertheless these polities do exist" (88b). Oresme believes that democracies and oligarchies—like tyrannies—are not merely theoretical systems but have real-world corollaries.

Oresme extends the Ciceronian understanding of imperfect regimes when he takes up the question of their operative principles of distributive justice, especially in the case of oligarchic and democratic systems. Aristotle in *Politics* 1280a8–1281a10 maintains that citizens in both of the latter constitutions profoundly misunderstand the nature of political justice, and thus that neither of their governmental structures qualifies as just. Oresme adopts a more conciliatory line. "In all constitutions, whether they be good or bad," he says, "they must agree that there is a certain right (*droit*) and ordinances or positive laws that approximate justice in some degree, for otherwise there could not be legal actions or entry into interrelations" (*Politiques* 89b). In support of this view, Oresme quotes *De officiis* 2.40 to the effect that justice so predominates in human nature that even the iniquitous partake of some small portion of it (89b–c). The reader is left to conclude that even the rules and principles by which imperfect regimes are governed may thereby incorporate some measure of justice. Indeed, slightly later in the discussion, Oresme states this conclusion overtly: one must admit that "there are many just laws that are common to both [perfect and imperfect] sorts of constitution," such as "commutative justice in contracts and in punishment and in other like matters" (90b). Once again, Oresme seems prepared to accommodate defective systems to a far greater extent than Aristotle. Justice is not an all-or-nothing proposition in political communities. Hence, the line between perfect and imperfect regimes begins to blur.

Oresme similarly adapted several other notable Ciceronian themes that he renders relevant to his interpretation of Aristotle. As already noted, one of the central aspects of the *Politics* is the doctrine that man is naturally born for life in civil community and thus is a "political animal" (*Politics* 1253a1–18). (The meaning of the latter phrase continues to be a subject of considerable controversy even today.[14]) In order to explicate the meaning of Aristotle's claim about the naturalness of political community, Oresme turns to Cicero's *De officiis*: "Just as a hand cannot truly be a hand if it is not attached to a man, so man is not properly man apart from a community of men. Cicero has stated that we are not born for ourselves alone, but for the continuity of our race, our city and our country" (*Politiques* 8d). In a later passage, Oresme develops the bodily analogy in considerably more detail, citing Cicero's account (44d). But the special importance of Oresme's reference to elements of Ciceronian naturalism, invoked to elaborate on Aristotle's teaching about the relation between individual and community, stems from his direct association of Cicero's organicism with his familiar doctrine of the range of the mutual human duties that we owe to one another. Near the close of the *Politics* commentary, he reiterates this Ciceronian teaching: "For a city or a community is like a body whose members or parts serve one another and principally the whole.... And for this reason, Tully says we are born not only for ourselves, but for our friends and our country" (295c). In contrast with Aristotle, Oresme quite evidently believes that the prioritization of various binding human relationships is a far more complex affair than Aristotle's valorization of citizenship in the *polis* as the ultimate form of human fulfillment.

Oresme returns to these features of Cicero's thought elsewhere in his *Politics* commentary. For instance, in a long excursus concerning a brief remark in Aristotle's *Politics* about the relationship between contemplative and active *eudaimonia* (1325b15–20), Oresme recasts Aristotle's well-known predilection for philosophical contemplation over action (as expressed in book 10 of the *Nicomachean Ethics* and elsewhere) in decidedly Ciceronian terms. Cicero had consistently praised the active life guided by justice as generally better than the leisured pursuit of wisdom.[15] In Oresme's extensive discussion of which form of existence is most fulfilling, he reminds us of Cicero's principle that "we are not born for ourselves but for our parents and our country," from which he concludes, on the authority of De officiis 1.4, that contemplation must be set aside when action is required for the maintenance of social and political bonds (Politiques 243a). A similar position is maintained in Oresme's commentary on the tenth book of the Nicomachean Ethics: "For as Tully says, speculation is no more great and noble than taking action in order to assist and protect against perils to the public good" (Èthiques 212c). In his remarks concerning the Politics, Oresme asserts that "a mixture of contemplative work and active work is more desirable and better than one that is entirely taken up with contemplation," which in turn permits him to praise the life of the prince (presumably someone like Charles V) as the best possible one on earth (Politiques 243d, 244c).

Further instances of Oresme's appeal to Cicero in the context of a naturalist theory are evident as well (Politiques 44d, 295c). Admittedly, Oresme's commentary on the Politics contains no sustained discussion of natural law (at least so far as I can find), only occasional and insubstantial references to it scattered across the text (Politiques 17c, 19d). Likewise, Oresme limits his citation of Cicero's views on justice to the discussion in De officiis 2.40 in support of the argument that even the most pernicious thieves possess a minimal sense of justice, otherwise they could never band together and they would be constantly in conflict with one another (Politiques 89b, 90a). However, the natural law foundation of justice is extensively addressed in Oresme's gloss on the Nicomachean Ethics with direct reference to Cicero (Éthiques 103d–109c). At Ethics 1134b18–35, Aristotle discussed a distinction between two different types of justice: one is natural, and one is conventional. The former, he says, is universal, applying to all men without exception; the latter principle of justice is specific to one or another political system. Aristotle's rationale for introducing this division of the dual meanings of justice seems to refute the argument that justice is utterly conventional and thus does not exist elsewhere than in positive law, which is specific to a given polis.[16] Where the text of the Ethics states simply "natural justice," Oresme adds "or natural law," clearly equating the two (Éthiques 103d). He then comments on the passage that human beings in a sense share natural law with other beasts, a direct echo of De officiis 1.11. What separates the nature of man from that of animal is the possession of reason, which permits human beings to move away from pure instinct and to construct a system of civil law grounded in natural law, a position that Oresme expressly ascribes to Cicero (*Éthiques* 104a).

Two additional dimensions of Ciceronian naturalism find their way into Oresme's commentaries. The first is Cicero's explanation of inequality among members of mankind. Cicero held that while all people are capable of employing their latent reason, many (indeed most) do not do so. Oresme adopts precisely the same viewpoint. Quoting the Latin of *Paradox Stoicorum* 5.33, and translating it into French, he asserts that "all wise men are free and all ignorant ones are serfs" (*Politiques* 12c) A few sections later, Oresme cites the same passage to identical effect, as he also does later in the commentary (17a, 192a). He places a Christian interpretation on this in order to reconcile Aristotle with the biblical teaching that all of humanity was born equal in the state of innocence: the wise are the virtuous and the unfree are tainted with vice (17a–d). In some sense, Cicero would probably not have disputed the overall validity of this position, since he himself believed human beings to be equal by nature yet unequal on account of their differential wisdom and virtue. But Oresme also faced the problem of lords who excessively exploit the servile, and he attributed to Cicero on more than one occasion in the *Politics* commentary the dictum that no seignorial power that greatly oppresses its people will last very long (*Politiques* 144d, 210b, 210d). Oresme maintained that a leveling of social and economic status, of the free and the slavish, is contrary to nature. Inevitably, however, oppression leads to revolt; he even mentions a specific example that resulted from such mistreatment—the Jacquerie, a violent peasant uprising in France that occurred in 1358 and thus would have been in the recent memory of his audience. Oresme offers Cicero's own proposal for avoiding such conflict in the future, as derived from *De re publica* (via Augustine's intermediation), namely, the model of musical consonance and harmony according to which each "voice" (that is, class of people) would sing in its own register (*Politiques* 149c). As a consequence, Oresme contends, "There would be a form of inequality that would be well measured and proportionate, and neither irregular nor excessive, but nearest to the middle. . . . And by appearance, the inequality of the citizens is middling and moderated" (149c–d). In Cicero, the idea of the concordant blending of unequals was closely associated with his defense of the Roman republican constitution as the ideal system of government. At present, however, it points to Oresme's adaptation of the Ciceronian idea that social inequality can exist without contradicting the principle of natural equality.

A final, and fascinating, instance of Oresme's reliance on a Ciceronian version of naturalism as part of his commentary on Aristotle's *Politics* pertains to religion. Aristotle had very little to say in the *Politics* about religious matters. Like his Greek contemporaries, he viewed the worship of the gods as essentially a civic activity, so his primary concern was with populating the priestly class (*Politics* 1329a25–34). By contrast, it was unavoidable for Oresme to expound upon matters of religion, which he did throughout his remarks on the seventh book of the *Politics*. He attacked the voluntary poverty of the mendicants, justified the church's taxation of the faithful and its exemption from secular imposts, praised papal supremacy in ecclesiastical governance, and endorsed canon law (*Politiques* 250d–51c, 265a–67a, 276a–77c). But he also integrated Cicero's naturalistic insights about divinity into his examination of the Christian religion. One facet of his appropriation in this regard was his endorsement of Cicero's position concerning the universality of the human recognition of a supernatural power. Citing both *De natura deorum* and *Tusculanarum disputationum*, he asserts that "knowledge of the deity is innate and inborn in us as a part of our natures" (*Politiques* 261b). Oresme reiterates this position somewhat later, referring to the same texts to support the claim that "our knowledge that God is or God exists is the law of nature" (266b). At the same time, he realizes the functional aspect of religion as a civilizing force: "The worship of the divine is necessary to human community in order to avoid adversities or to attain prosperity" (261a). Human beings, he thinks, are inclined toward evil actions, and fear of human law per se is insufficient to guide them toward the good (261a–b).

Citing Cicero's *Tusculanarum disputationum*, Oresme insists that, on account of practical considerations, "all of the ancient philosophers upheld the eternal soul and its duration after death and the fear of divine judgment that determines the penalties for evil or the rewards for merits committed in this life" (*Politiques* 261a). Beyond strict issues of true and false conceptions of the divine, Oresme agrees with Cicero that all forms of communal order, practically speaking, require a religious dimension if they are to persist, let alone exist at all. Yet Oresme also follows Cicero's caution in *De divinatione* against the superstitious elements of religion,

in particular, the dangers associated with the magical arts of prognostication. Such practices, in his view, exist "partly by nature, partly by deception
and fiction, and all are very doubtful, uncertain, and perilous" (*Politiques*
275b–c). In sum, many of the fundamental elements that characterize Cicero's attitude toward the supernatural realm and its implications for human
social and political life are echoed (on occasion loudly) in Oresme's work.

Oresme's thought also relies consistently on the Ciceronian conception
of friendship. In the context of the need for kings to rely upon counselors and officials, his *Politics* commentary discusses a problem common in
medieval political writings, namely, how to know when rulers ought to trust
those on whom they turn for advice. Aristotle seems entirely unaware of
this dilemma, saying merely that the king ought to differentiate between
those who are friendly toward him and those who are not (*Politics* 1313b29–
31). By contrast, Oresme considers the issue of judging royal counselors
from the perspective of flattery and invokes lessons drawn from *De amicitia*.
He makes an interesting distinction between those who are friends of the
kingdom and those who are friendly to the king. He worries that those who
care about the kingdom, but do not count the king among their friends,
"are not good." By contrast, those who are truly the king's friends will also
be counted among the friends of the kingdom. Oresme then cites Cicero's
view on friendship as a fundamentally interpersonal relationship: "For as
Tully says, the real friend never does anything dishonorable to his friend.
And for this reason anyone who counsels the king in order to please him to
do something contrary to the public good is not a friend of the king" (*Politiques* 120c). Thus, on Ciceronian grounds, the king must always consider
whether his advisors are merely flattering him or whether they indeed make
his well-being, and the kingdom, their priority.

Beyond the adaption of *De amicitia* in the *Politics* commentary, other
references to Cicero's concept of friendship may be found in Oresme's translation of and gloss on the pseudo-Aristotle *Economics*, *Livre de yconomique
d'Aristote*, where he remarks that "in adversity one discovers his true friend,"
followed somewhat later by the statement that "as Tully says, the first law of
friendship is that we should ask of our friends only righteous things: 'The
first law of friendship is to ask only honorable things from one's friends'"
(341b, 346c). Interestingly, both remarks pertain to the relationship
between husband and wife, suggesting that each partner is bound to the
other by the terms of friendship as conceived by Cicero. What makes this

fascinating is Oresme's apparent endorsement of Cicero's claim that friends must be equals in virtue, and thus that spouses possess (at least potentially) equal moral standing, the latter a view that Aristotle (or pseudo-Aristotle, in this case) would never have accepted. It should be noted, however, that despite the extensive treatment of friendship in the *Nicomachean Ethics*, Oresme does not appear to have cited relevant passages of *De amicitia* in his commentary thereon. In any case, it is possible to ascribe to Oresme a pronounced dependence upon the precepts articulated in *De amicitia*, in a manner consonant with other instances of his reliance on Cicero's thought.

CHRISTINE DE PIZAN

A generation after Oresme composed his commentaries, Christine de Pizan, another French author connected with the royal court, wrote several treatises that relied in equally intriguing ways on elements of Ciceronian social and political thought. While Oresme flourished during the period of Charles V's patronage of literary and philosophical activities in the vernacular, Christine's career largely spanned the reign of Charles VI, during whose lifetime France fell into a long-standing series of quarrels among members of the royal family, exacerbated by the king's bouts of madness. Christine's political writings in the French language in many ways reflected the tumultuous events of her time.[17] Moreover, Christine confronted and responded to the detractors of her status as a woman who spent most of her adult life supporting herself as a professional writer. She proved to be perhaps the most prolific author of political treatises during the Middle Ages, even as she also composed significant works of poetry and engaged in the ongoing dispute over the overt hostility to women found in earlier literature (especially her contributions to an ongoing quarrel concerning the thirteenth-century misogynistic poem *Le roman de la rose*). Moreover, Christine's many writings of an overtly political nature employed and adapted some key Ciceronian concepts that have already been examined in the present chapter. We know that many (perhaps most) of the sources for her thought derived from prior vernacular texts. For instance, she depended heavily on Latini's *Tresor* and probably knew much of her Aristotle from Oresme's translations and commentaries; she also drew on Denis Foulechat's French rendering of John of Salisbury's *Policraticus*, which was also commissioned during the reign of Charles V.[18] The extent to which she was directly familiar with Cicero's oeuvre in the original language remains a somewhat more speculative matter, although, as mentioned earlier, it now seems beyond doubt that she possessed sufficient linguistic skills to read Latin texts.

During the early 1400s, Christine wrote a notably large number of treatises on subjects addressing social and political issues, among which were several works regarded to be some of her most important contributions, namely, *Le livre de la cité des dames* (1405), *Le livre de corps de policie* (1406), and *Le trésor de la cité des dames* (also 1406). For present purposes, the *Trésor* demonstrates no particular cognizance of Cicero, while the *Corps de policie* cites *De officiis* and *De senectute* (once) only peripherally. By contrast, the *Cité des dames* includes an unmistakable, if unacknowledged, reworking of Cicero's account of the foundations of human association. Christine's overarching goal in the *Cité des dames* was to refute the judgment contained in "the treatises of all philosophers and poets and from all the orators ... that the behavior of women is inclined to and full of every vice" (1.1.1).[19] In line with this remark, the only direct reference to Cicero in the *Cité des dames* merely ascribes to him the view "that a man should never serve any woman and that he who does so debases himself, for no man should serve anyone lower than him" (1.9.3). That no such statement is to be found anywhere in the extant Ciceronian corpus is beside the point; her wish is to paint the great male authors of the past with the brush of misogyny.

Perhaps for this reason, Christine's own depiction of the emergence of social relations lacks any explicit citation of Cicero. Yet there are clear Ciceronian components to her account of the many achievements of the human race that are attributable to the activities of women. According to Christine, most of the arts typical of civilization, including organized society itself, were feminine in origin. The *Cité des dames* provides a lengthy accounting of "the earthly benefits accruing thanks to women ... who gave the sciences and arts to the world" (2.30.1). Among such arts invented by women, Christine mentions weaving, extraction of olive oil, cart construction, metalworking, agricultural cultivation, toolmaking, and gardening (1.34.1–1.36.2). All of these arts involve the existence of communal association, the formation of which she ascribes to Ceres, who assembled together human beings who had previously lived as beasts. Adapting the familiar story of social origination derived from *De inventione*, Christine recounts how Ceres "had the people of that time gather together in communities. They had traditionally lived scattered here and there in the forest and wilderness, wandering like animals. She taught them to build cities and towns of permanent construction where they could reside together. Thus thanks to this woman, the world was led away from bestial living conditions to a rational, human life" (1.35.1). This trope of the female source of social interaction recurs throughout Christine's presentation of Ceres's accomplishments. According to Christine, no one could

> ever acquire a more praiseworthy name than by leading wandering and savage men, living in the woods like cruel beasts without the rule of justice, to reside in cities and towns and by teaching them to make use of law and by securing better provisions for them than acorns and wild apples. . . . Because of this lady, humanity benefitted from the transformation of the harsh and untamed world into a civilized and urban place. She transformed the minds of vagabond and lazy men by drawing them to herself and leading them from the caverns of ignorance to the heights of contemplation and proper behavior. By organizing certain men to perform field labor, this woman made it possible for so many cities and towns to be populated and for their residents, who perform the other works necessary for life, to be supplied. (1.38.1)

Christine follows closely Cicero's story of the origins of fixed human association that posits a special leader who, on the basis of the power of reason, induces social relations among his fellows based on justice. Although she never expressly invokes the function of speech in the process of uniting human beings, the central elements of the Ciceronian narrative are nonetheless brought together by Christine, only now attributed to the singular abilities of one woman to draw the rest of hu(man)kind to the recognition and fulfillment of its natural but untapped aptitudes.

In similar fashion, Christine contends that Isis "handed down and instituted several good and upright laws; she instructed the people of Egypt, who had, until then, lived like savages, without law, justice or order, to live according to the rule of law" (*Cité des dames* 1.36.1). Christine thus credits women with the major achievements in the development of human culture and the improvement of the species' conditions of social and political existence. Christine admits that some thinkers may not view the development of the human race as a laudable accomplishment: "Several authors have argued that this world was better off when people lived only from haws and acorns and wore nothing more than animal skins" (1.39.3). She takes strong exception to such authorities, however. Living in an ordered community fulfills the divine plan, the realization of those capacities and faculties that God has granted to humanity: "God has wished to provide the world with many necessary and profitable things ... through these women" (1.39.1). Without women's innovations and contributions, she implies, humanity would have remained in a state of depredation and misery. Christine's language and account follow Cicero closely, even in the absence of attribution.

By contrast, Christine does not hesitate to invoke Cicero by name, and to employ significant elements of his thought, in her later book, *Le livre de paix* (apparently finished in late 1413). Composed in celebration of two (ultimately unsuccessful) truces between warring factions in France, the *Paix* was dedicated to Louis, Duke of Guyenne, the son of King Charles VI. Much of the work commends to Louis the qualities of his grandfather, Charles V, which rendered his reign so peaceful and worthy of praise. Why should such tranquility be attainable at all? Central to Christine's political thought in the *Paix* is the principle that human social interaction constitutes the natural condition for mankind. Borrowing from Latini's gloss on *De officiis* 3.26, she cites Cicero to the effect that "if for gain we do not mind stripping others of their goods or taking from them by force, it follows that the society formed by human love, in accordance with nature, will be sundered, where it should remain one" (*Paix* 2.25).[20] Sociability untroubled by conflict constitutes the natural and normal condition of humanity, so that contestation and warfare between people should be regarded as abnormal and unnatural.

In turn, responsibility for securing and maintaining peace pertains primarily to kings and other earthly lords. And Christine holds that foremost among the characteristics necessary for a ruler to maintain peace in his realm is the acquisition of virtue in a manner consonant with the teachings of nature and in accordance with reason. She remarks that "as all things here below be fallible, virtue alone, says Tully, has dominion over itself, which means that it has endurance; and because of this, one's reasons for living well should be founded in virtue" (1.4). Virtue for Christine is closely aligned with reason. A person "is rightly called lord and master of other men because of the noble workings of virtue. So, as Tully says, in view of the great fault and evil it is for such a noble animal as man, in whom reason should rule—otherwise he is defective and like a brute beast—he must guard against degrading his heart" (2.38). In the absence of such virtue, those who exercise power will use their positions in order to molest and rob their subjects with impunity.

Among the various virtues necessary for the ruler to possess in order to govern his realm peaceably, justice stands at the fore. In a striking analogy, Christine compares justice to "a faithful housekeeper who distributes and shares out to each person that part and portion that is due for their acts, whether they be good or bad. It is fitting for you to keep and work through her, for nothing is more pertinent for a king or prince" (2.5). Christine's own definition of justice is constructed in terms that directly echo Cicero in *De officiis*, namely, its dual character. It is "commanded by natural law," she says, that "justice involves two things in particular: one is that the judge have the will and desire to benefit all, and the other is not to harm anyone" (2.9). Christine makes reference in the *Paix* to Cicero's specific version of organic order to explain the functioning of justice. The absence of justice is "as if one part of the body possessed understanding and strove to draw to itself the blood, health and substance of its neighboring limb. This would cause the weakening and deterioration of the whole body, of which every limb needs its share of blood, humors and nourishment. So it is in human society: for just as nature grants that each part acquires what it needs for its betterment, she does not wish us to strip someone else to clothe ourselves" (2.25). Christine thus demonstrates a strong grasp of the natural foundations of justice according to Cicero and adapts his precepts to the problem of eliminating quarrels and discord in France. A ruler who governs on the basis of justice, in conformity with the dictates of nature and the bonds of human society, ensures that his realm will be peaceful. By contrast, no community can flourish if justice is not the principle according to which it is ordered. Christine's plea for peace throughout the country is inseparable from her appeal for the (re)institution of just rule there.

To reinforce the lesson that human beings are by nature harmonious in their relations, Christine appeals frequently to the Ciceronian idea of friendship. After quoting *De amicitia* 23, she observes, "It seems as if Tully was prophesying about the present time when he spoke the words above, which mean that we can now see how great is the power of friendship and concord over the evils that have come our way through dissension and discord" (2.7). Elsewhere she cites Cicero to the effect that nothing is more natural than to place friendship at the center of all human affairs (2.26).

Christine's interest in friendship is apparently twofold. First, she deems it extremely important for the king to maintain "amity" with and among the powerful men of France, so that they will prefer peace to internecine warfare (2.3). In line with her primary concerns, Christine recognizes that friendship is the complete opposite of hostility. Since those who are friends necessarily live together in peace, the wise ruler promotes and enhances the virtues required for the cultivation of solid friendships.

Second, and perhaps more crucially, Christine expresses considerable trepidation about how to distinguish between true and false friendships when making judgments concerning the reliability of the king's counselors. The fraught problem of royal reliance on advisors, especially in regard to the potential for flattery, so commanded her attention that she devoted seven chapters of the *Paix* to it. Although, as we have seen, Cicero himself regarded genuine friendship to exist only among equals, Christine modifies elements of his thought to address the problem of the trustworthiness of counselors and officials in their proffering of advice and aid to their superior. In this regard, she particularly emphasizes the importance of assuring that there is no ulterior motive on the part of persons on whom the king relies. Service done in the hope of some reward is a betrayal of the core of a properly virtuous relationship. "Powerful men," Christine remarks, "deceive themselves greatly, as Tully says, when they believe in times of prosperity that they are loved by those who lead them on with false blandishments, while everything appears different if ever fortune turns from sweet to bitter. As soon as power is lost, so too are such friends" (1.14). Cicero's critical discussion of the instrumental nature of many so-called friendships assists Christine in focusing on the hazards posed by untrustworthy advisors and thereby in identifying the qualities of virtue necessary to assure that members of the royal circle will serve their king honorably. Cicero's insights proved useful to Christine in counseling kings about the perils that they confronted.

CONCLUSION

In considering more generally the presence of Ciceronian elements in the vernacular considered in this chapter, it seems appropriate to raise, however briefly, the issue of the geographical and linguistic pattern of their diffusion. That many of Cicero's writings would have been attractive to thinkers resident in the Italian communes of the High and Late Middle Ages is sensible enough, both because of his avowed attachment to and advocacy of republican constitutions and virtues and of their instructional value in the skills associated with rhetorical success. Although Latini's *Tresor* had been composed in French during his period of exile, it nonetheless reflects its Florentine author's urban and republican sensibilities. By contrast, we might assume that the situation in France would be similar to that in contemporary England and the Holy Roman (German) Empire. In those locales, vernacular texts did address social and political issues and proposed remedies, but these took forms far different from those to be found in Oresme and Christine. Why? I will close this chapter with the simple speculation that the especially close connections between the French royal court and the University of Paris account for at least part of the reason that significant vernacular writing on theoretical topics (often constructed by employing Ciceronian materials) flourished in France as in no other Latin territorial kingdom prior to the Renaissance.

CHAPTER 7

Ciceronian Imperialism

From Cicero's lifetime onward, he has been heralded as the chief exponent of the values and institutions associated with ancient republican Rome. His reputation was cemented by a variety of factors, political as well as philosophical: his contention that the life of the statesman represents the highest human calling, his implacable antagonism toward threats of tyranny, and his oratorical defenses of fellow Romans against arbitrary abuses of power. Cicero's status in this regard formed a common theme among his devotees as well as his detractors. As Thierry Sol has exhaustively documented, a debate of major proportions raged in European political writing from the early fourteenth century through to the Italian Renaissance concerning the conflict between those who believed Cicero to be justified in opposing the "tyranny" of Julius Caesar (and in legitimating his assassination) and those who held that Caesar was the savior of the Republic, against whom Cicero's attacks were baseless and perhaps even self-serving.[1] As a social and political theorist, Cicero's authorship of the treatises *De re publica* and *De legibus*, as well as *De officiis* and other of his philosophical and rhetorical works and speeches, unquestionably identifies him as a quintessential republican of the Roman variety. Certainly, this reflected the attitude of the great "civic" humanists of the fifteenth and sixteenth centuries.[2] And, as discussed in chapter 4, a medieval republican such as Ptolemy of Lucca at the beginning of the fourteenth century found in Cicero a kindred spirit.

Yet, as with other instances already examined in this book, Cicero's ideas were also appropriated by thinkers who adopted views seemingly at odds with fundamental Ciceronian principles: in the present case, early European proponents of empire, understood as a universal world government modeled after imperial Rome. The very attempt to defend a world monarch may seem highly implausible, given the political realities of the later Middle Ages and the Renaissance: emerging territorial kings, self-governing urbanized republics, and the reduction of the Holy Roman emperor to little more than the king of Germany (with some vestigial authority in northern Italy). Even in the latter instance, the incumbent remained beholden to the electors (an elite body of nobles from "greater Germany," lay and ecclesiastical, who selected the possessor of the imperial office), or to the papacy (to which was ascribed the customary authority of crowning emperors), or to both. One might certainly conclude that the designation of emperor was little more than an honorific. And yet the propagation of the idea of the emperor as *dominus mundi* (lord over the entirety of the earth) persisted as a key theme in contemporary political theory.

To what may we ascribe this peculiar situation? A number of factors are relevant. Certainly, one pertains to what James Muldoon refers to as "apocalyptic," in the sense that the empire performed a function of fulfilling biblical prophecy concerning "end times."[3] Another significant element may be located in the very notion of the Christian faith, and thus the church, as unitary and universal. The assertion of a single *res publica Christiana*, guided by the pope in spiritual matters, was often presumed to entail a temporal authority of comparable magnitude competent to protect it: the Holy Roman emperor.[4] Authors argued over the question of which ruler—pope or emperor—was supreme, which was the main issue at stake, for instance, in Dante's widely read *Monarchia* as well as its forerunners and critics.[5] Certainly other explanations might be adduced for the lingering of imperial ideals well beyond their apparently practical utility. The point of the present chapter, however, is not to analyze these various accounts but instead to demonstrate how appeal to the social and political thought of Cicero constituted one important strategy on behalf of legitimizing world empire. Specifically, three thinkers illustrate the trend of putting Cicero to work in the cause of empire: Engelbert of Admont, an eminent schoolman and cleric who flourished around the turn of the fourteenth century; Aeneas Silvius Piccolomini, a highly educated humanist raised to the papal throne in 1458 as Pius II; and Nicholas of Cusa, an eminent fifteenth-century philosopher, theologian, and cardinal.[6] Each of these figures produced treatises lauding the Roman Empire that were clearly indebted to doctrines first

proposed in the context of the seemingly uncongenial teachings of Ciceronian republicanism.

ENGELBERT OF ADMONT

Among university-trained scholars who flourished during the late thirteenth and early fourteenth centuries, Engelbert of Admont was one of
the most prolific and intellectually wide-ranging. Educated primarily at
the universities of Prague and Padua, he followed the path of ecclesiastical
administration rather than academia, holding numerous and increasingly
important posts throughout central Europe.[7] G. B. Fowler, in his survey
of Engelbert's career from a number of years ago, demonstrated convincingly the intellectual breadth of a cosmopolitan and savvy churchman who
composed forty-four genuine works, with another twenty-five extant texts
attributed to him at one time or another.[8] The range of topics covered by
these treatises bespeaks the vastness of his interests, including theology, natural philosophy, ethical theory, aesthetics, and history. Given the breadth
and eclecticism of Engelbert's writings, as well as his practical experiences,
it is hardly surprising that he turned his pen to political matters as well. He is
credited with a tract entitled *De regimine principum* (ca. 1290), to which
James Blythe has drawn considerable attention in recent times,[9] and a *Speculum virtutum moralium*, which touches on social ethics.[10] Yet Engelbert's
treatise promoting the singular legitimacy of the universal Roman Empire,
De ortu et fine Romani imperii, stands as his most significant contribution
to political theory,[11] composed at a time when its author was enmeshed in
the machinations of imperial politics swirling around the early part of the
reign of the German king (and eventual emperor) Henry VII.[12]

Engelbert commences his investigation into the contemporary status
of the Roman Empire with a preface recounting the circumstances under
which *De ortu et fine* was written.[13] According to him, he had entered into
a conversation with some friends who expressed doubts about the validity
of the Roman ruler's claims to exercise universal jurisdiction in the past
as well as about the relevance of the empire given the realities posed by
the autonomy of "diverse kingdoms and principates and people," in other
words, the precise situation mentioned above (*De ortu et fine*, 37). Engelbert
resolved to compose a tract that considers and responds to these objections.
Initially, he states that he will employ the Aristotelian investigative method
as laid out in the opening section of the *Politics* in order to establish the

basis of natural superiority and inferiority, from which flows the necessity of the subjection of the latter to the former (37–38).[14] From the very first paragraph, however, he departs from Aristotle and turns instead to Cicero in order to ground the distinction between the inferior and the superior. It rests, Engelbert says, on a matter of reason: "Man naturally excels man according to the fact that one man is better than another—or many others—through intellect and reason" (38). Yet Engelbert does not deny, as did Aristotle, that certain people's capacity for the exercise of rational faculties is somehow so defective that they are unable to make judgments about their own condition. Rather, "Those who are inferior in intellect naturally are subjects and obey them [i.e., 'those who thrive naturally by intellect and reason'] as better, more worthy, and more powerful to save and preserve themselves by means of those men" (38–39). Precisely such an inegalitarian principle explains the origins of government within human society, according to Engelbert. On this point, Cicero is invoked:

> And so the first origin of kingdoms and principates, according to this order and way of nature, was thus from the beginning: that men from the first age of the world, as if instigated by nature and reason and compelled by the natural experience of need, having fixed more secure places and boundaries—within which they dwell together, gathered as one under a conformity of language, life, and customs— set up someone among themselves by reason and intellect to rule, save and preserve the rest of the multitude, obey and accept having themselves ruled, saved and preserved, as Tully clearly writes at the first part of the *Rhetoric* [*De inventione*]. (39)

Having come together out of necessity for their own survival, human beings voluntarily submitted themselves to a ruler, a man of superior reason and virtue, who would protect them and govern for their well-being. For Engelbert, the assembly of human beings in a community and the establishment of a basic system of governance are the products of the "reason and intellect" of those party to the process of social and political cohesion. As Cicero posits, all humans possess a latent rational capacity sufficient to recognize that they are better off living socially with one another.

Engelbert thus relies on the typically Ciceronian view that nature, reason, and virtue are intimately connected. On several occasions throughout *De ortu et fine*, he proposes that reason and art imitate nature (e.g., 38,

68). By this, Engelbert appears to mean that nature (which he sometimes equates with divine providence, in line with the medieval formula *natura, id est, Deus*) provides the standard against which the innovations introduced by the efforts of men are to be evaluated: "The society of men (*sociatate hominum*) comes from art and reason, which are the directive principles of human acts" (64). The rational and inventive dimensions inherent in mankind, applied in accordance with nature, lead to the creation of social order and with it the authorization of a ruler necessary for its maintenance. Consequently, the governance of the many (who do not live according to the reason they possess) by a wise man—that is, kingship—is a human construct, yet is wholly in accord with nature. Engelbert remarks that "primordial kingdoms seem commendable on account of their origin," namely, "on account of the goodness of the kings, because they were promoted to being kings not by way of ambition for power but by way of election based on their virtue and probity" (39). *De ortu et fine* effectively echoes Cicero's account of the need for human beings to cooperate with nature by the exercise of their rational powers in order to institute all of the features of social and political life. This impression is reinforced later in the work, when Engelbert cites with approval Cicero's definition from *De re publica* (as replicated by Augustine) of a people as "the multitude of men associated as one by common consent" (65). He, however, modifies the force of the Ciceronian definition of a people, and thus a republic, by insisting that the consent given is to divine and human law. Since the law of God is singular, and "all human law derives its authority and foundation from divine law," Engelbert concludes that the consent of a people requires that there is "only one republic of the whole Christian people. Therefore, there will be of necessity only one true prince and king of that republic" (65–66). Simply put, the logic of agreement by the people to their governance entails that they will, if they employ their reason in a manner consonant with nature, endorse kingship—whether primordial or imperial—and no other form of rule.

Engelbert thus begins with essentially Ciceronian premises and repurposes them to suit his own pro-imperial position. Certainly, Cicero and Engelbert both assert that the earliest form of government is monarchic, and that the person chosen to be king will possess outstanding virtue. Likewise, each author maintains that kingship, at least in its primitive state, comes into existence by means of the exercise of human reason in order to uphold fair and equitable social intercourse among men. And, finally, they acknowledge that virtuous kingly rule will inevitably devolve across generations into tyranny. It is the case, Engelbert observes, that "from the beginning of the origin of kingdoms, there were good kings and good and just kingdoms and that, later, as if succeeding and prevailing over that which is according to nature, that which is against nature prevailed.... Consequently, too, that primeval good and equity of the first kings and kingdoms and peoples was changed in the process successively into the malice and evil of succeeding kings and kingdoms" (42). Such corruption among primordial rulers occurs when they begin to privilege passion over reason and virtue, so that the very purpose for which kings are created and obeyed becomes utterly perverted (41). An important token of the transformation from kingship to tyranny is the alteration of the aim of warfare. Citing *De officiis*, Engelbert distinguishes between defensive and offensive uses of martial violence. It is perfectly valid, in his view, to protect one's property and *patria* by military means. Indeed, true kings ought to take up arms "on account of the security of their kingdoms, because the kingdoms of individuals were confined within the fatherland of each" (40). By contrast, expansionistic war is a primary mark of tyranny, inasmuch as the peace of early kingdoms was replaced by "violent invasion and oppression of neighbors and iniquitous expansion of borders and the transgression of external boundaries" (43). Once aggressive armed conflict directed externally becomes the norm, a breakdown of order within the tyrannically governed territory occurs, with the emergence of discordant factions fighting one another as well as their ruler, and the strong oppressing the weak.

Engelbert thus concurs with Cicero that the primary good of civilized peoples is peace: "Peace, then, is the end on account of which every community and society of men (*omnes communitas et societas hominum*) is established and the form according to which it is ruled and the reason or cause on account of which it endures and is preserved" (63). Beyond this point in their respective arguments, however, Engelbert and Cicero diverge. For Cicero, the primary assurance of peace is the formulation of civil laws on the basis of reason in accord with justice founded on natural law, which for him involves constitutional government. Engelbert's solution for the elimination of conflict is instead the institution of world empire. Engelbert recognizes that differences among various localized political groupings reflect natural, cultural, linguistic, and geographic diversity. But he points out that such differences inevitably generate competition, conflict, discord, and ultimately warfare. The disturbance of the peace and spread of injustice resulting from a localized organization of political institutions thus violate the very purposes for which government was created (66–80). By contrast, the presence of a unitary global regime eliminates discord and promotes an established system of justice and rectification. Engelbert carefully considers the counterarguments favoring the emerging territorial political systems in Europe, yet he finally refutes them as incongruent with the telos of politics itself. He forcefully advocates the preferability of a single, universal form of imperial rule in comparison with individual, separate kingdoms and republics. The ordering of both the natural and the supernatural worlds points to the validity of submitting to the rule of a single, universally acknowledged empire and emperor in the political realm as well.

Once the submission of all people on earth to a single *dominus mundi* is accomplished, the attendant fruits of peace will be attained. According to *De ortu et fine*, human happiness may only be achieved under world monarchy. Happiness is understood by Engelbert as the greatest good of any regime. A community may be counted happy when its ruler is contented with his possessions and station and thus has a quarrel neither with his own subjects nor with other countries. Such happiness exists when three conditions are met: sufficiency, tranquility, and security. If a ruler is materially self-reliant, undisturbed by complaints, and assured in his office, the conduct of public affairs will accord with human happiness in the political sphere. The Roman Empire distinctively meets these criteria. Its existence is not, in Engelbert's view, the consequence of violent domination. Rather, it affords the quintessential example of a regime that fulfilled the dual goals of both justice in the acquisition of power and justice in administration. All Roman territorial expansion resulted from either just war, inheritance, or voluntary subjection. Moreover, once acquired, these territories were always governed justly. But *De ortu et fine* reaches these imperialist conclusions by commencing with and embracing a framework originally meant to justify a very different form of social and political organization, namely, the republicanism advocated by Cicero. And Engelbert was not alone in applying Ciceronian ideas to the defense of empire.

AENEAS SILVIUS PICCOLOMINI

By the middle of the fifteenth century, as a result of the efforts of Italian Renaissance humanists, Cicero had become thoroughly entrenched as the leading philosopher of antiquity in matters of social and political theory. His central place within humanism has, as noted previously, often been assimilated to a "civic" and urban model of republican constitution that stood firmly opposed to the imperial form of government he propounded as well as the personal example he set. Simply stated, "For the humanists, the Roman prototype of the ['ideal citizen'] was Cicero, the defender of the republic . . . who is *optimus* through virtue and intelligence."[15] Consequently, there have been negligible efforts to reevaluate, let alone sever, the general relationship between *quattrocento* humanism and the political climate of the Italian cities.[16] At the same time, some humanists utilized Cicero in ways entirely antithetical to urban republican institutions and practices. Aeneas Silvius Piccolomini provides a prominent example of how Cicero could be invoked by an Italian humanist to support the cause of the Holy Roman Empire, a polity far different from the self-governing cities of Italy.

Aeneas received a fine humanist education. He was an almost exact contemporary of some of the most notable figures of the fifteenth-century Renaissance, such as Palmieri, Valla, and Patrizi, and he enjoyed a reputation similar to theirs for his writings. His letters, in particular, compare favorably in their style and substance to the best of humanist literature.[17] A man of action and faith as well as letters, Aeneas's career included lengthy service to Emperor Frederick III as a secretary and diplomat, as well as appointment to the bishoprics of Trieste and Siena. He was ultimately elevated to the papal seat in 1458 as Pius II,[18] in which office he has come to be regarded as both the first "humanist pope" and as a leading disseminator of Italian Renaissance values to northern and central Europe.[19] Yet Aeneas's name is consistently absent from surveys of Renaissance political thought.[20] The reason for this, simply stated, is that Aeneas's main treatises on secular politics are almost exclusively concerned with defending and promoting a universalistic, imperial, and even absolutist ideal of government under the banner of the Holy Roman Empire. Consequently, his political thought is treated (at least implicitly) as an anachronistic reversion to outdated constructs and categories rather than as the reflection of an authentically Renaissance perspective on politics. Why? Presumably on the assumption just discussed that Renaissance humanism was fundamentally incompatible with the advocacy of an imperial ideal.

Yet the evidence provided by the social and political ideas of Aeneas suggests that this position is mistaken. The main body of his thought is to be found in two treatises, the *Pentalogus de rebus ecclesiae et imperii* of 1443 and

De ortu et auctoritate imperii Romani, composed three years later. The first of these is primarily a book of practical advice to the emperor containing recommendations for the reunification of Europe and the reconquest of the Holy Lands.[21] Consequently, the *Pentalogus* is of interest to the modern reader for more purely historical rather than theoretical reasons. By contrast, one may detect in *De ortu et auctoritate* the presence of a coherent philosophical argument of demonstrably Ciceronian provenance.[22] Scholars have seldom acknowledged a Ciceronian component within *De ortu et auctoritate,* let alone investigated the significance and depth of Cicero's impact upon Aeneas's political theory.[23] It may be argued, indeed, that Aeneas more nearly approaches the philosophical core of Cicero's own thought than did *quattrocento* humanists. I say this because Aeneas recognizes that Cicero's own work involved an unresolved tension between what might be termed localism and a universalism that might be used to found a theory of world empire. On Aeneas's account, localism stimulates the disintegration of the principles of mutual association and common benefit upon which society itself is built. Localism is incompatible with the rational foundations of social and political life stemming from human nature, a claim that arises directly out of Aeneas's adherence to Ciceronian premises. By contrast, he holds that only a universal empire performs the functions necessary for the maintenance of social bonds among human beings and is therefore uniquely consistent with the natural endowment of mankind.

To the extent that Aeneas's work seeks to develop and refine a set of philosophical precepts derived from the writings of Cicero, the presumed incongruity between his humanist intellectual commitments, on the one hand, and his imperialism, on the other, becomes considerably less tenable. Admittedly, *De ortu et auctoritate* occasionally refers to the divine ordination of the Roman emperor and his successors. But such remarks are largely tangential to the main features of Aeneas's argument; they augment his position rather than establish its premises. If we instead view his theory as characteristically Ciceronian in orientation, however, we may more readily understand how a dedicated humanist could, without self-contradiction, arrive at an ostensibly "anachronistic" conception of political life as ultimately universalistic in character. So what exactly is the ambiguity that Aeneas exploits? He seeks to demonstrate that lingering within Cicero's conception of human association is an unresolved tension arising from the Ciceronian conception of human association. Aeneas unequivocally asserts that Roman dominion "derives its origin from the rational faculty of human nature which is the best guide of how to live and which all must obey" (95).[24] The Christian commitments that compelled him to acknowledge the sinful condition of postlapsarian man did not intrude into his account of the origins of human social and political relations. Aeneas observes that "once our first parents had been driven out of the paradise of delights," men were condemned to "roaming the fields and woods like beasts and preserving their existence with the meat of wild animals" (95). Thus the Fall induced among men a solitary existence, bereft of whatever forms of association might have existed in paradise—in sum, a state of primeval isolation.

Such a presocial world corresponds to the description of the "original" circumstances of mankind sketched by Cicero in his rhetorical works in order to explain the role played by oratory in uniting dispersed individuals. But Aeneas never appeals directly in *De ortu et auctoritate* to men's linguistic faculties. Rather, adopting the framework of the mature Cicero, who somewhat downplayed language in relation to rationality, he identifies reason as the unique source of man's social tendencies.

> Man observed—since God created him to share in His rational faculty—that to draw man together with man for the maximally good life, a society would be of great necessity. Therefore, those who had previously lived their lives separate from one another in the forests, like wild animals, whether at nature's behest or by the will of God who directs all nature, came together in the same place, established societies, built houses, surrounded their communities with walls, discovered practical skills, and, when one man ministered to the convenience of another, the civic way of life was astonishingly pleasing for individuals, and the companionship of neighbors and friends, which had previously not been known, seemed exceedingly sweet. (95–96)

Aeneas here recapitulates the main points emphasized by Cicero in *De officiis* and elsewhere. Human beings in their pristine state all possessed by nature the same capacity for reason that led them to unite. Underlying Aeneas's argument for superior and inferior human beings is the premise of the equality of rationality that derives from the Ciceronian account of social intercourse.

Aeneas also shares with Cicero a pronounced doubt about the permanence of such a primitive social arrangement founded solely on reason and nature. He explicitly cites the dictum of *De officiis* that "just as many advantageous things are acquired by man for his fellow man, so there is no evil which is not brought about by man to his fellow man" (*De ortu et auctoritate*, 96). He proceeds to describe a condition of existence not so far removed from a Hobbesian state of nature, in which neither wealth and possessions, nor families, nor even personal safety can be assured and that hence knows no social bond. Aeneas ascribes this breakdown of communal harmony to the vice of "cupidity" ("the rival of peace") which could "not suffer the justice of a pure society to endure inviolate for long" (96). The rationality that stimulates men to join together into a community gives way to passion and the pursuit of narrow self-interest that proves to be the ultimate enemy of social relations. In such a context, justice may too readily be ignored even when it is acknowledged to govern the communal order. Individuals cannot be counted upon to exercise self-restraint and moderation consistently and thereby to respect the rights of their fellows.

Initially, the "justice of a pure society" drives the oppressed to seek out an "individual, outstanding in virtue, who would prevent injuries being done to weaker men, who, established by equity, would bind the greatest together with the least with an equal law" (96). This event, Aeneas says, occurred not in just one locale, but in many. The function of these men of superlative virtue, who came to be called kings, was the enforcement of "justice," which "is a civil institution, guarding the bonds of human society so long as it punishes the iniquity of evildoers or confers rewards on good men" (96). Such civil justice is essential to uphold all forms of social cooperation. If peaceful relations could have been maintained by men in a purely social setting, political power would never have been conferred upon kings in the first place (a fact that, for Aeneas, guides the subsequent imposition of political power over communities). The king is regarded in Ciceronian terms as the personification of justice: his moral character outshines that of his fellows, and so he does not require law as the foundation of his rule, since his judgments are so rooted in a sense of justice and equity that they enjoy the force of law. Hence, the introduction of royal government represents an extension of the principles of natural reason: "Nature disposed that the varying impulses of individual men should be moderated by the just governance of kings" (97). Kingship accords with nature inasmuch as it permits human beings to live that sociable existence toward which they are naturally inclined but with which the vice of cupidity interferes. For this reason, kings are never excused from the duty to enforce the precepts of justice.

Thus far, Aeneas has worked along strictly Ciceronian lines. But he begins to diverge from this path when he addresses the disintegration of primitive kingship. It may be recalled that Cicero premised the replacement of such rulers on the acquisition of the crown by persons of evil character; a system of law replaced the initial kingship to combat the vicissitudes of arbitrary personal government. As described by Cicero, this process is entirely contingent. So long as a succession of good men occupies the throne, there is no reason for kingship to be supplanted by the rule of law. By contrast, Aeneas thinks that he detects an inherent weakness in political arrangements associated with kingship, regardless of the moral qualities of a particular royal incumbent. He had already pointed out that the creation of the king was not a unique or isolated event: "The world had many kings" (97). Thus we confront a plurality of territorial units. As these kingdoms defined and expanded their geographical boundaries or spheres of jurisdiction, they inevitably came into conflict. And since there was no means of arbitration among such coequal powers, the resolution of disputes between them occurred by means of armed engagements.

Two points flow from Aeneas's observation. First, it is clear that the ensuing conflicts that arise from the proliferation of royally governed territories are directly the function of an inescapable structural limitation endemic to localized or regional governance per se. It is not morally corrupt rulers alone who are held responsible for clashes over lands and rights. Instead, any king who is performing his proper duties will, Aeneas supposes, inevitably enter into contention with another king and will be compelled to turn to warfare (97). This suggests a second consequence: the political model of an independent network of kingships is incompatible with the very purpose for which civil justice was instituted, namely, the maintenance of harmonious relations among human beings. As Aeneas remarks, "With wars clattering and raging, republic was unable to meet together with republic, nor territory with territory, and that sweetest commerce of human society was obstructed" (97). The decentralized distribution of royal power ultimately produces an effect that is exactly contrary to that intended. Empowered as the agent of social harmony, kingship proves to be its enemy, confounding rather than reinforcing the associative propensities within human nature.

Sociability is deemed, in Ciceronian fashion, to be a universal human attribute. The particularity of royal regimes runs afoul of this universality of nature, and the ordained end of political power will thereby never be achieved.

On this score, Aeneas renders explicit a tension lurking beneath Cicero's own account of social and political organization. He confronts a question with which Cicero had declined to deal: are certain political forms more or less consistent with the purpose of political power as upholding justice and social order? Aeneas's answer is that the universality of human society founded upon justice requires the concomitant universality of political rule—that is, a single world empire. Nature itself authorizes such a universal arrangement of political power: "The beneficent providence of human nature [viz., reason], which strives by its very nature toward the best, not wishing present or future circumstances to be badly disposed, was at hand. Therefore, under its influence, it was resolved that individual rulers should be brought back under a single will, which the Greeks call monarchy and we call empire" (97). In empire alone does political power finally attain a form consistent with the universalistic tendencies of sociability implicit within human nature. Rational reflection about the common good will inevitably lead us to acknowledge that imperial rule is necessary for the maintenance of the basic principles of human association.

Aeneas only moves beyond a naturalistic Ciceronian perspective when he attempts to justify the specific claim of the Roman emperors and their heirs to global predominance. At that point, the tone of his argument shifts markedly, emphasizing instead a combination of historical and religious factors. He recounts the failure of various pre-Roman empires and of the Roman Republic. He asserts in teleological fashion that these other nations and forms of government were a kind of prelude to the best regime—the imperial system founded by Julius Caesar and consolidated by Augustus (98). The superiority of the rule of a single man over the entire world is confirmed by the deeds and words of Jesus, as well as by the teachings of the church, all of which afford the Roman Empire special rights and prerogatives (98–100). Although Aeneas sometimes implies that nature itself has sanctioned the authority of the Roman rulers and their Frankish and German successors (101–2), his ultimate conclusion about the relation between the natural basis of imperial power, on the one hand, and the historicoreligious foundations of specifically Roman dominion, on the other, is more subtly stated: "Since natural reason itself showed that a single ruler was required—one who would resolve disputes, administer justice, watch over the peoples in peace, and preside over all temporal matters—it is clear that the dignity of this task is fit for the Roman King, who, it is agreed, has had this task in his keeping for a long time" (102). Reason instructs us in the necessity of the rule of one imperial authority over all human affairs; historical experience and divine intervention indicate to us that this authority should be vested in the Roman emperor. Thus Aeneas implicitly recognizes that the Ciceronian framework has an essentially philosophical bearing: it can tell us which arrangement of political power is best (and why) but not which historical configuration must be obeyed. To justify the latter, other criteria of a nonphilosophical sort (such as tradition and divine ordination) must be invoked.

The Ciceronian dimension does not thereafter disappear from Aeneas's argument, however. Rather, he returns to a fundamentally naturalistic approach when he addresses the central theme of *De ortu et auctoritate*, namely, the explicit critique of the claims made on behalf of localized regimes to be independent of imperial control. He observes that one of two grounds is ordinarily advanced for such an exemption from subjection to the empire: either liberty has been conceded by the superior authority of an emperor, or it has been earned by meritorious virtue. In both instances, the case for autonomy rests on a readiness to shatter the bonds of human sociability, the maintenance of which is the primary purpose of the exercise of political power. Even admitting that an emperor might have ceded some of his prerogatives to inferior governments, still all such grants are cancelled because of their incompatibility with the natural law dictates of universal justice:

> Since, as we have shown previously, it is agreed that empire was established in accordance with the law of nature and that monarchy is necessary to the preservation of peace and the administration of justice, it is certain that concessions of the sort which confer power upon a multitude of authorities have no validity. For discord is born of this, robbery frequently occurs, murder in various forms and countless numbers is committed, since once the peace has been upset wars spring up everywhere, because there is no individual greater than all others who could impose a limit on discord with

the rule of law. If we were living under one head, if we owed obedience to a single person, if we recognized only one supreme ruler in temporal affairs, the best sort of peace would flourish everywhere on earth and we would all enjoy sweet harmony. (103)

Society itself crumbles when divided by concessions of liberty, reverting to those conditions that obtained in the past before the multitude of kingdoms was replaced by a single world empire. But since political power is pointless or arbitrary unless it contributes to the promotion of communal intercourse, such reversion cannot be justified by even the most thoroughly documented and complete grant of freedom given by an emperor to a nation or its rulers.

Similar considerations exclude merit as a legitimate rationale for the assertion of the independence of territorial governance. Aeneas allows that during the dark days of the empire, certain men may have recovered imperial territories from barbarian domination and thereby claimed hegemony over a given province as the reward for their courage and skill. He does not deny that such a liberator and his heirs should be permitted to serve in the role of imperial vicar in these reclaimed lands. But the authority enjoyed by those who recover imperial territories is at best that of a protectorate; *de facto* possession and rule does not confer *de jure* lordship (*dominium*) (104). Indeed, if such *dominium* were claimed, these men would be thieves and usurpers rather than defenders of the empire. No merit of persons or families can displace the fact that political power must be exercised according to a universal plan if it is be employed in a manner congruent with the legitimate standards of reason and justice. The application of authority independent of the emperor, by even the most virtuous individual, "shatters the dignity of monarchical power, produces schism within the empire, and takes away all the concord of human society" (104). The emperor is thus obliged to assert his imperial rights over any lesser ruler who believes that he has earned autonomous power over a realm because of his own good deeds or those of his ancestors. If the division of the empire into localized units is not to be destructive of social order, the governors of territories must acknowledge their lack of independence and their primary duty to defer and submit to their imperial master.

In this way, a Ciceronian conception of the natural foundations of society might well yield the philosophical premises for a critique of localized and civic government. The validity of this conclusion is in no way undermined by Aeneas's further devotion to an absolutist model of imperial rule, according to which the emperor's will has the force of law and he also enjoys the right to appropriate the private property of his subjects (106). Indeed, while these doctrines may be utterly anathema to the views espoused by Cicero, Aeneas's account suggests that the two perspectives may not be so incompatible, at least logically, as they would seem at first glance. He endeavors to elucidate the imperial powers of appropriation and legislation in terms consonant with Ciceronian teachings. In the instance of an emperor's claim upon the goods of his subjects—which is in any case limited to "when necessity demands it for the republic"—Aeneas connects his position with Cicero's remarks in *De finibus*, *De officiis*, and elsewhere in his corpus that our duties extend beyond ourselves to the political community of which we are a member.[25] *De ortu et auctoritate* proclaims, "If a citizen will give everything he possesses for his safety, by how much more will he do this for the sake of the republic, for which we ought to develop our wealth no less than for ourselves?" (106). Inasmuch as the "republic" in question can only be the empire, because it is the only legitimate political structure, Aeneas posits the duty of all persons to surrender their material goods without objection to the emperor when required for the common welfare. He repeatedly stresses the obligation of individuals to prefer the benefit of the community to any private gain. At this juncture, Aeneas invokes a version of the organic analogy that Cicero himself employed in *De officiis*:

> For, just as certain limbs are amputated should they atrophy and, as it were, begin to lack spirit, lest they harm the remaining parts of the body, so too some men must suffer for the sake of the republic, although they appear to have merited no evil, if the state, which will be safe without them, perishes with them. . . . Nor should it seem a grave thing, if, for the sake of the body's health, we say that a foot or a hand, as citizens are in the republic, must be cut off, for the prince, who is the head of the body of the republic, is bound, when the common safety demands it, to lay down his life. (*De ortu et auctoritate*, 107)

For Aeneas as for Cicero, the overriding interests of the individual in the maintenance of society authorize any sacrifice necessary for the public good. The mere fact that *De ortu et auctoritate* lapses into the language of *res publica* is highly suggestive of the extent to which Aeneas is overlaying Ciceronian precepts on his defense of the Roman Empire.

The theory of legislation in *De ortu et auctoritate* perhaps affords still clearer insight into Aeneas's extension of Ciceronian ideas to support imperial absolutism. He accepts that under ordinary circumstances the emperor should regard himself to be bound by the same laws that he enforces over his subjects, restating the traditional *digna vox* formula (108). Yet Aeneas also insists that the main purpose of imperial rule prohibits the permanent enforced submission of the emperor to statutory law. The reason is that the Roman Empire and emperor exist for the sake not of imposing law but of disseminating justice. Justice composes the essential fabric of society, and in its absence communal disorder necessarily ensues. But what, then, of the case (envisaged by Cicero himself) in which justice and statutory law conflict? Aeneas declares that it is precisely our ability to raise this question that indicates the need for the emperor to stand above law and to dedicate himself to "equity, that which is just beyond the scope of written law. If a law instructs one course and justice argues some other course, it is right that the emperor tempers the force of law with the check of equity; it falls to the emperor alone to interpose an interpretation between the letter of the law and the spirit of justice" (108).[26] Relying upon an awareness of the historicity of law, the growth of which was central to Renaissance humanism, Aeneas explains that statutes "which were once just have been rendered unjust, ineffective, harsh or iniquitous" (109). Consequently, he believes that the emperor must possess the authority to abrogate or change the law when such incongruities emerge. The emperor is not granted carte blanche to legislate arbitrarily or for personal gain. Rather, he acts at times above the law in order to secure that end for which his office and political power generally were instituted: to uphold the harmonious order of society by enforcing justice. Since it is not always assured that "the legal" is coextensive with "the just," the emperor as the agent of the universal bonds of community must be permitted to exercise his discretion in revising or dismissing unjust decrees. To deny him this jurisdiction would be to imperil the perpetuation of human association itself. Once again, Ciceronian premises can be seen to underpin a political doctrine that admittedly shares little with Cicero's own vision of politics.

We are thus justified in rejecting as a false dichotomy the distinction that has been repeatedly drawn within the scholarship on Aeneas between

his Renaissance humanist inclinations and his imperialist political propensities.[27] Rather, the reconciliation of this apparent antinomy may be
located in Aeneas's subtle extension and recasting of the theoretical framework provided by Cicero in directions that the Roman himself had not
envisaged. Aeneas's Ciceronianism is vital inasmuch as it treats Cicero's
ideas as materials to be transformed and fashioned according to their inner
logic as well as external political exigencies. *De ortu et auctoritate* wrests the
substance (if not the intent) of Cicero's political thought away from the
exclusive control of urban and Republican authors. In doing so, Aeneas
revitalized a long-standing debate about the proper relations between the
Roman emperor and other European polities by translating its terms into
a Ciceronian vocabulary accessible to *quattrocento* humanists of all orientations. In sum, dedication to the principles of Italian Renaissance humanism
was not incompatible with advocacy of a theory of empire.

NICHOLAS OF CUSA

Scholars have widely maintained that the *De concordantia catholica* of Nicholas of Cusa (composed in 1433–34) also fits the mold of universal imperialism. Writing at the Council of Basle, in the context of the Great Schism,
Cusa produced his treatise in defense of legitimate conciliar supremacy
in the ultimate determination of matters of orthodoxy and in ecclesiastical governance. One key element of his argument required that the ruler
who occupied the office of emperor (in this specific instance, the current
emperor-elect Sigismund) possessed the authority to convoke a General
Council in the absence of an undisputed papal incumbent. Given this
polemical context, the ascription to Cusa of a commitment to universalism
appears quite reasonable. Thus Paul Sigmund remarked that "the yearning
for a universal empire and universal church, and the hopes for the universal agreement among men that characterized *De concordantia catholica*,
remained with Nicholas until his death."[28] Likewise, Morimichi Watanabe
lamented Cusa's "failure to recognize the emergence of the nation-state,
which had been gradually gaining ground in Europe."[29] Jeannine Quillet
located in Cusa "a basis and sanction for the progressive development of
a 'universal commonwealth' as the utopian conclusion of an ecumenism
whose theoretical foundations he propounded with a boldness that goes
well beyond Dante's anticipatory ideas."[30] And Bernard Guenée implicated

Cusa in a renewal of "the old idea of universal empire" from which "confusion was created which was ultimately responsible for the persistence of the German dream of universal hegemony."[31] On the face of it, then, there seems to be little that distinguishes Cusa's political doctrines from the preceding advocates of universal empire surveyed earlier in this chapter. It turns out, however, that the story is more complicated than the easy assimilation of his thought to other imperialists of his time, such as Aeneas, might suggest.[32] In contrast to his pro-imperial contemporaries, Cusa envisioned a specific and limited application of imperial governance. Yet his position was built upon Ciceronian foundations just as surely as the theories encountered elsewhere among more full-blooded advocates of the universal authority of the latter-day heir to the office of Roman emperor.

De concordantia is composed of three books. The first concerns the harmonious organization of the Christian church, the second contains an explication and defense of conciliar supremacy over the church and especially the pope, and the third investigates the role of the emperor in convoking and participating in a General Council. It has been recognized that the opening sections of book 3 (268–91, termed a "preface")—almost certainly added to the text at a later time than the composition of its main body—were clearly indebted to various chapters of Marsiglio of Padua's Defensor pacis.[33] Without doubt, Cusa was familiar with the Defensor, because near the end of book 2 of De concordantia he says that he had "seen [it] after writing this volume" (197, sec. 256),[34] and he explicitly condemns the ecclesiological doctrines found therein as "pernicious" and "not true" (203–4, sec. 265). Having made such a pronouncement, it may surprise us that he purloins material from Marsiglio's Dictio 1, an appropriation that occurs without mention of his source. Although he usually attributes his discussion of secular social and political theory to Aristotle, he apparently did not consult the Politics directly, instead borrowing various citations employed by Marsiglio.

Yet, as has already been repeatedly demonstrated, ascription of a claim to Aristotle's Politics or Ethics (even filtered through an intermediary source such as Marsiglio) by no means assured its accuracy or veracity. This is evidently the case in De concordantia's references to Aristotle, which mask its author's debt to Ciceronian doctrines. Despite his reliance on the Defensor, Cusa's employment of Cicero's thought differed markedly from Marsiglio's. That Cusa knew of the Roman's work is unquestionable, since he mentions

Cicero alongside Plato, Aristotle, "and all the other philosophers who have written" about political topics (*De concordantia*, 205, sec. 268; see also 249–50, sec. 378). And it is beyond dispute that Ciceronian ideas are fundamental to his account of communal order. Indeed, Cusa at times acknowledges the derivation of his views from Cicero in preference to Aristotle:

> Natural laws precede all human considerations and provide the principles for them all. First, nature intends every kind of animal to preserve its physical existence and its life, to avoid what would be harmful and secure what is necessary to it, as Cicero concludes in the first book, third [fourth] chapter of *De officiis*. For the first requirement of essence is for it to exist. Therefore, for any essence to exist, it possesses inborn faculties designed for this purpose—instinct, appetite, and reason. Hence it happens in different ways in nature that various means are implanted by natural instinct for the purpose of existence and self preservation. (205, sec. 268)

The Ciceronian elements in this passage are unmistakable. Despite the fact that Cusa's reference to *De officiis* is cribbed from *Defensor* 1.4.2, he moves well beyond Marsiglio, specifically, by reference both to natural law and to inborn faculties. Neither of these precepts are to be found in the relevant section of the *Defensor*, making it difficult to conclude that Cusa's Ciceronian appropriations were simply derived from Marsiglio's text.

De concordantia reinforces this impression by immediately explaining that, in spite of the impetus toward self-preservation that is found in all sentient creatures, men possess one faculty distinct to their species: their endowment with reason. (Again, no parallel statement is to be found in the corresponding passage in the *Defensor*.) The special significance of the human rational capacity, Cusa asserts, is its realization that mankind requires social and political relationships in order to survive. On account of "the exercise of their reason," men recognized that "association and sharing are most useful—indeed necessary—for their self preservation and to achieve the purpose of human existence" (205, sec. 269). Natural reason impels people to create civic bodies, laws, and government, all of which are necessary to secure them against "the corrupt desires of many [that] would have prevented this union from improving human life" (205–6, sec. 269). This account very closely resembles Cicero's, especially when Cusa incorporates consent into his formula: "By a marvelous and beneficent divine law"—Cusa treats natural and divine law as mutually interdependent, in line with common medieval usage (for example, 229 sec. 328 and 230 secs. 331–32)—"infused in all men, they know that associating together would be most beneficial to them and that social life would be maintained by laws adopted with the common consent of all" (206, sec. 270). The Ciceronian account of the origin of social relations involves agreement by those party to a communal order extended on the basis of the exercise of their reason. The theme of consent runs throughout the preface to book 3 as well as later chapters. In turn, Cusa connects the consensual nature of society based on men's possession of reason—inhering in them by means of nature and God—to fundamental human equality. "All legitimate authority arises from elective concordance and free submission. There is in people *a divine seed* by virtue of their common equal birth and the equal rights of all men so that all authority—which comes from God as does man himself—is recognized as divine when it comes from the common consent of subjects" (230, sec. 331, emphasis added). Clearly, Cusa means for his audience to see the triad of reason, consent, and equality as bound tightly together. This contrasts notably with Aristotle but adheres quite closely to Ciceronian principles.[35] In addition, Cusa also throws natural law into the mix as the ultimate basis of the rational capacity that renders all of mankind equal and thus competent to consent to the terms of their rule. Already in book 2, Cusa had insisted that "all legislation is based on natural law and any law which contradicts it cannot be valid. . . . Hence, since natural law is naturally based on reason, all law is rooted by nature in the reason of man," which entails that "every governance whether it consists in a written law or is living law in the person of the prince . . . can only come from the agreement and consent of the subjects" (98, sec. 127). Conceptually as well as linguistically, echoes of Cicero resound.

Yet Cusa's appeal to reason is a double-edged sword, since he also maintains that the utilization of the rational faculties is unequal among human beings. He remarks that some people are "better endowed with reason," so that these "wiser and more outstanding men are chosen as rulers by the others to draw up just laws by the clear reason, wisdom and prudence given to them by nature and to rule the others by these laws" (98, sec. 127). Consequently, Cusa posits a strict distinction between the wise few and the foolish multitude, which dictates that the latter ought to play no direct role in their own rule. He says, "Almighty God has assigned a certain natural servitude to the ignorant and stupid so that they readily trust the wise to help them preserve themselves" (206, sec. 271.) Reason dictates the dominance of the few over the many, and thus the rule of a small governing elite over the subjected masses. Strange as it may seem, Cusa does not see any conflict between this position and his insistence upon the equality of human reason and the concomitant requirement of consent. The "enslavement" of the ignorant to the wise does not undercut the volitional character of political arrangements. It may be true that "those better endowed with reason are the natural lords and masters of the others but not by any coercive law or judgment imposed on someone against his will" (98, sec. 127). Submission is entirely voluntary, arising from what Cusa terms "a certain natural instinct" by means of which the relationship between the intellectual elites and their incompetent subjects "is harmonized through common laws that have the wise as their special authors, protectors, and executors, and the concurrent agreement of all the others in voluntary subjection" (208, sec. 275). This suggests, at minimum, that their status as superiors does not exempt the wise from obedience to the same laws by means of which they govern their subjects.

For Cusa, however, the consensual basis of social and political community is not deemed to be participatory.[36] Whatever the impact of the *Defensor pacis* upon *De concordantia* may be, Cusa moved very far from Marsiglio's conception of active and constant communal consent. Nor is this position ascribable to Aristotle, despite references to the *Politics*. Rather, the division between the wise and the ignorant does fit rather well with Cicero's view that, despite the equal natural potential for rational reflection, most men are so corrupted by their passions and desires that they thereby abdicate their ability to use their inbred reason, from which virtue blossoms. It is similar with Cusa. "The foolish man cannot control himself," he states, "and unless he had someone to direct him he would fail in his efforts" (207, sec. 272). There is no contradiction in this position, at least not in Cusa's mind. Nor does Cusa ever appeal to Aristotle's conception of the slave by nature. In fact, he explicitly rejects that doctrine: "For nature does not make a slave, but ignorance, nor does manumission make one free, but learning" (207, sec. 272). He echoes the key Ciceronian theme that the basic endowment of reason in humans does not imply that they will deploy it in identical fashion. Cusa apparently recognizes, as does Cicero, that education is the linchpin for overcoming servitude, since it involves the grooming of reason from which emerges the virtues that liberate men. In summary, men are sufficiently competent intellectually that they recognize their commonality as realized by social relations and political institutions. Yet their shared reason is minimal, inasmuch as most of them cannot resist the ardor stirred up by their addiction to the flesh.

What has all of this to do with the Romanist universalism so often imputed to Cusa? Simply stated, the Ciceronian rationalism on which Engelbert and Aeneas relied was antithetical to Cusa's identification of the foundation of the specifically imperial form of government, which he claimed derives from its spiritual calling. In making this case, Cusa posits a hierarchy of historical regimes stretching from the "king of the Tartars"—who "is the least worthy because he governs through laws least in agreement with those divinely instituted"—through Islamic governance to Christian monarchs. On top of the pyramid, "according to the standard of holiness of rule, I maintain that the authority of the empire is the greatest" (237, sec. 348). He reasons that the chief purposes of all rulers, and especially of Christian kings, are the maintenance of religion and the promotion of eternal ends; all other goals of government are "subservient." Thus "our Christian empire outranks the others, just as our most holy and pure Christian religion in highest in holiness and truth. And as every kingdom and prince should care for his kingdom, so the emperor should care for the whole Christian people" (237–38, sec. 349). Other Christian princes are therefore beneath the Roman emperor and must submit to him in matters concerning the protection of Christ's church (239, sec. 349). Cusa's support of the efforts of Emperor Sigismund to intervene in the Council of Basle rested on the view that to the emperor pertains the duty to enforce conciliar decrees (250–67, secs. 380–424). Hence, imperial authority must extend to all Christian believers: "Because he is guardian of the universal faith and the protector of universal statutes [canons] which could not be effectively executed without a ruler over all, and since the universal statutes respecting the Christian faithful bind all faithful Christians to maintain and apply them, all are subject to the emperor's rule insofar as he is established to maintain those directives" (239–40, sec. 355). Such a universal jurisdiction stems from the fact that "the whole Christian people" transferred power to him to act as enforcer of canon law and "guardian of the universal faith" (238, sec. 349; 239, sec. 355). In these matters, little room would appear to be afforded for national governments to exist as anything other than local agents of the emperor.

Yet Cusa is careful to stipulate that the honor due to the empire, and hence its universalistic character, refers only to its status and functions in the spiritual realm. To the extent that political rule naturally and necessarily involves nonreligious functions that properly pertain to Christian and non-Christian regimes alike, all rulership is legitimate insofar as it performs the tasks necessary for ensuring survival of the incompetent multitude in accordance with voluntarily agreed-upon common laws. In the performance of such purely temporal duties, the emperor's authority derives not from God and the Christian people but from the natural, rational justification for governance previously discussed. Cusa's distinction between the spiritual role performed by the emperor and the earthly responsibility of rulers in general undercuts universalism at the latter level, and it even sanctions localized variations in government. Because political order and law depend upon human volition, valid regimes must always be traced to public consent apart from spiritual authorization. This also implies that political arrangements are historically mutable and capable of reorganization over time. Volition in accordance with reason, then, becomes the touchstone of local diversity in political rule. The emperor's "power to command," Cusa asserts, "does not extend beyond the territorial limits of the empire under him," citing a decree of the Carolingian emperor Louis, who, although he "describes himself as Emperor, . . . issues commands only to the inhabitants of the kingdom of France and the Lombards who were his *de facto* subjects" (235, sec. 343). Even the claim made on behalf of the Roman emperor "to be lord of the world as ruler of the empire that the Romans once conquered by their valor" must be tempered by the fact that Rome never extended its conquests to the larger part of Asia and Africa that, if not heavily populated [to Cusa's knowledge], are of great geographic expanse" (235–36, sec. 344). The emperor's duty as protector of the Catholic faith has no corollary in a secular responsibility for all the peoples of the earth, because the latter requires public consent that has not been given, whereas the permission of the body of Christian believers authorizes the former.

All of this casts doubt on the universalism that scholars have ascribed to Cusa. In terms of the present chapter's focus on the Ciceronian dimensions of imperialism, Cusa offers a rather interesting alternative to Engelbert and Aeneas. *De concordantia* relies upon many of the same materials derived from Cicero that are found in these other theorists of empire: natural law, human reason, equality, virtue. Yet these lead Cusa not to endorse an imperial ideal but rather to posit a disanalogy between naturalistic and spiritual justifications of world government under the Roman emperor. Certainly, he values political universality as a quality necessary for the sake of maintaining the church's unity. Yet the naturalistic dimensions of Cicero's thought upon which Cusa depends—in particular, the principle of consent—undercut any appeal to the Christian foundations of universal empire as a justification of Roman global dominance. Given the shifting and wholly conventional character of the political volition Cusa infers from his Ciceronian premises, a permanent worldwide temporal government cannot be christened "best" or "ideal." Cusa's chastened conception of the pretensions of universal empire finds just as much validation in Cicero as did the vastly more expansive views expounded by Engelbert and Aeneas.

CONCLUSION

Once again, Ciceronian premises can be seen to underpin a political doctrine that shares little with Cicero's own vision of politics. The very idea that his theories might be put to extensive use to advocate universal empire seems oxymoronic at best. Yet Engelbert, Aeneas, and Cusa evidently had no qualms about converting the principles of republican Cicero (and surely they knew that he was that) into a form of imperialism that would have been odious to the Roman. So it makes little sense to invoke the former perspective of "authentic" Ciceronianism, just as the three figures in question did not. Quite without recognizing it, Cicero's political theory opened up possibilities unimaginable to him. This is perhaps especially shocking in the cases of Aeneas and (to a lesser extent) Cusa. Both were associated with Renaissance humanism, which for many scholars equates to a "civic" sensibility associated with cities (especially, although not exclusively, Florence), a position associated most famously with Hans Baron, as noted in the introduction. Based on the evidence examined above, the so-called Baron thesis lacks merit. A Ciceronian of the fifteenth or sixteenth century could, with no less merit or plausibility, defend a "globalized" Roman Empire rather than a civic republic.

A further conclusion follows from this point. The identification of a significant Ciceronian component within the arguments presented by Engelbert, Aeneas, and Cusa illustrates the futility of interpretations that appeal to an unresolved tension or tragic conflict between "medieval" and

"Renaissance" (or early modern) forms of political theory. From the early fourteenth century until the middle of the fifteenth, pro-imperial authors deployed similar tools in order to pursue their intellectual and political agendas. A scholastic such as Engelbert had more in common with the humanists Aeneas and Cusa than with, say, contemporaries like Ptolemy or Marsiglio, not least because of the concordant fashion in which they utilized Cicero's ideas.

CHAPTER 8

Cicero Against Empire

Bartolomé de Las Casas

If the fourteenth- and fifteenth-century debates surrounding the status of world lordship (*dominus mundi*) might seem to us abstract and arcane, the European encounter with the indigenous populations of the Americas occasioned a new chapter in the story of Western imperialist theory as well as practice. On the face of it, the peoples of the "Indies" seemed to sixteenth-century thinkers to stand at a considerable remove from the traditions and practices of Mediterranean religions, even of pre-Christian paganism. Not only did the inhabitants of the Americas worship many gods and engage in palpable idolatry, but they also lacked a literate (text-based) faith and performed rites, such as human sacrifice, deemed incompatible with a "civilized" way of life. In sum, to many Europeans, native Americans were simply "barbarous" and therefore "barbarians," a term that, with its Aristotelian connotations, implied their natural servitude: people incapable of governing themselves and hence susceptible to legitimate domination by a superior (Christian European) race.[1] The justification of conquest and subjugation took on an urgency in the Christian West that perhaps had not been experienced since the era of the Crusades. If the indigenous populations of the Americas were to be enslaved or massacred, historical as well as conceptual grounds for these acts would prove useful, if only to salve the tender consciences of those who might find genocide incompatible with "civilized" or "Christian" values.

Yet there were authors prepared to question and criticize pointedly the treatment of native Americans, primarily by Spain.[2] In this context, several of Cicero's leading social and political ideas would prove extraordinarily useful. The preeminent example of a writer employing Ciceronian thought to criticize European imperialism in the Americas was Bartolomé de Las

Casas. Las Casas provides an especially compelling case, because he began his career as a member of the conquering Spanish elite but renounced his own holdings in "New Spain," joined the Dominican order, and achieved the office of bishop of Chiapas.[3] He observed the conquest firsthand, which permitted him to draw on empirical as well as philosophical evidence to refute justifications of Spanish imperialism. In more than half a century of concerted attack on Spanish dominion over the indigenous population of the Americas, he unleashed a broad array of arguments against the policies and conduct of his fellow Spaniards, contained in a stunningly prolific and wide-ranging body of works in defense of the "Indians": polemical tracts, historical and anthropological treatises, and a famous refutation of Juan Ginés de Sepúlveda's scholastic *Apologia* for Spanish conquest. In recent times, Las Casas's writings have been the object of considerable study—and controversy—in both academic and polemical spheres. For some, like the Peruvian Dominican Gustavo Gutiérrez, he was lauded as a hero (if not a saint) who prefigured the modern liberation theology movement.[4] For others, he was little more than an advocate and perpetrator of European colonization.[5] The literature focused on Las Casas has grown formidably in a relatively brief span of time, to the extent that it can only be noted rather than considered and assessed in the context of the present chapter.[6]

A large measure of scholarship on Las Casas has concentrated on the sources of his writings, which utilize multiple conventions of philosophy, politics, and law current during his time (often depending upon the audience to whom he was writing). Some commentators have emphasized his appropriation of the philosophical frameworks of Aristotelianism and Thomism to serve the cause of protecting Indian culture.[7] Other readers stress his reliance upon medieval canon law and indeed ascribe to him a "subjective natural rights" theory derived from canonist thought.[8] Less frequently noted, however, is Las Casas's employment of key elements of Cicero's theory in his analysis of the indigenous peoples of the Americas. At best, scholars have paid lip service to the Ciceronian dimensions of his treatises.[9] However, throughout his corpus—in his polemical tomes and especially his anthropological studies—Las Casas returned repeatedly to central themes of Ciceronian texts, citing and quoting from them copiously.

Specifically, Las Casas relied heavily upon the strand of Cicero's thought that upheld the principle of fundamental human equality. For Las Casas, as for Cicero, human beings are distinguished by the ability to reason, to associate in an organized fashion, and to perceive divinity. By arguing that these capacities define indigenous peoples as members of the human race and accord them basic individual and cultural rights, Las Casas establishes that the use of force in order to "civilize" so-called barbarians (or alternatively, to destroy them) is both inhumane and uncivilized. To employ coercion is inhumane because it fails to take into account that humanity is defined by the possession of certain inborn, but imperfectly realized, potentialities; it is uncivilized because it mistakes European cultural development for a singular process that no other people is capable of recapitulating, except perhaps at the point of a sword. One can make no sense of Las Casas's attack on European justifications of imperialism in the Americas without recognizing its reliance on Ciceronian social and political principles.

PRINCIPLES OF EQUALITY

Las Casas's familiarity with Cicero rivaled that of any contemporary. In the course of his works, he cites a full range of Cicero's philosophical treatises available during the early sixteenth century—including *De officiis, De legibus, De natura deorum, Tusculanarum disputationum*, and *De divinatione*—as well as treatises on rhetoric (*De inventione, De oratore*) and various speeches and letters. In many instances, Las Casas mentions Cicero simply as a source of historical information about the beliefs and rituals of ancient religions in Greece, Rome, and the wider world. *Apologética historia sumaria*, in particular, relies heavily on Cicero's works for evidence about the names and natures of Greek and Roman deities; about the forms of superstition, idolatry, sacrifice, and divination employed by the ancients; and about the diverse rites and sacraments that Mediterranean and Near Eastern peoples practiced.[10] Las Casas's purpose is to demonstrate the extraordinary number of parallels between classical religions and those faiths found among the American "Indians," consequently deflecting the Eurocentric view that the inhabitants of the "New World" are incorrigibly primitive and thus unworthy of respect. To uphold the latter position, he implies, is to deny the humanity of the pagan forebears of Christian Europeans and the presence among them of a mature civilization, inasmuch as the Greco-Roman world subscribed to many of the same beliefs and rituals as indigenous Americans. Likewise, the pagans of the West were susceptible to conversion by the gentle and patient teachings and good examples of Christianity, and hence capable of cultural development without recourse to coercion or decimation. Policy toward the aboriginal peoples of the Americas should follow suit.

Las Casas bolsters the empirical force of this case by reference to a set of theoretical arguments, derived from Cicero, about the natural equality of the human race. He has been hailed by modern scholars for his repeated declaration that "all the nations of the world are human beings."[11] More rarely noticed is that he ordinarily asserts this claim in the context of a discussion of Ciceronian principles of human nature. Indeed, Las Casas's most extensive defense of the doctrine of equality, in *Apologética historia sumaria*, ascribes the idea expressly to Cicero himself: "Tully posited in Book 1 of *De legibus* [that] ... all the nations of the world are human beings, and all human beings and each one of them form no less the definition [of humanity] than any other, and this is that they are rational" (1:257). Las Casas then enumerates the psychological qualities on the basis of which human beings are deemed to possess reason—some suggested by Cicero (the senses, the capacity for knowledge and virtue), others supported by Christian teaching (free will). The passage underscores the Ciceronian provenance of human reason by advancing an extensive (if at times extraneous) series of quotations from *De legibus*. The phrase "all the nations of the world are human beings" is entirely Las Casas's own invention. Yet it crystallizes his appropriation of Cicero: the powers of the human mind being identical in all cases, and the faculty of reason being therefore universal, "all the lineage of humanity is one, and all human beings as regards their creation and natural existence are alike" (*AHS*, 1:257–58). The ascription of human equality Las Casas finds in Cicero's writings becomes the cornerstone of his defense of Indian peoples against European oppression.

This egalitarian precept effectively undercuts any attempt to withhold the status of humanness from certain peoples on the grounds that their conditions of life are barbarous. Although Las Casas does not overtly invoke Cicero's authority on this point in his reply to Sepúlveda—since he confines himself there largely to the languages of his opponent, namely, Aristotelianism and scholastic theology—the principle of equal human reason is evident in the *Apologia*,[12] helping to explain its apparently idiosyncratic understanding of Aristotle's concept of the barbarian (see 28–53). Las Casas takes for granted what Aristotle manifestly did not: that a certain uniformity exists within the natural world such that the qualities of human nature are distributed more or less equally and without ethnic, racial, or cultural distinction. Hence, Las

Casas denies that any people as a whole could be barbarian in the strict Aristotelian sense of "slaves by nature," incapable of self-governance. As he concludes in *Apologética historia sumaria*, "It is an impossibility of all impossibilities that an entire nation may be incapable or so barbaric and of little judgment and or lesser or diminished reason that it does not know how to govern itself" (1:260; see also *Apologia*, 28). Underlying this claim is the Ciceronian conviction that human nature is inherently and universally rational.

One might still object that Las Casas is simply addressing the condition of entire populations rather than of discrete individuals.[13] That is, the wording of his treatises might suggest a concern with the equality of groups, not of each of their particular members. But on occasion Las Casas explicitly specifies that his claim about the equal powers of reason applies to persons as individuals: "Human beings are more rational than other creatures and are conferred in their souls, upon their creation, with the seeds and beginnings and natural inclinations of the senses and the virtues, and they are by no means deficient in the exercise of these qualities . . . ; and the entire human race and *every individual member of it* [possesses] . . . all these characteristics, dispositions and natural human inclinations [that] are natural and universally the same in all human beings, as was affirmed above by the declared judgment of Tully" (*AHS*, 2:362, emphasis added).

The essentially invariant presence of a rational faculty among individual human beings is confirmed for Las Casas by the extreme rarity of persons who are impeded in their use of reason. He maintains in both the *Apologia* and *Apologética historia sumaria* that those few persons whose souls do not equip them to exercise reason are to be counted among the monstrosities of nature, comparable to people born with extra limbs or organs, whose existence is commonly explained by reference to divine (extranatural) causes (*AHS*, 1:259; see also *Apologia*, 34–35). That such deformities—whether of the body or the soul—occur so infrequently simply provides further proof that nature is consistent in granting the same properties, psychological as well as physiological, to each and every human being. Only God's direct intervention in nature can disrupt this pattern.

REASON AND CIVILIZATION

While Las Casas upholds the principle of human equality, he is by no means insensitive to or unrealistic about differences among the world's cultures and peoples. He admits that some of the inhabitants of the Americas apparently lack the defining marks of the most rudimentary civilization: they "are found to live separately and remotely, and have no dwelling-place in the form of a city, ... but live vagrantly without order like savages" (*AHS*, 1:260), ignorant of political affairs, law, commerce, friendship, and the other salient characteristics of civilized life.[14] While Las Casas does not shy away from describing some indigenous nations of the "New World" as "primitive," "crude," "uncivilized," indeed, "barbarous," he concludes that their present condition is not a permanent or intractable state. Rather, he discerns a universal process of historical progress, a recognizable pattern of cultural development, followed by all peoples of the world, Europeans no less than "Indians," stemming from the natural faculties possessed by each and every human being. Inasmuch as human knowledge is grounded in reason, all members of the race possess an identical capacity to attain a fully civilized life, although these potentialities are realized in a historically contingent fashion. Thus it may be said of even the most ostensibly primitive peoples "that they would not fail to be rational human beings, and reducible to order and reason, but that they still have not begun and are in such a pristine rude state that they are earlier than all the other nations that exist" (*AHS*, 1:260). While Las Casas doubts that many completely primordial groups remain to be discovered, he maintains that, should such a nation be encountered, it will still exhibit just as great a potential for achieving a civilized way of life as any European population.

In part, Las Casas founds his account of the historicity of the civilizing process on psychological observations about human ontogeny. Individuals in their earliest stages of life are governed by "sensuous and animalistic" inclinations, such as "eating and drinking and other acts that are common to ourselves and beasts, without any time or work or deliberation or application of reason"; by contrast, "rational [activities] require time, work, deliberation, and the application of reason" (*AHS*, 1:260). In other words, all human beings move from a prerational to a rational stage, maturing intellectually through passage of time and effort. "The acts of reason are more recent and less used, because we do not know nor can we use reason until we are older, nine, ten, or eleven years; and as a consequence, certain acts are performed more easily, and those of reason with difficulty, and thus, for acting in certain ways we do not need any guide, aid, tutor and director, and for others for which a guide, attractor, aid, and persuader is required, we have a great need" (*AHS*, 1:258–59). Prerational modes of action are, in effect, instinctual and unlearned, whereas the use of reason depends upon tuition and practice. Las Casas's implication is clear: phylogeny recapitulates ontogeny. Human civilizations progress towards completion as they replace their animalistic standards of behavior with a set of rational precepts—social, political, legal, and religious. Just as no person is born with the powers of reason entirely operative, so no people begins its communal life in a fully formed condition but rather undergoes a process of collective education.

This psychological claim correlates directly with Cicero's account of the foundations of human society in *De inventione*, according to which human beings in their most primitive state lived a quasi-bestial existence, depending on physical strength instead of reason, ignorant of religious worship, social institutions, morality, and law, until the persuasion and instruction of a wise and eloquent man led them to discover and implement all the fruits of communal life. In the course of his writings, Las Casas returns time and again to Cicero's narrative of social development. For example, his first published work, *De unico modo*, presents a sketch of a wise philosopher who, employing considerable art, induced primitive human beings (who lived in a savage state very similar to wild animals) to a more human life, to education, to instruction in good morals, to knowledge of God and worship of divine religion in the form in which they then existed. Eventually, they united and convened in a communal life, manifested in the institutions of the community and the city. He persuaded them of the individual utility and fruits that result from a more human life, attracting them by his eloquence and graceful oration, and thus by art.[15]

Thereafter, Las Casas quotes the relevant passage from the prologue of *De inventione* in its entirety and then highlights what he takes to be the salient lessons of Cicero's account. First, if human beings are found in a condition of savagery or wildness, this does not reflect their "true" nature but rather is a consequence of "second nature"—that is, custom. Primitive human existence is not a "state of nature" but an aberration thereof. Second, the ferocity of primordial people can be tamed, and the seeds of civilization can be cultivated in them, "through the force of natural reason" supplemented by the persuasion of "honeyed, sweet, and patient words." Finally, any transformation from a primitive to a civilized condition is only properly achieved by "compelling the human intellect rationally . . . not by armed attack or violence."[16] All of these conclusions have considerable import for the key theme of *De unico modo*: that the sole valid and efficacious way of converting the inhabitants of the Americas to Christianity is through "the persuasion of the understanding by means of reason."[17] Las Casas's appeal to Cicero supports the position that no people is so undeveloped that it is unable to receive the words of Christian preachers, and thus it should not be subjected to the alternatives of enforced conversion or extinction. Rather, the most "natural" method of spreading Christianity among the "Indians" is to recapitulate the educative process by which their social order was first formed.

The deployment of Cicero's account of social development in *De unico modo* remains focused, however, on Las Casas's polemical aims and as such never receives full statement as a theoretical principle. In his historical and anthropological treatises, by contrast, the Ciceronian reconstruction of the origins of communal life assumes a more central place in the argument. For instance, *Historia de las Indias*, a work that primarily chronicles the early Spanish voyages of discovery, prefaces its detailed recounting of European contact with the "Indians" by reminding its audience of the historical experience common to all peoples. Las Casas initially presents his view of the civilizing process as simply an inductive generalization that may be gleaned by anyone who takes "notice of the ancient histories, not only the divine and ecclesiastical ones, but also the profane ones" (1:14).[18] He frames his reading of these historical accounts in overtly Ciceronian language. "No generation or nation of the past, neither before nor after the deluge," he observes, was so advanced "that at its beginnings it did not suffer from very many flaws of wildness and irrationality, such that it lived without politics (*policia*)" (1:14). And yet, although all the peoples of the earth first "lived without houses and without cities and as brute animals," still "they came together by the use of reason and took hold of those things pertaining to human capacity" (1:14). In this connection, Las Casas introduces a favored metaphor: that human beings in their primitive state are like "uncultivated land" that yields "thorns and thistles," but when domesticated through persuasion and instruction, they are capable of producing the most useful and pleasing fruits (1:14–15).

As authority for these broad assertions, Las Casas quotes but a single source—the preface to *De inventione*—and proceeds to expand upon and extrapolate from it at length. On the basis of this analysis of Cicero's doctrine, he announces the principle that will guide his investigations throughout the considerable body of *Historia de las Indias*:

> And thus it appears that although human beings at the beginning were totally uncultivated, and, as they did not work the land, ferocious and bestial, but by the natural discretion and talent that was innate in their souls, since God created them rational creatures, being ordered and persuaded by reason and love and good industry, which is the proper way for rational creatures to be attracted to the exercise of virtue, there is no nation whatsoever, nor could there be, regardless of how barbarous, wild and depraved its customs may be, that cannot be attracted and ordered to all the political virtues and all the humanity of domesticated, political and rational human beings, and notably to the Catholic faith and Christian religion. (1:16)

As an illustration of this theoretical point, Las Casas reports that no less a civilized nation than Spain itself originated out of a "barbaric" people whose ferocity rivaled that ascribed to the "Indians." If the Spanish could arrive at a mature culture, he implies, then so surely can the indigenous inhabitants of the Americas (1:16–19). While Las Casas may have intended to invoke such a comparison in order to provoke and even shock his fellow Spaniards, one may notice that it follows quite directly from his antecedent proposition that all societies emerge gradually from barbarism into a civilized condition.

By far the most pronounced use made by Las Casas of this Ciceronian framework may be found in *Apologética historia sumaria*, his contribution to what Anthony Pagden terms "comparative ethnology."[19] There Cicero's teaching about the historicity of civilization is not only stated at greater length than in any of Las Casas's other writings, but is reiterated throughout. In addition to the sheer extent of the recitation of the Ciceronian account of human development in *Apologética historia sumaria*—couched not primarily in quotations from *De inventione*, but in the words of Las Casas himself—several factors distinguish that presentation from the appropriations he makes elsewhere. First, Las Casas weaves together the principle of human equality derived from *De legibus* (and other Ciceronian works) with the doctrine of cultural evolution borrowed from *De inventione* into a single coherent and seamless account. Having narrated the pattern according to which human beings are transformed from bestial to civilized creatures, he asserts that the "truth" of this view rests upon the antecedent claim of Cicero that human beings are united—across all geographical and cultural divides—by reason (*AHS*, 1:257). Because people invariably possess the capacity for rationality, they are susceptible to "sweet words and the vehement force of powerful reason," by means of which they "come together out of their dispersion in mountains and fields, one with the others, to a certain place in order to live in company and assemble themselves in society" (*AHS*, 1:249). Equality of reason thus entails for Las Casas that every nation experiences an identical process leading to full human association, including political institutions and, eventually, worship of the true God.

Once again, he employs the analogy of the barren field: a "wild" people is "like uncultivated land that produces simply weeds and useless spines, but has within itself such natural virtue that it may, by work and cultivation, yield healthy and advantageous domesticated fruits" (*AHS*, 1:258). Yet, at the same time, Las Casas stresses the contingency of the occurrence of communal organization. It did not happen at the same time among all the peoples of the world nor was the transition necessarily a smooth one. Rather, "rudeness, coarseness, and quasi-bestiality lasted much later" among some nations than among others, depending upon a wide range of entirely unpredictable local circumstances (*AHS*, 1:250). Las Casas emphasizes that the formation of human societies was by no means an inexorable, unconscious event. It depended instead upon art—in particular, the persuasive skill of the primitive wise orator in overcoming the habitual behavior of uncivilized people unaccustomed to social order and harmony. When and where such talented speakers might appear, and how arduous their labors might be, are matters that resist systematic human explanation. The most that can be said is that all human beings share the potential to achieve a completely acculturated way of life, and all nations follow essentially the same pattern in attaining this condition.

Las Casas concludes that if all people (and peoples) possess rudimentary reason, as well as the potential to partake of civilized association, then every nation must be left to follow its own "natural" and appropriate route to maturity. And the use of coercive force—either to destroy supposedly incorrigible barbarians or to speed the process of cultural evolution—is wrong and self-defeating: no population is so brutish that it cannot be improved, yet the sole way in which this may be achieved is through patient, rational persuasion. There is no set timeline for this process, just as there is none for the course of human development generally. Las Casas bids his fellow Europeans to extend respect to the "Indians," then, on the basis of the universality of humanity. Not only do circumstances in the Americas closely resemble those in the West during earlier times, but the potential for civilized development is identical among all the world's peoples. To foreclose this potential by violent conquest is, in effect, to deny that Latin Christianity possesses an intrinsic rationality and truth superior to other forms of belief. Las Casas's repeated insistence upon rational persuasion as the "only way" of inducing the "Indians" to enter the Christian fold reflects his belief that Christianity is the most humane religion, the confession most consonant with human nature (conceived in Ciceronian terms), and that coercion is antithetical to this human nature. To treat the "Indians" differently than, say, the Spaniards were treated by early Christian missionaries would be to affront and ultimately to invalidate the very basis of the superiority that Las Casas claims for Christianity (*AHS*, 2:362–63).

RELIGION AND SOCIAL ORDER

A related token of equality for Las Casas is the universal human acknowledgment of the existence of a divine being or supernatural power. His argument does not rely merely on induction; it is a theoretical case framed in expressly Ciceronian language. The most extensive articulation of this position is located in *Apologética historia sumaria*, where Las Casas quotes lavishly from *De natura deorum* as well as from *Tusculanarum disputationum* and *De legibus*, in support of the claim that "all the nations in the world, no matter how barbarous and wild they may be, can and may be moved to know and understand that some Lord exists, a creator, mover and consecrator of all things, who is more excellent than humanity, whom all human beings call God" (*AHS*, 2:374). Such "knowledge of the gods," Las Casas insists (on Cicero's authority), "is naturally formed, impressed and carved upon the souls of human beings" (*AHS*, 2:372). This awareness of divinity, in turn, depends upon "the light of reason and the agency of understanding"—that is, natural properties of "all human beings of the world, no matter how barbarous, uncivilized and wild and isolated on lands or islands or far-flung places they may be" (*AHS*, 2:375). To the extent that human reason is universal, knowledge of the divine manifests itself without exception.

Consequently, evidence of the worship of some deity or deities can be found throughout human history in all cultures, including that of the "Indians," without regard for their locale. As Las Casas remarks in the *Apologia* against Sepúlveda (again, with reference to *De legibus* and *Tusculanarum disputationum*), "No matter how wild or barbarous a nation may be, it cannot live without the worship of the true or of a false deity" (75). The connection between reason and the knowledge of divinity was postulated by Cicero on identical grounds. This is consonant with the Christian teaching that people have intellect and understanding because "they are formed in the image and likeness of God" (*AHS*, 1:257). The shared quality of reason extends to the whole of the human race and is reflected in the universal awareness of the divine presence regardless of the contingent differences of culture that divide humankind. Hence, the worship of deities that one encounters at all times and places constitutes for Las Casas one of the primary signs—indeed, perhaps the preeminent token—of natural human equality.

In turn, the human propensity for engagement in religious rites, whether the cult of false gods or of the one true God, has direct implications for social and political order, according to Las Casas. One of the standard reasons adduced by those seeking to justify the Spanish conquest of the Americas was the indigenous religious convention of sacrificing innocent human life to the deities. Christians supposedly have a duty on the basis of natural law to protect the slaughter of innocents. Somewhat ironically, however, Las Casas proposes that the practice of human sacrifice demonstrates the very humanity of native societies. He reasons that appeasing the gods by rendering unto them that which they hold most precious (namely, human life) reflects their quite rational deduction that worship is paramount to the maintenance of the social compact upholding political order and tradition. Las Casas remarks that "by a natural inclination, men are led to worship God according to their capacities and in their own ways ... by natural law, men are obliged to honor God by the best means available and to offer the best things in sacrifice" (*Apologia*, 227, 228). Yet the choice of sacrifice is a matter of particular cultural conventions: "The things to be offered to God are a matter of human law and positive legislation. For this reason this matter is either left to the whole community or those who represent it, such as the ruler" (230). Among indigenous societies, which operate according to the light of natural reason alone, this sanctions "the most difficult type of repayment, that is, human sacrifice in God's honor" (237). Indeed, any member of such a community regards it as his civic duty "to expose his life so that God's honor and glory may not be diminished, since God wants every man to die in defense of His glory" (237). Cicero and numerous early

European Ciceronians held much the same view about the sacrifice of one's life in the service of a greater common good.

Las Casas justifies this assertion by reference to an organic analogy that echoes Cicero to the effect that each and every part of the body must be prepared to endanger its own well-being, even its existence, for the sake of the preservation of the whole. A sense of divinity (including of those deities taken to be the true God) requires that "any outstanding citizen is obliged to give his life for the sake of the state (this welfare, according to the erroneous opinion of the pagans, was thought to consist of the worship of the gods)" (*Apologia*, 235). However much it may horrify us, Las Casas refuses to shrink from the conclusion that human sacrifice stemming from the valid dictates of an established civil religion should be regarded as entirely legitimate, even glorious:

> For, since each legislator has the authority to make laws not from himself but from the people or the community, he can oblige subjects to do or undergo something by law only as it is conducive to the welfare and happiness of the whole state or community, in proportion to the needs of the state. He must keep in mind the truth that the condition of each citizen should be regulated or preserved for as long a time as possible. But if the need of the state demands that a man do or undergo all that he is capable of, that is, that he expose his life to the danger of death for the welfare of the state, undoubtedly the legislator, by his command, can lawfully obligate each suitable citizen to do so. And the citizen is obliged by the natural law to obey the mandate. . . . For, since the citizen is part of the whole state and his happiness or welfare depends on the welfare and good of the state, he is obliged to love the common welfare and good more than his private welfare, and therefore, in order to preserve that common welfare, he is obliged by the natural law to do and suffer all he can, even by sacrificing his life. (238)

Las Casas insists upon the sanctity of the apparently cruel practices of Indian communities (judged by contemporary European values) on the grounds that their religious rites reveal their humanity as reflected in their communal beliefs. Since all peoples possess rudimentary reason and knowledge of the divine, every nation must be left to follow its own "natural" and appropriate route to the worship of its deities.

Given Las Casas's theoretical commitment to the equal natural distribution of human reason and its ties to religiosity, as well as the necessary foundations these provide for social and political systems, the legitimacy and inviolability of non-Christian indigenous societies must be upheld. Indeed, Las Casas sometimes insists that those who would oppress a populace with violence are in fact enemies of humanity who have renounced the right to be treated peacefully. The connection between a Ciceronian conception of human nature and the propriety of resisting those who would act contrary to such nature is drawn explicitly, for instance, in *Historia de las Indias*. Las Casas asks whether there exists "any reasonable people or nation in the world that, through the authority of natural law and reason, would not" respond to the violence of the Spanish conquest with force. He then immediately proclaims the universality of human nature with reference to *De legibus* and concludes that no community would be unjustified in responding to oppression, since all people by nature "hate evil and shun the painful and the harmful" (*Historia de las Indias*, 2:396–97). Las Casas writes in an analogous manner in his other tracts, remarking with approval that "Tully understands that all human beings are obligated by natural *ius* to defend their God, or gods taken for the true God."[20] Likewise, he observes elsewhere, "When some people, kingdom or city suffers oppression or molestation from some tyrant, it can justly contest him who tyrannizes over it, and be freed from its weighty yoke by killing him, according to Tully, *De officiis*, Book 3," from which he then quotes.[21] Las Casas clearly intends to convey, at minimum, that the close connection between religious rite and civil order licenses human beings to defend their communal way of life against violent invasion and persecution—a claim equally valid for all peoples alike, non-Christian as well as Christian. The warrant for this assertion, in turn, derives from the central principle that all human populations, inasmuch as they are rational, must and will embrace a belief in and worship of divinity in order to sustain their communities. Therefore, an external attack on a people on account of its religious rites, no matter how supposedly well-meaning, may legitimately be repelled by force.

CONCLUSION

What may be the most surprising aspect of the pro-imperialism addressed in chapter 7 and the anti-imperialism discussed in the present chapter is the extent to which both rely upon many identical features of Cicero's social and political thought. For instance, each posits the fundamental rationality inhering in human beings and some basic equality arising therefrom, even if this equity in some cases leads to the inequitable distribution of power. Both posit a latent human propensity toward sociability that remains undeveloped in a primeval period but is drawn out by a process of recognition that leads to the formation of social, and later political, institutions. And in Las Casas, as well as in Engelbert, Aeneas, and Cusa, Ciceronian principles are wedded to Christian doctrine (albeit very different interpretations thereof). I mention these resemblances to reinforce a central claim of this book, namely, that the appropriation of Ciceronian precepts in early European social and political theory could and did produce multiple and divergent understandings of human beings and their relationships with one another.

Conclusion

I write these final remarks in the winter of 2018–19. Over the course of the years that I have toiled on *The Bonds of Humanity*, I have observed the political culture of the United States—and indeed, many other nations to which we attach the moniker of "liberal democracy"—become deformed and degraded almost beyond the point of recognition. I fully realize that works of serious historical scholarship are more or less forbidden to engage directly with the times in which they are written, on pain of the accusation of presentism. Yet it strikes me that something right and valuable results from considering Cicero in terms not so distant from the many ways his earlier audiences regarded his ideas during the five centuries or so that I have covered in this volume. The sensibility of Ciceronians from a far different era pushed them in the direction of engagements with humanity and recognition of human dignity. These bonds might be narrow, including parents or family or friends, or more expansive, reaching to fellow citizens or mankind or divinity. But all of them reflect deeply rooted and profound connections beyond the self and toward others, grounded in the realization of our common natures as creatures who form and sustain associations that thereby arise.

The Ciceronian recognition of the diversity of goods typical of humanity clashes markedly with the sheer parochialism of the sort I find Aristotle and most forms of Aristotelianism guilty. For an Aristotelian, Christian or not, there is only a single path to human fulfillment and flourishing designated by the Greek term *eudaimonia*. In the ethical/political realm, this is realized by learning and exercising virtue (at least for those who are capable of acquiring it). The very point of politics, and thus of "political science,"

is to make men good, to which the Christian philosopher would presumably add "and to save their souls." I do not mean to imply by way of contrast
that Ciceronians of the medieval and early modern period were unconcerned with matters of salvation. But it is noteworthy that the elements
of Cicero's thought that were generally appropriated by subsequent social
and political theorists pertained mostly to myriad earthly obligations to
our fellow human beings. Again, it is worth stressing that various adherents
to Cicero highlighted or focused on different aspects of his ideas about
what we owe to others and how we perform our duties attached thereto,
expressed by friendship, country, humanity, and so forth. What Ciceronians
of early Europe did share is awareness that human interactions of all kinds
are ultimately rooted in mankind's fundamentally associative nature, arising
from a common set of innate qualities.

Cicero and Ciceronians may appear to be unsystematic in the way in
which they array the range of men's relationships, but this very disorga-
nization, and the loose multiplicity that it supposes, constitutes one of
the defining characteristics of Ciceronianism across the board—one that
distinguishes it from Aristotelianism. Aristotelian social and political theory requires buying into a rather strict epistemological and metaphysical
framework.[1] The Ciceronian outlook eschews such orderliness in favor of
the acknowledgment that the many sorts of human associations may be
arranged differently from man to man and time to time, giving our due
to family, parents, family, friends, country, and humanity as circumstances
seem to require. And contra Aristotelianism, the performance of these
duties can never be fully determined in advance or ranked hierarchically.

One final property that may be attributed to Ciceronians in medieval and early modern Europe as a loose group is dedication to the life of
action rather than that of contemplation. In some ways, this may be the
most salient feature of Ciceronian social and political thought. As we have
seen, Cicero devoted himself first and foremost to his responsibilities as a
Roman citizen and statesman. To label his theoretical orientation "practical philosophy," as Walter Nicgorski has done, seems entirely appropriate.[2]
This orientation permeates the early European theorists who walked in his
footsteps. Like Cicero, many of them take their writing to constitute a form
of political activity and even of advocacy. They regard philosophical reflection and the world that supports it (the university, the monastery) as second best. The plain divergence of Ciceronianism from other approaches to

politics proposed by ancient Greco-Roman philosophers and schools—both before and after Cicero's lifetime—provided an attractive exemplar to many of the medieval and early modern authors surveyed in the present volume, who were often engaged in church or temporal affairs or in both. One can readily recognize the affinities between the mind-set reflected in the Ciceronian corpus and the theories propounded by politically active thinkers such as John of Salisbury and Marsiglio of Padua, Christine de Pizan and Bartolomé de Las Casas.

To be clear, not every author whom I have counted as a Ciceronian possessed a preponderance of the intellectual proclivities that I have identified, although some did. Whereas the systematic character of Aristotelianism renders it reasonably simple to distinguish between Aristotelian and non-Aristotelian social and political thinkers, the same cannot be said of Ciceronianism. (Indeed, this may be an important reason why scholarship has largely overlooked the Ciceronian contribution to the social and political theory in the period considered here.) Should some scholar attempt to locate a specific "core" property or properties of a Ciceronian perspective in order to discern "genuine" from "inauthentic" commitments to it, she shall surely despair in the end. Rather, it may be useful to adapt some insights afforded by the twentieth-century Austrian-English philosopher Ludwig Wittgenstein, whose major work, *Philosophical Investigations,* demolishes the (characteristically Platonic) position that words (and attendant concepts) have essences, "true" and precise meanings. He illustrates the problem at stake by analysis of the noun "game," which properly denotes a vast range of activities. Can we find a common quality or nature to all games? Games such as chess or baseball, for example, might seem to share the property of winning and losing. The nursery school game Ring a Ring o' Roses, however, lacks exactly this characteristic. Wittgenstein's point is that a general word that we might presume to possess one and only one meaning—a single essentiality—turns out to have no such thing. Instead, he says, "We see a complicated network of similarities overlapping and crisscrossing; sometimes overall similarities, sometimes similarities of detail."[3] He calls such networks "family resemblances," in the sense that members of a biological family each have certain common features (nose, chin, eye color, and so on), but none is identical to one or the other parent or sibling.[4] The word "game," Wittgenstein insists, illustrates just such a family resemblance.[5] And no single game is quintessential or archetypal. Wittgenstein advises, "*Look and see* whether there is anything common to all.—For if you look at them you will not see something that is common to *all*, but similarities, relationships, and a whole series of them at that. To repeat: Don't think, but look."[6] In just the same way, we may move beyond an otherwise intractable debate about the chief properties of Ciceronianism. The Ciceronian characteristics that I have suggested do not require reference to a "core"; there is no "ideal" proponent who embodies Ciceronianism to be found in Europe from the twelfth to the sixteenth century—or indeed ever.[7]

Yet, to a large swath of medieval and early modern social and political theorists, Cicero mattered. Whatever else distinguished the diverse receptions of Ciceronian philosophy—and there was much—good reasons exist to suggest that its highlighting of social solidarities appealed to his long-ago readers. Cicero opened up spaces for considered reflection on social and political problems that permitted later generations of theorists to engage with the ever-present threat that various forms of interaction natural to human beings might be undermined or at least endangered. The early European recipients of Ciceronian ideas and ideals, however intellectually elite they might seem, nonetheless confronted practical quandaries posed by the various breakdowns of engagement. Many facets of Ciceronian philosophy—not simply his ruminations on the varied forms of communal fellowship in which we participate—attracted early European authors. Historical scholarship is charged with investigation into these appropriations, as I seek to do in this volume.

We might also take a small tip from Cicero himself. The pursuit of wisdom, in whatever form it might adopt, is beneficial only if it ultimately betters the conditions of the members of the associations—small and large—that define our humanity. The men and women for whom Cicero's ideas mattered many centuries ago are not so different in their predicaments and perplexities than those of us who struggle with the same in the present. If *The Bonds of Humanity* realizes the aim of the intellectual historian to make sense of the ideas of the past, I hope that it thereby also demonstrates the enduring value of Cicero's plea to avoid the infancy of those who fail to appreciate how they are "woven into the life of our ancestors by the records of history."

Introduction

1. Moore, *First European Revolution*.

2. Throughout the present volume, I shall generally use the term "early Europe," rather than "Middle Ages," to describe the period from circa 1100 to circa 1550 that it covers. My reasoning for this nomenclature stems from the recognition by recent historians of political thought (the present one included) that the customary division between "medieval" and "early modern" is often untenable. J. H. Burns remarked in his introduction to *Cambridge History of Political Thought, 1450–1700* that scholars have increasingly challenged the idea of "a watershed between 'medieval' and 'modern' European history [that] has conventionally been located in the late fifteenth century and the beginning of the sixteenth. . . . The period from the late fifteenth century to the end of the seventeenth saw neither innovation nor even the unfolding of what had been implicit or latent, but rather the fuller and faster development of tendencies already explicitly present in late medieval society" (2, 3). See also my *Lineages of European Political Thought*.

3. An excellent overview of the complex transmissional history prior to 1000 C.E. may be found in Reynolds and Wilson, *Scribes and Scholars*.

4. See Nederman, "Aristotelianism and the Origins of 'Political Science,'" and Nederman, "Meaning of 'Aristotelianism.'"

5. See especially Ullmann, *Medieval Political Thought*, 159–228.

6. Among the important studies associated with this development are Renna, "Aristotle and the French Monarchy"; Dunbabin, "Reception and Interpretation of Aristotle's *Politics*"; Black, *Political Thought in Europe*, 7–12; Canning, *History of Medieval Political Thought*, 125–34.

7. See, for instance, Tierney, *Religion, Law*, 29, 30; Blythe, *Ideal Government and the Mixed Constitution*, 8; Sullivan, "Bonds of Aristotelian Language."

8. In addition to the scholarship cited in note 12 below, see Digeser, "Citizenship and the Roman *Res publica*"; Coyle, "Cicero's *De officiis*"; Atkins, "*Officia* of St. Ambrose."

9. I am not counting here the *Rhetorica ad Herennium* that was widely but incorrectly thought to originate from Cicero's hand. See Murphy and Winterbottom, "Raffaele Regio's 1492 *Quaestio*."

10. The extent to which a substantial range of Cicero's writings were not merely known but available before 1000 C.E. is documented in Reynolds and Wilson, *Scribes and Scholars*, 80–110.

11. Thomson, *William of Malmesbury*, 9.

12. Colish, *Stoic Tradition*, 2:156–58 and the accompanying footnotes. An exhaustive survey of Augustine's familiarity with and use of Cicero's writings is found in Testard, *Saint Augustin et Cicéron*; the first volume addresses Cicero's impact on Augustine, while the second contains a comprehensive listing of all of the Saint's references to his predecessor's works. Clavier has discussed the importance of Ciceronian rhetoric and related themes for Augustine in *Eloquent Wisdom*, 25–85. For a detailed examination of the complexities surrounding the medieval manuscript tradition of Cicero, see the chapter on him by Rouse in "Survival of the Latin Classics," 54–142, as well as the useful discussion in Rouse and Rouse, *Authentic Witnesses*, 61–98. Also of some significance in this regard is Macrobius's commentary of the sixth book of *De re publica* (otherwise known as the *Somnium Scipionis*), chapter 18 of which briefly summarizes some of the distinctive features of Cicero's social and political thought; see Macrobius, *Commentary on the Dream of Scipio*, 120–24. *Les Études Philosophiques* 99 (2011) contains a thematic issue devoted to "Le Songe de Scipion

de Cicéron et sa tradition," several articles of which address the fundamentally apolitical character of Macrobius's presentation.

13. For instance, Coleman states flatly that by the close of the thirteenth century "Aristotle had come to replace Cicero . . . as the 'master' of the science of politics and its related rhetorical strategies of public persuasion. Cicero continued to be cited, but mainly in those areas of moral philosophy known as *ethica* and *privativa*, that is, the government of the self and the government of the household" (*History of Political Thought*, 63). A primary purpose of this book is to demonstrate that nothing could be farther from the truth.

14. Carlyle and Carlyle, *History of Mediæval Political Theory*, 1:8, 9. An interesting, although I think ultimately unsuccessful, critique of this position was offered some years ago by Rifkin in "Aristotle on Equality," 276–83.

15. Sabine, *History of Political Theory*, 114–15; McIlwain, *Growth of Political Thought*, 165.

16. Carlyle and Carlyle, *History of Mediæval Political Theory*, 1:17.

17. Cumming, *History and Human Nature*, 1:234 n. 74; see also 1:135–36.

18. Wood, *Cicero's Social and Political Thought*, 10.

19. Stuurman, *Invention of Humanity*, 89–96. This point is made more forcefully still by Annas, "Aristotelian Political Theory."

20. Straumann, *Crisis and Constitutionalism*, 247–55.

21. Saccenti, *Debating Medieval Natural Law*.

22. The *locus classicus* is Baron, "Cicero and the Roman Civil Spirit."

23. A noteworthy exception is Kennedy, "Cicero's Oratorical and Rhetorical Legacy."

24. Hankins provides an extensive overview of the controversies surrounding Baron's position in "'Baron Thesis' After Forty Years." See also Hankins, *Renaissance Civic Humanism*.

25. Witt, though, has made a real start at outlining the contours of such a project in the final three chapters of and conclusion to his book *In the Footsteps of the Ancients*,

338–507. A very comprehensive general bibliography of Ciceronian thought during the early modern period has been compiled by Kallendorf in "Ciceronianism."

26. Skinner, "Limits of Historical Explanation," 210.

27. Skinner, "Meaning and Understanding," 75–76 (originally published in 1969). For another, even more strident, version of this argument, see Condren, *Status and Appraisal of Classic Texts*, esp. 129–41.

28. Oakley, *Politics and Eternity*, 172.

29. De Pourcq, "Classical Reception Studies," 220.

30. Extensive overviews of the field may be found in Martindale and Thomas, *Classics and the Uses of Reception*, and Hardwick and Stray, *Companion to Classical Receptions*.

31. Martindale, "Introduction," 1–2.

32. Kempshall, *Rhetoric and the Writing of History*, 17. Just as I was completing this volume, I encountered a perfect example of the approach I have in mind: Keeline, *Reception of Cicero*.

33. Nederman, "Meaning of 'Aristotelianism.'"

34. I heartily endorse and adopt Fox's wise admonition, in *Cicero's Philosophy of History*, to forego the use of abbreviation or the standard nomenclature of classicists. I stand with Fox when he says, "My aim here has been clarity and ease of reading, so that readers dipping into this book will not need to adjust themselves to a convention, nor have their reading disrupted" (ix).

35. Pighius, *Hierarchiae ecclesiastica assertio*, book 5.

Chapter 1

1. Carlyle and Carlyle, *History of Mediæval Political Theory*, 1:3.

2. Wood, *Cicero's Social and Political Thought*, 11.

3. Perelli, *Pensiero politico*.

4. Nicgorski, *Cicero's Practical Philosophy*, 1–2.

5. Powell, *Cicero the Philosopher*, 1.

6. In addition to the books edited by Nicgorski and Powell just mentioned, a sampling of this renewal of interest in Cicero's social and political thought, either directly

or in its central place in Roman theory more generally, includes (in chronological order): Powell and North, *Cicero's Republic*; Radford, *Cicero*; Steel, *Cicero, Rhetoric, and Empire*; May, *Brill's Companion to Cicero*; Harries, *Cicero and the Jurists*; Fox, *Cicero's Philosophy of History*; Connolly, *State of Speech*; Hammer, *Roman Political Thought and the Modern*; Baraz, *Written Republic*; Steel, *Cambridge Companion to Cicero*; Atkins, *Cicero on Politics*; Hammer, *Roman Political Thought*, 26–94; Zarecki, *Cicero's Ideal Statesman*; Maso, *Grasp and Dissent*; Nicgorski, *Cicero's Skepticism*; Du Plessis, *Cicero's Law*; Remer, *Ethics and the Orator*; Connolly, *The Life of Roman Republicanism*; Smith, *Political Philosophy and the Republican Future*; Atkins, *Roman Political Thought*; and even a web presence (!) called Cicero on Line (http:// www.ojs.unito.it/index.php/COL).

7. Kennedy, "Cicero, Roman Republicanism and the Contested Meaning."

8. See Kapust, "*Advenit Cicero*," and Kapust, "*Ecce Romani!*"

9. Cox and Ward, *Rhetoric of Cicero*, and Ward, "What the Middle Ages Missed," and the notes therein.

10. Kempshall, "*De re publica* I.39."

11. Fidora and Pastor, "Cicero and the Middle Ages."

12. The *Rhetorica ad Herennium* (also known as the "new rhetoric") is clearly a forgery, although it was treated as genuine throughout the Middle Ages and was subject to a large body of commentary. See Ward, *Classical Rhetoric in the Middle Ages*. The authenticity of the *Genus optima oratore* has been questioned (see Ward, "What the Middle Ages Missed," 310 n. 17, although in an email exchange, Dr. Ward admitted that his skepticism may not be entirely warranted). See also the entry on Cicero in Howatson and Chilvers, *Concise Oxford Companion to Classical Literature*, 124.

13. I follow the dating by MacKendrick, *Philosophical Books of Cicero*, although I acknowledge that his chronology is open to challenge. On rare occasions, I will refer to Cicero's speeches, when directly relevant to his rhetorical and philosophical ideas. Of course, as noted previously, *De re publica*

(with the exception of book 6, the so-called *Somnium Scipionis*, which lacks significant political content) was only known in small fragments by way of intermediary classical and Christian sources until the early nineteenth century. Indeed, there were vast and concerted (and always frustrated) quests over the centuries to locate the full text. Thus my references to *De re publica* will include only those passages of which medieval and early modern thinkers might reasonably have cognizance.

14. See Perelli, *Pensiero Politico*, 24–27.

15. An appraisal of the union between philosophy and oratory according to Cicero is provided by Ballacci, *Political Theory*, 51–83.

16. This very serious issue is addressed in two contemporary works of scholarship: Kapust, "Cicero on Decorum," and Remer, *Ethics and the Orator*.

17. Goodman, "'I Tremble with My Whole Heart.'"

18. See also *De legibus* 1.24–25 and *De natura deorum* 2.12.

19. Quoted by Augustine, *Epistolae* 104.7.

20. See Goodman, "Political Society."

21. Quoted by Augustine, *De civitate Dei* 2.21.

22. In the subsequent sections, the status of the tribune in relation to the violence of the plebs is debated at some length.

23. Quoted by Lactantius, *Divinae institutiones* 5.14.3–5.

24. Quoted by Augustine, *De civitate Dei* 2.21; 19.21; *Epistolae* 138.2.10.

25. Nussbaum, "Duties of Justice," 187.

26. Viroli, *For Love of Country*, 26–34 and passim; Nussbaum, "Duties of Justice," 186–87.

27. See also *De officiis* 3.43.

28. For example, *De legibus* 1.34, 49; *De finibus* 2.72, 78–79; *De natura deorum* 1.22.

Chapter 2

1. Haskins, *Renaissance of the Twelfth Century*.

2. Ibid., 111.

3. Ibid.

4. A useful compendium of early receptions is Young, *Twelfth-Century Renaissance*. A comprehensive overview of the literature

on the topic may be found in Mulve, "'Revolt of the Medievalists.'"

5. James, *Two Ancient English Scholars*, 21–23.

6. Thomson, *William of Malmesbury*, 50–53.

7. Ibid., 55, 86–87.

8. Ibid., 53, 55.

9. Ibid., 143.

10. The most comprehensive examination of this literature may be found in Ward, *Classical Rhetoric in the Middle Ages*.

11. On the background to Thierry's commentary, see Fredborg, "Commentary of Thierry of Chartres," and Ward, "Date of the Commentary on Cicero's '*De inventione.*'" The commentary is available in a critical edition edited by Fredborg, *Latin Rhetorical Commentaries*, 45–215. By my rough estimation, nearly 10 percent of Thierry's commentary concerns the prologue to *De inventione*, whereas it occupies only 3.5 percent of Cicero's total text. On the wider context for Thierry's commentary, see Cox and Ward, *Rhetoric of Cicero*. A partial translation may be found in Copeland and Sluiter, *Medieval Grammar and Rhetoric*, 416–36.

12. References to Thierry of Chartres's *Commentarius super De inventione* cite page numbers in Fredborg's edition.

13. In support of this conclusion, I refer the reader to Ward, *Ciceronian Rhetoric*.

14. See Pennington and Müller, "Decretists," 121–22, 125.

15. Ibid., 135–36.

16. Somerville and Brasington, *Prefaces to Canon Law Books*.

17. Ibid., 191–92.

18. Ibid., 192.

19. O'Donovan and Lockwood O'Donovan, *From Irenaeus to Grotius*, 300.

20. Ibid., 300–301.

21. Ibid., 301.

22. Cochrane, *Christianity and Classical Culture*, 39.

23. See Burns, *Cambridge History of Medieval Political Thought*, 323–24, and Muldoon, *Empire and Order*, 105–6.

24. References to Otto of Freising's *Chronica* cite the page numbers of the Evans and Knapp edition, *The Two Cities*.

25. In the following paragraph, Otto also quotes the pseudo-Ciceronian *De Herennium* to make a historical point, which further confirms his knowledge of Cicero's rhetorical treatises, genuine or not (*Two Cities*, 131).

26. McGuire, *Friendship and Community*, 231.

27. Haseldine, "Friendship Networks in Medieval Europe"; especially useful is the comprehensive bibliography. Also of importance is Haseldine, *Friendship in Medieval Europe*, although a few of the chapters cover periods strictly beyond the Latin Middle Ages.

28. Haseldine, "Understanding the Language of *Amicitia*," 237–60.

29. Cotts, *Clerical Dilemma*.

30. Nederman, "Friendship in Public Life."

31. An overview of the state of recent scholarship on Aelred may be found in Dutton, *Companion to Aelred of Rievaulx*.

32. On the latter aspect of Aelred's career, see Truax, *Aelred the Peacemaker*.

33. References to Aelred of Rievaulx's *De spirituali amicitia* cite the chapter and section numbers in the Dutton translation, *Spiritual Friendship*. I generally follow this translation, although occasionally I have altered it slightly in line with the Latin text found in his *Opera omnia*, ed. Hoeste and Talbot, 1:287–350.

34. I explicitly use a gender-neutral word here in light of a persuasive argument that Aelred adopted a gender-inclusive perspective; see Truax, *Aelred the Peacemaker*, 96–129.

35. See Coyle, "Cicero's *De officiis*," and Atkins, "*Officia* of St. Ambrose's *De officiis*."

36. McGuire, *Friendship and Community*, 297. Beyond initial agreement about our mutual point of departure, our arguments diverge quite substantially.

37. Although Aelred made good use of Ambrose's *De officiis ministrorum*, there is no resonance in the text of the former of the ideas of the latter that will be highlighted at present.

38. Cicero, *De amicitia* 27–28, 32; Aelred, *De spirituali amicitia* 1.50–56.

39. Cicero, *De amicitia* 20, 23, 69, 80, 100; Aelred, *De spirituali amicitia* 1.21, 1.46–49, 2.41.

40. Cicero, *De amicitia* 26–27, 30–31, 49–51; Aelred, *De spirituali amicitia* 1.42–44, 3.68.

41. Cicero, *De amicitia* 38–44, 91; Aelred, *De spirituali amicitia* 2.38–40, 3.105–5.

42. Cf. Cicero, *De amicitia* 69, which is supposedly Aelred's exemplar.

43. On the complex relationship between "friendship" and "charity," see Pezzini, "Sermons of Aelred of Rievaulx."

44. Dutton, introduction, 49.

45. A general sense of its context may be found in Schulze-Busacker, *Didactique profane.*

46. Holmberg, *Das "Moralium Dogma Philosophorum,"* 7–8 (foreword). Subsequent citations of the *Moralium* in the text refer to page numbers in this edition. Please note that the foreword is paginated with consecutive Arabic numerals, starting with page 1, and the main text restarts at page 1. To avoid confusion, I will indicate when the page number is from the foreword section.

47. The controversy was thoroughly surveyed by Williams, "Authorship of the *Moralium Dogma Philosophorum.*" For a bibliography of more recent literature concerning the controversy about authorship, see Lapidge, "Stoic Inheritance," 96 n. 87, although Lapidge is comfortable with the attribution to William of Conches.

48. Williams, "Authorship of the *Moralium Dogma Philosophorum,*" 411. Twenty-six years later Williams returned to the topic and arrived at the same conclusion in "Quest for the Author."

49. See the list in the entry on William of Conches in *Les Archives de littérature du Moyen Âge* https://www.arlima.net/eh/guillaume_de_conches.html.

50. Williams, "Authorship of the *Moralium dogma philosophorum,*" 392.

51. Lapidge, "Stoic Influence," 96.

52. Holmberg, *Moralium,* 9–10 n. 3 (foreword).

53. Friendship seems most important to the author; see *Moralium,* 22, 26. On the latter page, he quotes from *De amicitia.*

54. See *De officiis* 1.11–14; *De inventione* 2.161–62. The only passage in the *Moralium* I can locate that refers to eloquence (on 21) is taken from *De officiis* 2.51, where the author

quotes the text almost exactly but leaves out the phrase "a natura."

55. "Cohabitation" recurs in *Moralium,* 16.

56. For the following, see *De officiis* 3.21–22.

57. The sources may be found in *De officiis* 3.24–29; 3.81–82; 3.36–38; 3.77.

Chapter 3

1. A brief overview of John's life and writings is Nederman, *John of Salisbury.* More extensive analysis may be found in Grellard and Lachaud, *Companion to John of Salisbury.*

2. As is indicated, for instance, by the title of Hans Leibeschütz's classic study *Mediaeval Humanism.* See also Nederman, *John of Salisbury,* 41–43.

3. See Grellard, *Jean de Salisbury.*

4. References to John of Salisbury's *Metalogicon* cite the page numbers of the Hall edition.

5. There are multiple partial English translations of the *Policraticus: Statesman's Book of John of Salisbury,* trans. Dickinson; John of Salisbury *Frivolities of Courtiers,* trans. Pike; *Policraticus: Of the Frivolities of Courtiers,* trans. Nederman. In the present chapter, I make use of all of these translations, although with occasional modifications as warranted by the Latin text, the only complete edition of which is by Webb, *Policraticus.* Subsequent citations of the *Policraticus* refer to book and chapter numbers, followed by the name of the relevant translator and page number(s) in the English version.

6. See Nederman, "Aristotelian Doctrine of the Mean."

7. See Maso, *Grasp and Dissent,* and Nederman and Bollermann, "'Extravagance of the Senses.'"

8. As examined by Munk-Olsen, "Humanisme de Jean de Salisbury."

9. Thomson, *William of Malmesbury,* 143 and n. 25.

10. As Thomson himself admits in ibid., 27–28.

11. A useful analysis of the question is offered by Tobin, "Cornifician Motif."

12. *Policraticus* 4.prologue, 6.21, 8.18; Nederman 27, 122, 201.

13. See Struve, *Die Entwicklung der organologischen Staatsauffassung*, 123–48, and Briguglia, *Corpo vivente dello Stato*.

14. Martin summarizes the evidence for this in "John of Salisbury as Classical Scholar," 194–96.

15. Struve, "Importance of the Organism," 304–7, and Hale, *Body Politic*, 26–32.

16. On John's attitude toward ancient Rome generally, see O'Daly, *John of Salisbury*.

17. See *Policraticus* 5.9, 5.11, 5.17, 6.1, 6.8, 6.20; Nederman 84, 91, 94, 101, 104, 116, 126.

18. A particularly compelling example of John's views on the commission of tyrannicide is afforded by John's adaptation of the story of the biblical Judith; see *Policraticus* 8.20 (Nederman 207–9). This tale is discussed in Bollermann and Nederman, "Sword in Her Hand."

19. This is addressed in some detail by van Laarhoven, "Thou Shall NOT Slay a Tyrant," 320.

20. For a thorough survey of the controversies surrounding John's doctrine of tyrannicide, see Nederman, "Duty to Kill," 365–89.

21. This does not, however, make John a theocrat or a hierocrat, as has been demonstrated by Nederman and Campbell in "Priests, Kings, and Tyrants."

22. See also *Policraticus* 5.4; Dickinson 77–78.

23. See Silk, "Numa Pompilius"; Silk, "John of Salisbury"; Grellard, "Le sacré et le profane"; Grellard, "Religion comme technique de gouvernement."

24. On John's employment of this trope, see Dox, *Idea of the Theater*, 87–92.

25. Nearly all of the contents of the letter collections were compiled by John himself. The most recent editions are Millor, Butler, and Brooke, *Letters of John of Salisbury*, vol. 1, and Millor and Brooke, *Letters of John of Salisbury*, vol. 2. The first volume contains Letters 1–135, the second Letters 136–325. Although I have relied on these editions, I have altered translations when I deemed this appropriate.

26. Brooke, "Adrian IV and John of Salisbury."

27. See Letters 15, 17, 18, 46, 50, 52, 113, 128. (When I quote from or cite a particular passage, I will employ the number of the letter with the volume and specific page in parentheses; otherwise, I will refer to the number of the letter only.)

28. See Letter 260.

29. Letters 138, 162.

30. Letter 261 (2:528).

31. Letter 254 (2:512).

32. Most prominently in Letters 34 and 35.

33. Letter 31 (1:50).

34. Letter 41 (1:76). This is consistent with *Policraticus* 6.24, where John recounts an interview with Pope Adrian (formerly Cardinal Nicholas Breakspear, the only Englishman ever to hold papal office) in which he openly speaks of the corruption that exists in the Roman curia; Adrian's reply is instructive, since it demonstrates the receptive tone appropriate among friends.

35. Letter 97 (2:149).

36. Letter 43 (1:78).

37. Letter 13 (2:243).

38. Letter 234 (2:426–28).

39. Letter 95 (1:146).

40. Letter 95 (1:148).

41. See Letters 171, 188, 192, 212, 220, 241, 254, 263, 273.

42. Letter 261 (2:528).

Chapter 4

1. Schmidt, "Raven with a Halo."

2. A fine study of the Western reception of the *Politics* is Christoph Flüeler, *Rezeption und Interpretation*.

3. See Schabel, *Theological Quodlibeta*, and Bazán, Wippel, Fransen, and Jacquart, *Questions disputées*.

4. A useful survey may be found in Van Engen, *Learning Institutionalized*.

5. For an overview of the current state of the debate, as well as an important contribution to it, see Toeste, "Naturalness of Human Association," esp. 114–20; also Sullivan, "Political Science and Paradigms."

6. See Tuck, *Philosophy and Government*, 12, and Coleman, *History of Political Thought*, 63, 72.

7. See Rand, *Cicero in the Courtroom*.

8. For example, Corso de Estrada, "Proyecciones de la concepción ciceroniana."

9. See Keyes, *Aquinas, Aristotle, and the Promise*, and Seagrave, "Cicero, Aquinas, and Contemporary Issues."

10. Some instances are provided by Corso de Estrada, "Proyecciones de la concepción ciceroniana," 345.

11. Keyes, *Aquinas, Aristotle and the Promise*, 70 n. 11.

12. Although Aquinas's authorship of *De regno* has been quite convincingly called into question, I will for the present consider it to be authentic, not least because it was known as such during the rest of the Middle Ages. See Blythe's introduction to his translation of Ptolemy of Lucca, *On the Government of Rulers*, 3–5, and Kempshall, *Common Good*, 132 n. 13.

13. The current state of scholarship on Henry's career and thought may be gleaned from the chapters contained in Wilson, *Companion to Henry of Ghent*.

14. A point about which none of the contributors to Wilson, *Companion to Henry of Ghent*, appears cognizant.

15. References to Henry of Ghent's *Quodlibetal Questions* cite the page numbers of the Teske edition.

16. This point has evidently been lost on the scholars who have focused on Henry's preference for the *vita activa*. See Leone, "Moral Philosophy in Henry of Ghent," and the literature cited in n. 9 of her chapter.

17. Kempshall, *Common Good*, 200–201.

18. This theme was widely addressed among scholastic thinkers; see Toiavanen, "Beasts, Human Beings, or Gods?"

19. As is the case with Corey and Charles, *Just War Tradition*, 53–65.

20. This is emphasized by John von Heyking in "Taming Warriors."

21. Hence, I concur with Kempshall, *Common Good*, 201: "If Cicero provides a consistent point of reference for Henry's analysis of the relationship between individual and community, this provides a contrast with Henry's sporadic citation of Aristotle in the same context."

22. The most extensive case for this position has been made by Blythe in *Thought and Worldview of Tolomeo Fiadoni*, but it is hardly an unusual view. See, for example,

Black, *Political Thought in Europe*, 122–23, and Skinner, *Foundations of Modern Political Thought*, 1:53–55, 79, 82.

23. As observed by Nederman and Sullivan, "Reading Aristotle Through Rome," 223–40; Nederman and Sullivan, "Polybian Moment." See also Straumann, *Crisis and Constitutionalism*, 248–49, who, curiously, evinces no awareness of the two aforementioned articles.

24. References to *De regimine* cite book, chapter, and section numbers.

25. See *De regimine* 2.8.4, 3.6.3, 3.12.5, 3.20.3, 4.1.4, 4.7.4.

26. Straumann, *Crisis and Constitutionalism*, 255.

27. A superb job of tracking the transformation of this trope is offered by Kempshall, "*De re publica* I.39." Kempshall notes that if "Cicero's definition of *res publica* was being read though a distinctly Augustinian filter in the Middle Ages, then the strength of such an interpretation can be gauged by the fact that this was still the line which was being pursued in the thirteenth century, by no less a scholar than Thomas Aquinas" (108).

28. See *De regimine* 4.3.11.

29. The paucity of knowledge about John's life is affirmed by Jones, "John of Paris."

30. The most up-to-date scholarship on John's nonpolitical thought may be found in several of the chapters in Jones, *John of Paris*.

31. This commonplace view has been questioned, or at least moderated, by both Coleman and Ubl, whose views about the appropriate context for John's composition are usefully summarized by Theng, "Why Did John of Paris Write?"

32. John's views have been placed into such a comparative framework by Renna, "Aristotle and the French Monarchy."

33. References to John of Paris's *De potestate* are to Watt's edition, *On Royal and Papal Power*.

34. The development of this theme in later French political thought is examined by Keohane, *Philosophy and the State*, and Wood, "State and Popular Sovereignty.'"

35. A recent survey of this theme in *De potestate*, and the debates about its interpretation, may be found in Moreno-Riaño, "John of Paris, Private Property."

36. Sylvain Piron pointed out to me that there are roughly 150 instances in which Cicero used the term *industria*, spread through the entirety of his corpus.

37. Perhaps most notably by Coleman, "*Dominium*."

38. A useful discussion of his career is Ypma, "Recherches sur la carrière."

39. The background is surveyed by Dyson, "*De regimine christiano* and the Franco-Papal Crisis."

40. A fact not lost on James's latest editor, Dyson, who prefaces his critical edition and English translation of *De regimine* with the observation that scholars have overlooked that text in preference to the treatise by Giles. See James of Viterbo, *De regimine christiano*, ed. Dyson, xxi.

41. Burns, *Cambridge History of Medieval Political Thought*, 400, 401, 640; Miethke, *De potestate papae*.

42. Canning, *Ideas of Power*, 38–47.

43. For example, see Guenée, *States and Rulers*, 40; Black, *Political Thought in Europe*, 51; Canning, *Ideas of Power*, 40, 42.

44. Citations of James of Viterbo's *De regimine christiano* refer to the page numbers (facing Latin and English) in the Dyson edition.

45. See Damiata, *Alvaro Pelagio*, 134, and Kempshall, "*De re publica* 1.39," 111–12.

46. As has recently been affirmed by Oakley, *Emergence of Western Political Thought*, 2:79–80.

Chapter 5

1. The most recent scholarship on Marsiglio and his ideas may be found in Moreno-Riaño, *World of Marsilius of Padua*, and Moreno-Riaño and Nederman, *Companion to Marsilius of Padua*.

2. Gewirth, *Marsilius of Padua*, 32–44.

3. Ibid., 32.

4. Important studies from the past century of all of these potential sources abound. Among those who have investigated Marsiglio's Averroism are: Grabmann, "Studien über den Einfluss"; Troilo, "Averroismo di Marsilio da Padova"; Quillet, *Philosophie politique de Marsile de Padoue*, 59–71; Quillet, "Aristotélisme de Marsile de Padoue et ses

rapports"; Gogacz, "L'homme et la communauté"; Grignaschi, "Ideologia Marsiliana"; Bertelloni, "Filosofía explica la revelación." On Marsiglio's Augustinianism, see Mulcahy, "Hands of Augustine"; Mulcahy, "Marsilius of Padua's Use of St. Augustine"; Scott, "Influence or Manipulation?" For discussions of Marsiglio's Aristotelianism, see de Lagarde, "Adaptation de la politique d'Aristote"; Grignaschi, "Rôle de l'Aristotélisme"; Quillet, "Aristotélisme de Marsile de Padoue," 696–706; Enrico Berti, "'Regnum' di Marsilio"; Olivieri, "Teoria Aristotelica"; Cesare Vasoli, "'Politica' di Aristotele"; Sturner, "Adam und Aristoteles"; Mulieri, "Against Classical Republicanism."

5. Previté-Orton, "Authors Cited in the *Defensor Pacis*."

6. See, for example, Quillet, *Philosophie politique de Marsile de Padoue*; de Lagarde, *Defensor pacis*; di Vona, *I principi del Defensor pacis*; Damiata, *Plenitudo potestatis e universitas civium*; De Rossi, *Marsilio de Padua*; Dolcini, *Introduzione a Marsilio da Padova*; Garnett, *Marsilius of Padua and "The Truth of History"*; Briguglia, *Marsilio da Padova*.

7. Maiolo, *Medieval Sovereignty*, 186–87; Lee, *Political Representation*, 80–81.

8. Skinner, *Foundations of Modern Political Thought*, 1:55; Gewirth, *Marsilius of Padua*, 91 n. 31.

9. See McIlwain, *Growth of Political Thought*, 305, and Myers, *Medieval Kingship*, 288.

10. A noteworthy exception is Syros, *Marsilius of Padua at the Intersection*, which builds upon his 2003 University of Heidelberg doctoral dissertation.

11. In the present chapter, I shall follow the two-volume edition of the *Defensor pacis* edited by Scholz (1932). Citations in the text will be to the discourse, chapter, and section numbers. Translations are based (with occasional alterations) on the English version rendered in *The Defender of Peace*, edited by Gewirth (1956). Although there exists a more recent translation, *The Defender of the Peace*, edited by Brett (2005), I have declined to follow it on some of the grounds I noted in my review of her version in *Political Studies Review*.

12. The third discourse, usually over-looked, has lately been examined in detail by Moreno-Riaño, "Marsilius of Padua's Forgotten Discourse."

13. The phrase "Regnum Italicum" is discussed by Quillet, *Philosophie politique de Marsile de Padoue*, 37–38, 76–77.

14. This interpretation was initially propounded by Segall in *Der "Defensor pacis"* and by Condren in "Democracy and the *Defensor Pacis*" and *Status and Appraisal of Classic Texts*, 189–97.

15. Gewirth, *Marsilius of Padua*, 54–56, 88–91; Quillet, *Philosophie politique de Marsile de Padoue*, 64–66; di Vona, *I principi del Defensor pacis*, 379–80.; Mulieri, "Against Classical Republicanism."

16. For instance, Quillet, *Philosophie politique de Marsile de Padoue*, 80 and, more recently, Lee, *Political Representation in the Later Middle Ages*, 99–100.

17. This represents a clear divergence from Aristotle, for whom the village is simply the first association outside of the *oikos*, and thus the earliest unit of intercourse to address more than immediate physical needs (*Politics* 1252b).

18. For the responsibilities of the *pars principans*, see *Defensor* 1.4.4.

19. Two proponents of this view are de Lagarde, *Naissance de l'esprit laïque*, 2:164–74, and Gewirth, *Marsilius of Padua*, 132–75.

20. This point, crucial to the refutation of Marsiglio's positivism, has been stressed by Lewis, "'Positivism' of Marsiglio of Padua." Lewis's position has been reaffirmed recently by Pawlak, "Teoria prawa Marsyliusza z Padwy."

21. Cicero also equates divine and natural law in *De officiis* 3.23, as he did as part of his account of *ius naturale* in *De re publica* 3.33 (with which Marsiglio was, however, unfa-miliar). By contrast, Lewis's attribution of Marsiglio's "confusion" of divine and natural law to his use of canonistic sources seems less convincing ("'Positivism' of Marsiglio of Padua," 553 n. 49).

22. On the significance of the distinction between "immanent" and "transient" acts, see Nederman, "Community and Self-Interest."

23. On Marsiglio's theory of "natural habit," see Nederman, "Character and Community."

24. The former view is defended by Gewirth in *Marsilius of Padua and Medieval Political Philosophy*, 301–15; the latter position has been asserted by Condren, "Marsilius of Padua's Argument from Authority," 206–7, 213–14.

Chapter 6

1. See Coleman, *History of Political Thought*; Canning, *History of Medieval Political Thought*; Oakley, *Emergence of Western Political Thought*. This proclivity goes at least as far back as the six volumes of the encyclopedic Carlyle and Carlyle, *History of Mediæval Political Theory*.

2. As argued quite persuasively by Mews, "Latin Learning of Christine de Pizan."

3. Oresme, *Livre de éthiques d'Aristote* 2a, ed. Menut, 101; Oresme, *Livre de politiques d'Aristote* 4b, ed. Menut, 44–45. I shall henceforth refer to these texts as *Éthiques* and *Politiques*, respectively.

4. As Antony Black might say; see his *Political Thought in Europe*, 9.

5. Paul Barnette and Spurgeon Baldwin have recently produced both an edition of *Tresor* (Latini, *Livres dou trésor*, 2003) and an English translation of it (Latini, *Book of the Treasure*, 1993). Still useful, especially for its critical apparatus, is the earlier version of *Tresor* edited by Carmody (Latini, *Livres dou trésor*, 1947). I shall generally follow the Barnette and Baldwin translation, with occa-sional modifications. References in the text will be to book, chapter, and section number.

6. An overview of the complexities of Florentine politics, including some reference to Latini's place in it, during the period may be found in Najemy, *History of Florence*, 63–95.

7. Latini, *La rettorica*, ed. Maggini. An English translation of *La rettorica* by Stefania D'Agata D'Ottavi is now available. For an especially useful overview of Latini's reliance on Cicero, see Alessio, "Brunetto Latini e Cicerone."

8. Compare also Latini, *Tresor* 3.2.20 and 3.52.11 with Cicero, *De oratore* 1.5.7.

9. Addressed by Post, *Studies in Medieval Legal Thought*, 37–39.

10. Images from Oresme's beautifully illuminated presentation manuscript of the *Politics* commentary to Charles V, along with an accompanying discussion of the text, are provided by Sherman, *Imaging Aristotle*.

11. The standard examination of Oresme's *Politiques* is Babbitt, *Oresme's "Livre de Politiques."* Kaye has placed Oresme within the broader contours of scholastic thought in *History of Balance*, 345–97, esp. 366–97.

12. Oresme, *Politiques*, ed. Menut, 11. Translations from the Old French are mine. Citations refer to Minut's section numbers and letters.

13. For further instances of the Ciceronian influence on Oresme's reading of the Aristotelian constitutional scheme, see *Politiques* 49b–c and 130d–31a.

14. See Nederman, "Puzzle of the Political Animal," 283–304.

15. For instance, *De officiis* 1.19; *Tusculanarum disputationum* 5.72; *De divinatione* 2.6–7. Many other examples might be adduced.

16. For an extensive and insightful discussion of Aristotle's position, see Burns, *Aristotle and Natural Law*.

17. On Christine's life and political ideas, see Forhan, *Political Theory of Christine de Pizan*.

18. See ibid. for extensive discussion of Christine's sources.

19. References to Christine de Pizan's *Cité des dames* cite the book, chapter, and section numbers given in the Richards edition, *Book of the City of Ladies*.

20. References to Christine de Pizan's *Le livre de paix* cite the book, chapter, and section numbers given in the Green, Mews, and Pinder edition, *Book of Peace*. This volume contains not only an English translation of Christine's text but also an edition of the French original.

Chapter 7

1. Sol, *Fallait-il tuer César*.

2. The position famously advocated by Baron, whose final statement of it may be found in "Memory of Cicero's Roman Civic Spirit," 1:94–133, 134–57. Another dimension

of Cicero's impact on the political ideas of the Italian Renaissance has been explored by Ceron, *Amicizia civile*.

3. Muldoon, *Empire and Order*, 101–5.

4. As explicated by Black, *Political Thought in Europe*, 87–90.

5. A useful review may be found in Burns, *Lordship, Kingship, and Empire*, 97–123.

6. Cusa and Aeneas were not only almost exact contemporaries but their careers intersected on a regular basis. See Housely, "Aeneas Silvius Piccolomini," and Naegle, "Ratgeber des Königs."

7. The most up-to-date biography is to be found in the introduction to the excellent critical edition of Engelbert's *De ortu et fine*, ed. Schneider, Fowler, and Zinsmeyer, 1–4.

8. Fowler, *Intellectual Interests of Engelbert of Admont*, 183–221.

9. Blythe, *Ideal Government and the Mixed Constitution*, 118–38.

10. Edited by Ubl in the second volume of *Die Schriften des Alexander von Roes*. See Briggs, "Scholarly and Intellectual Authority."

11. A thorough bibliography of secondary scholarship is compiled in the preface to the Latin edition of *De ortu et fine*, xi–xxxvii.

12. On contextual issues, see the introduction to ibid., 23–30.

13. I generally follow the translation of *De ortu et fine* contained in *Three Tracts on Empire*, ed. Izbicki and Nederman, which was published in 2000 prior to the new Latin critical edition. As a result, I consult this edition and make adjustments to the English as appropriate. The most pronounced difference between the recent edition and the 1614 version printed by Melchior Goldast on which the English translation is based concerns the renumbering of the chapters in the former, starting with chapter 13, such that an additional chapter is introduced. References cite page numbers from Izbicki and Nederman's edition.

14. Cf. Aristotle, *Politics* 1252a.

15. Rubinstein, "Political Theories in the Renaissance," 173. See the survey by Rabil of the major contributions to the debate: "Significance of 'Civic Humanism.'"

16. A recent noteworthy exception is Lee, *Humanism and Empire*.

17. Aeneas's accomplishments have been surveyed thoroughly by Kisch, *Enea Silvio Piccolomini*, and Widmer, *Enea Silvio Piccolomini*. More recently, Izbicki, Christianson, and Krey have compiled and translated a substantial collection of Aeneas's letters in *Reject Aeneas, Accept Pius*.

18. The standard biography of Aeneas is by Georg Voigt, *Enea Silvio Piccolomini als Papst Pius*. A more abbreviated account of Aeneas's career, albeit concentrating on his activities on the papal throne, is provided by Mitchell in *The Laurels and the Tiara*.

19. The former judgment is addressed by Partner in *Renaissance Rome*, 14, and D'Amico, *Renaissance Humanism in Papal Rome*, 8; the latter opinion may be found in Brann, "Humanism in Germany," 2:126–27, and Lencek, "Humanism in the Slavic Cultural Tradition," 2:348–49.

20. For example, his political ideas receive no attention from Skinner, *Foundations of Modern Political Thought*; Baron, *In Search of Florentine Civic Humanism*; Skinner, "Political Philosophy"; Harding, *Medieval Law*. Aeneas is discussed in more specialized studies of medieval imperialism, such as Burns, *Lordship, Kingship, and Empire*, 114–17; Muldoon, *Empire and Order*, 110–12.

21. The text of the *Pentalogus* was included in Pez, *Thesaurus antecdotorum novissimus*, 3:637–744. On its dating and substance, see Hallam, "Der Pentalogus des Aeneas Silvius Piccolomini."

22. I shall employ the translation of *De ortu et auctoritate imperii Romani* in Izbicki and Nederman, *Three Tracts on Empire*. The Latin text has been edited by Wolkan, "Der Briefwechsel des Eneas Silvius Piccolomini." Another Latin version (along with a German translation) is available in Kallen, *Aeneas Silvius Piccolomini als Publizist*, 52–100. The references are to the pages in the English translation.

23. An important exception is Black, *Political Thought in Europe*, 106–7, which offers a brief discussion of some Ciceronian elements contained in *De ortu et auctoritate*.

24. The phrasing of this statement is unmistakably Ciceronian; cf. *De finibus* 2.34.

25. See Cicero, *De officiis* 1.22 and *De finibus* 2.45.

26. The formula is derived from Codex 1.14.4.

27. Indeed, my ascription to Aeneas of a doctrine of "imperial" humanism seems emblematic of what D'Amico identified as the "Roman" version of Ciceronianism, which constituted "the chief means of expressing Roman humanism's authoritarian and imperial associations. . . . Roman humanists neglected the political side of Cicero's life and teachings. . . . [T]hey preferred to look at Cicero as the great Latin stylist rather than as a politician and defender of the Republic' (*Renaissance Humanism in Papal Rome*, 126, 125).

28. Sigmund, *Nicholas of Cusa and Medieval Political Thought*, 292.

29. Watanabe, *Political Ideas of Nicholas of Cusa*, 144.

30. Quillet, "Community I," 544–45.

31. Guenée, *States and Rulers*, 17.

32. See Muldoon, "Nicholas of Cusa, the Papacy, and World Order," 172–90.

33. Sigmund, "Influence of Marsilius of Padua."

34. I follow the translation of Nicholas of Cusa's *De concordantia catholica* by Sigmund, *Catholic Concordance*. The Latin text is Nicholas of Cusa, *Opera omnia*, vol. 14, *De concordantia catholica*, ed. Kallen, which I have employed very occasionally to amend Sigmund's rendering. References are to page and section numbers from Sigmund's translation.

35. Contra Oakley, who regards "as new" Cusa's connection between equality and consent; see *Emergence of Western Political Thought*, 3:203.

36. See Nederman, "Rhetoric, Reason, and Republic," 261–62.

Chapter 8

1. General treatments of European attitudes toward the newly encountered peoples of the Americas are afforded by Hanke, *Spanish Struggle for Justice*; Hanke, *Aristotle and the American Indians*; Pagden, *Fall of Natural Man*.

2. Pagden surveys primarily the arguments against violent conquest of the Americas proposed in a purely academic setting by Francisco de Vittori and his followers (*Fall*

of Natural Man, 57–108). Vittori's position, however, tended to be paternalistic within the Christian context of *caritas*.

3. There are several thorough biographical treatments of Las Casas in Spanish. In English, see Wagner, *Life and Writings of Bartolomé de las Casas*. Also useful are the studies contained in Friede and Keen, *Bartolomé de las Casas in History*.

4. Gutiérrez, *Las Casas*.

5. E.g., Castro, *Another Face of Empire*.

6. A sampling of scholarship in English alone includes (in chronological order) Todorov, "Toleration and the Intolerable"; Cornish, "Spanish Thomism and the American Indians"; Sastre, "National Prejudice and Religion"; Terraciano, "Spanish Struggle for Justification"; Vickery, *Bartolomé de las Casas*; Clayton, *Bartolomé de las Casas*; Brunstetter, *Tensions of Modernity*. This is in addition to the scholarly writings cited throughout the present chapter. The literature in Spanish is exponentially larger.

7. Pagden, *Fall of Natural Man*, 122. Similar views have been espoused by Hanke, *Aristotle and the American Indians*; André-Vincent, "Concrétisation de la notion classique"; Cornish, "Spanish Thomism and the American Indians."

8. Tierney, "Aristotle and the American Indians," 299. See also Pennington, "Bartolomé de las Casas," and Muldoon, *Popes, Lawyers, and Infidels*, 132–52.

9. Hanke makes no reference at all to Cicero in either of his classic books. Pagden (*Fall of Natural Man*, 140) and Tierney ("Aristotle and the American Indians," 319) make only fleeting mention of Las Casas's use of Cicero. Anthony Pagden (*Lords of All the World*, 19–23) discusses Las Casas in a Roman context, but never returns to the impact of his thought in later times.

10. Las Casas, *Apologética historia sumaria*, ed. O'Gorman, 1:256, 391, 392, 397, 400, 409, 410, 414, 547, 549, 550, 567, 599, 600, 610,

615, 618, 630, 698; 2:7, 38–39, 45–46, 55, 59, 67, 85–86, 101–2, 149, 249, 319, 320, 340, 411, 460. *Apologética historia sumaria* is hereafter abbreviated *AHS* and cited according to the volume and page numbers of the O'Gorman edition. All translations from Spanish and Latin (except for the *Apologia*) are mine.

11. Las Casas, *Historia de las Indias*, ed. Millares Carlo, 2:396; see also *AHS* 1:257, 258. Las Casas's egalitarianism is stressed by Todorov, "Toleration and the Intolerable," 141–42.

12. Parenthetical citations of Las Casas's *Apologia* refer to pages in Poole's translation, *In Defense of the Indians*.

13. André-Vincent, "Concrétisation de la notion classique," 205.

14. He enumerates these tokens of civilization in *Apologia*, 42–43.

15. Las Casas, *De unico vocationis modo omnium gentium*, ed. Millares Carlo, 98.

16. Ibid., 100.

17. Ibid., 6.

18. References to Las Casas's *Historia de las Indias* cite the volume and page numbers of the Millares Carlo edition.

19. Pagden, *Fall of Natural Man*, 122.

20. Las Casas, *Disputa o controversia*, 1:408.

21. Las Casas, *Tratado comprobatorio del imperio soberano*, 2:1008–10.

Conclusion

1. A point that I made in "Meaning of 'Aristotelianism.'"

2. Nicgorski, *Cicero's Practical Philosophy*, 8–9.

3. Wittgenstein, *Philosophical Investigations*, trans. Amscombe, sec. 66.

4. See McGinn, *Truth by Analysis*, 15–34.

5. Wittgenstein, *Investigations*, trans. Amscombe, sec. 67.

6. Ibid., sec. 66.

7. Nelson adopts the same approach in his study of republicanism in *Greek Tradition*, 17–18.

Aelred of Rievaulx. *De spirituali amicitia.*
In *Opera omnia*, edited by A. Hoste
and C. H. Talbot, 1:287–350. Turn-
hout: Brepols, 1971.
———. *Spiritual Friendship.* Edited by Mar-
cia L. Dutton. Collegeville, Minn.:
Liturgical Press, 2010.
Alessio, Gian Carlo. "Brunetto Latini e Cice-
rone (e i dettator)." *Italia Medioevale e
Umanistica* 22 (1979): 123–69.
André-Vincent, Philippe. "La concrétisation
de la notion classique de droit naturel
à travers l'oeuvre de Las Casas."
In *Las Casas et la politque des droits
de l'homme*, 203–13. Aix-en-Provence:
Institut de études politiques, 1974.
Annas, Julia. "Aristotelian Political Theory in
the Hellenistic Period." In *Justice and
Generosity: Studies in Hellenistic Social
and Political Philosophy.* Edited by
André Laks and Malcolm Schofield,
74–94. Cambridge: Cambridge
University Press, 1995.
Aristotle. *Nicomachean Ethics.* Translated
by C. D. C. Reeve. Indianapolis:
Hackett, 2014.
———. *Politics.* Translated by C. D. C. Reeve.
Indianapolis: Hackett, 2017.
Atkins, Jed W. *Cicero on Politics and the Limits
of Reason.* Cambridge: Cambridge
University Press, 2013.
———. "The *Officia* of St. Ambrose's *De offi-
ciis.*" *Journal of Early Christian Studies*
19 (2011): 49–77.
———. *Roman Political Thought.* Cam-
bridge: Cambridge University Press,
2018.
Babbitt, Susan M. *Oresme's "Livre de Poli-
tiques" and the France of Charles V.*
Transactions of the American
Philosophical Society 75, part 1. Phil-
adelphia: American Philosophical
Society, 1985.

Ballacci, Guiseppe. *Political Theory Between
Philosophy and Rhetoric.* London:
Palgrave Macmillan, 2018.
Baraz, Elena. *A Written Republic: Cicero's
Philosophical Politics.* Princeton:
Princeton University Press, 2012.
Baron, Hans. "Cicero and the Roman Civil
Spirit in the Middle Ages and Early
Renaissance." *Bulletin of the John
Rylands Library* 22 (1938): 72–97.
———. "The Florentine Revival of the
Active Political Life." In *In Search of
Florentine Civic Humanism*, 1:134–57.
———. *In Search of Florentine Civic Human-
ism.* 2 vols. Princeton: Princeton
University Press, 1998.
———. "The Memory of Cicero's Roman
Civic Spirit in the Medieval Centu-
ries and the Florentine Renaissance."
In *In Search of Florentine Civic
Humanism*, 1:94–133.
Bazán, Bernardo C., John W. Wippel, Gérard
Fransen, and Danielle Jacquart.
*Les questions disputées et les questions
quodlibétiques dans les facultés de
théologie, de droit et de médecine.*
Turnhout: Brepols, 1985.
Bertelloni, Francisco. "La filosofía explica
la revelación: Sobre el 'averroismo
politico' en el *Defensor pacis* de Mar-
silio de Padua." *Educação e Filosofia
Uberlândia* 25 (2011): 475–500.
Berti, Enrico. "Il 'regnum' di Marsilio tra
la 'polis' Aristotelica et lo 'stato'
moderno." *Medioevo* 5 (1979):
165–81.
Black, Antony. *Political Thought in Europe,
1250–1450.* Cambridge: Cambridge
University Press, 1992.
Blythe, James M. *Ideal Government and the
Mixed Constitution in the Middle Ages.*
Princeton: Princeton University
Press, 1992.

————. *The Thought and Worldview of Tolomeo Fiadoni (Ptolemy of Lucca)*. Turnhout: Brepols, 2009.

Bolgar, R. R. *The Classical Heritage and Its Beneficiaries*. Cambridge: Cambridge University Press, 1954.

Bollermann, Karen, and Cary J. Nederman. "The Sword in Her Hand: Judith as Anglo-Saxon Warrior and John of Salisbury's Tyrant Slayer." In *Thinking Politics in the Vernacular from the Middle Ages to the Renaissance*, edited by Gianluca Briguglia and Thomas Ricklin, 23–41. Freiburg: Academic Press Freiburg, 2011.

Brann, Noel L. "Humanism in Germany." In *Renaissance Humanism*, edited by Albert Rabil, 2:123–55. 3 vols. Philadelphia: University of Pennsylvania Press, 1988.

Briggs, Charles. "Scholarly and Intellectual Authority in Late Medieval European Mirrors." In *Global Medieval Mirrors of Princes Reconsidered*, edited by Regula Foster and Neguin Yavari, 26–41. Boston: Ilez Foundation, 2015.

Briguglia, Gianluca. *Il corpo vivente dello Stato: Una metafora politica*. Pavia: Bruno Mondadori, 2006.

————. *Marsilio da Padova*. Rome: Carocci, 2013.

Brooke, Christopher N. L. "Adrian IV and John of Salisbury." In *Adrian IV The English Pope (1154–1159)*, edited by Brenda Bolton and Anne J. Duggan, 3–13. London: Routledge/Ashgate, 2003.

Brunstetter, Daniel R. *Tensions of Modernity: Las Casas and His Legacy in the French Enlightenment*. New York: Routledge, 2012.

Burns, J. H., ed. *The Cambridge History of Medieval Political Thought, c. 350–c. 1450*. Cambridge: Cambridge University Press, 1988.

————, ed. *The Cambridge History of Political Thought, 1450–1700*. Cambridge: Cambridge University Press, 1991.

————. *Lordship, Kingship, and Empire: The Idea of Monarchy, 1400–1525*. Oxford: Oxford University Press, 1992.

Burns, Tony. *Aristotle and Natural Law*. London: Bloomsbury, 2011.

Canning, Joseph. *A History of Medieval Political Thought, 300–1450*. 2nd ed. London: Routledge, 2005.

————. *Ideas of Power in the Late Middle Ages, 1296–1417*. Cambridge: Cambridge University Press, 2009.

Carlyle, A. J., and R. W. Carlyle. *A History of Mediæval Political Theory in the West*. 6 vols. Edinburgh: William Blackwood & Son, 1913–36.

Castro, Daniel. *Another Face of Empire: Bartolomé de Las Casas, Indigenous Rights, and Ecclesiastical Imperialism*. Durham: Duke University Press, 2007.

Ceron, Annalisa. *L'amicizia civile e gli amici de principe: Lo spazio politico dell' amicizia nel pensiero del Quattrocento*. Macerata: EUM, 2011.

Christine de Pizan. *The Book of Peace*. Edited by Karen Green, Constant J. Mews, and Janice Pinder. University Park: Pennsylvania State University Press, 2008.

————. *The Book of the City of Ladies*. Edited by Earl Jeffrey Richards. Rev. ed. New York: Persea Books, 1998.

Clavier, F. M. *Eloquent Wisdom: Rhetoric, Cosmology and Delight in Theology of Augustine of Hippo*. Turnhout: Brepols, 2014.

Clayton, Lawrence A. *Bartolomé de Las Casas and the Conquest of the Americas*. Chichester, U.K.: Wiley-Blackwell, 2011.

Cochrane, Charles Norris. *Christianity and Classical Culture*. Oxford: Oxford University Press, 1944.

Coleman, Janet. "*Dominium* in Thirteenth and Fourteenth-Century Political Thought and Its Seventeenth-Century Heirs: John of Paris and Locke." *Political Studies* 33 (1985): 73–100.

————. *A History of Political Thought from the Middle Ages to the Renaissance*. 2 vols. Oxford: Blackwell, 2000.

Colish, Marcia L. *The Stoic Tradition from Antiquity to the Early Middle Ages*. 2 vols. Leiden: Brill, 1985.

Condren, Conal. "Democracy and the *Defensor pacis*: On the English Language Tradition of Marsilian Interpretation." *Il Pensiero Politico* 13 (1980): 301–16.

———. "Marsilius of Padua's Argument from Authority: A Survey of Its Significance in the *Defensor Pacis*." *Political Theory* 5 (1977): 206–14.

———. *The Status and Appraisal of Classic Texts*. Princeton: Princeton University Press, 1985.

Connolly, Joy. *The State of Speech: Rhetoric and Political Thought in Ancient Rome*. Princeton: Princeton University Press, 2007.

Corey, David D., and J. Daryl Charles. *The Just War Tradition: An Introduction*. Wilmington, Del.: ISI, 2012.

Cornish, Paul J. "Spanish Thomism and the American Indians: Vitoria and Las Casas on the Toleration of Cultural Difference." In *Difference and Dissent: Theories of Toleration in Medieval and Early Modern Europe*, edited by Cary J. Nederman and John Christian Laursen, 99–117. Lanham, Md.: Rowman & Littlefield, 1996.

Corso de Estrada, Laura. "Proyecciones de la concepción ciceroniana de naturaleza en la ética escolástica del s. XIII: M. Tulio Cicero y Tomás de Aquino." *Annuario Filosófico* 34 (2001): 323–45.

Cotts, John D. *The Clerical Dilemma: Peter of Blois and Literate Culture*. Washington, D.C.: Catholic University of America Press, 2009.

Cox, Virginia, and John O. Ward, eds. *The Rhetoric of Cicero in Its Medieval and Early Renaissance Commentary Tradition*. Leiden: Brill, 2006.

Coyle, Alcuin F. "Cicero's *De officiis* and *De offiiciis ministrorum* of St. Ambrose." *Franciscan Studies* 15 (1955): 224–56.

Cumming, Robert Denoon. *History and Human Nature*. 2 vols. Chicago: University of Chicago Press, 1969.

Damiata, Marino. *Alvaro Pelagio: Teocratico scontento*. Florence: Edizioni Studi Francescani, 1984.

———. *Plenitudo potestatis e universitas civium in Marsilio da Padova*. Florence: Edizioni Studi Francescani, 1983.

D'Amico, John F. *Renaissance Humanism in Papal Rome*. Baltimore: Johns Hopkins University Press, 1983.

De Pourcq, Maarten. "Classical Reception Studies: Reconceptualizing the Study of the Classical Tradition." *International Journal of the Humanities* 9 (2012): 219–25.

De Rossi, Guido. *Marsilio de Padua: Profeta de la politica moderna*. Lima: Mosca Azul Editores, 1976.

Deusen, Nancy van, ed. *Cicero Refused to Die: Ciceronian Influence Through the Centuries*. Leiden: Brill, 2013.

Digeser, Elizabeth Depalma. "Citisenship and the Roman *Res Publica*: Cicero and a Christian Corollary." In *Republicanism: History, Theory and Practice*, edited by Daniel Weinstock and Christian Nadeau, 7–21. London: Frank Cass, 2004.

Di Vona, Piero. *I principi del Defensor pacis*. Naples: Morano Editore, 1974.

Dolcini, Carlo. *Introduzione a Marsilio da Padova*. Rome: Laterza, 1995.

Dox, Donnalee. *The Idea of the Theater in Latin Christian Thought: Augustine to the Fourteenth Century*. Ann Arbor: University of Michigan Press, 2004.

Dunbabin, Jean. "The Reception and Interpretation of Aristotle's *Politics*." In *The Cambridge History of Later Medieval Philosophy*, edited by Norman Kretzmann, Anthony Kenny, Eleonore Stump, and Jan Pinborg, 723–37. Cambridge: Cambridge University Press, 1982.

Du Plessis, Paul J., ed. *Cicero's Law: Rethinking Roman Law of the Late Republic*. Edinburgh: Edinburgh University Press, 2016.

Dutton, Marcia L., ed. *A Companion to Aelred of Rievaulx*. Leiden: Brill, 2017.

———. Introduction to Aelred of Rievaulx, *Spiritual Friendship*, 13–50. Translated by Lawrence C. Braceland. Edited by Marsha L. Dutton. Cistercian

Fathers Series 5. Collegeville, Minn.: Liturgical Press, 2010.

Dyson, R. G. "*De regimine christiano* and the Franco-Papal Crisis of 1296–1303." In *A Companion to James of Viterbo*, edited by Antoine Côté and Martin Pickavé, 331–56. Leiden: Brill, 2018.

Engelbert of Admont. *De ortu et fine Romani imperii.* Edited by Herbert Schneider, George B. Fowler, and Helga Zinsmeyer. Wiesbaden: Harrassowitz Verlag, 2016.

Engen, John van, ed. *Learning Institutionalized: Teaching in the Medieval University.* Notre Dame: Notre Dame University Press, 2000.

Fidora, Alexander, and Jordi Pardo Pastor, eds. "Cicero and the Middle Ages." *Convenit Selecta* 7 (2002).

Flüeler, Christoph. *Rezeption und Interpretation der aristotelischen Politica im späten Mittelalter.* 2 vols. Amsterdam: B. R. Grüner, 1992.

Forhan, Kate Langdon. *The Political Theory of Christine de Pizan.* Burlington, Vt.: Ashgate, 2002.

Fowler, G. B. *Intellectual Interests of Engelbert of Admont.* New York: Columbia University Press, 1947.

Fox, Matthew. *Cicero's Philosophy of History.* Oxford: Oxford University Press, 2007.

Fredborg, Karin M. "The Commentary of Thierry of Chartres on Cicero's *De inventione.*" In *Cahiers de l'Institut de Moyen Âge Grec et Latin*, 1–27. Copenhagen: University of Copenhagen, 1971.

———. *The Latin Rhetorical Commentaries of Thierry of Chartres.* Toronto: Pontifical Institute for Mediaeval Studies, 1988.

Friede, Juan, and Benjamin Keen, eds. *Bartolomé de Las Casas in History: Toward an Understanding of the Man and His Work.* DeKalb: Northern Illinois University Press, 1971.

Garnett, George. *Marsilius of Padua and "The Truth of History."* Cambridge: Cambridge University Press, 2006.

Gewirth, Alan. *Marsilius of Padua and Medieval Political Philosophy.* New York: Columbia University Press, 1951.

———. "Republicanism and Absolutism in the Thought of Marsilius of Padua." *Medioevo* 5 (1979): 23–48.

Gogacz, Mieczyslaw. "L'homme et la communauté dans le 'Defensor pacis' de Marsile de Padoue: Le problème de l'inconséquence de l'averroïsme comme aristotélisme néoplatonisant." *Medioevo* 5 (1979): 189–99.

Goodman, Rob. "'I Tremble with My Whole Heart': Cicero on the Anxieties of Eloquence." *European Journal of Political Theory* (forthcoming 2019).

Grabmann, Martin. "Studien über den Einfluss der aristotelischen Philosophie auf die mittelalterlichen Theorien über der Verhältnis von Kirche und Staat." *Sitzungberichte der Bayerischen Akademie der Wissenschaft, Philosophisch-Historische Abteilung* 2 (1934): 41–60.

Grellard, Christophe. *Jean de Salisbury et le renaissance mèdièvale du scepticisme.* Paris: Les Belles Lettres, 2013.

———. "La religion comme technique de gouvernement chez Jean de Salisbury." *Cahiers de Civilisation Médiévale* 53 (2010): 237–54.

———. "Le sacré et le profane: Le statut des laïcs dans la *Respublica* de Jean de Salisbury." In *Les laïcs dans les villes de la France du Nord au XIIe siècle*, edited by Patrick Demouy, 167–87. Turnhout: Brepols, 2008.

Grellard, Christophe, and Frédérique Lacaud, eds. *A Companion to John of Salisbury.* Leiden: Brill, 2015.

Grignaschi, Mario. "L'ideologia Marsiliana si spiega con l'adesione dell'autore all'uno o all'altro dei grandi sistemi filosofici dell'inizio del Trecento?" *Medioevo* 5 (1979): 201–21.

———. "Le rôle de l'aristotélisme dans le 'Defensor pacis' de Marsile de Padoue." *Revue d'Histoire et de Philosophie Religieuses* 35 (1955): 301–40.

Guenée, Bernard. *States and Rulers in Later Medieval Europe*. Translated by Juliette Vale. Oxford: Blackwell, 1989.

Gutiérrez, Gustavo. *Las Casas: In Search of the Poor of Jesus Christ*. Translated by Robert R. Barr. Marynoll, N.Y.: Orbis Books, 1993.

Hale, David George. *The Body Politic: A Political Metaphor in Renaissance English Literature*. The Hague: Mouton, 1968.

Hallam, H. J. "Der Pentalogus des Aeneas Silvius Piccolomini." Ph.D. diss., University of Cologne, 1951.

Hammer, Dean. *Roman Political Thought*. Cambridge: Cambridge University Press, 2014.

———. *Roman Political Thought and the Modern Political Imagination*. Norman: University of Oklahoma Press, 2008.

Hanke, Lewis. *Aristotle and the American Indians*. Chicago: Henry Regnery, 1959.

———. *The Spanish Struggle for Justice in the Conquest of America*. Philadelphia: University of Pennsylvania Press, 1949.

Hankins, James. "The 'Baron Thesis' After Forty Years and Some Recent Studies of Leonardo Bruni." *Journal of the History of Ideas* 56 (1995): 309–38.

———, ed. *Renaissance Civic Humanism: Reappraisals and Reflections*. Cambridge: Cambridge University Press, 2000.

Harding, Alan. *Medieval Law and the Foundations of the State*. Oxford: Oxford University Press, 2002.

Hardwick, Lorna, and Christopher Stray, eds. *A Companion to Classical Receptions*. Oxford: Blackwell, 2008.

Harries, Jill. *Cicero and the Jurists: From Citizens' Law to the Lawful State*. London: Duckworth, 2006.

Haseldine, Julian P. *Friendship in Medieval Europe*. Stroud, U.K.: Sutton, 1999.

———. "Friendship Networks in Medieval Europe: New Models of a Political Relationship." *Journal of Friendship Studies* 1 (2013): 69–88.

———. "Understanding the Language of *Amicitia*: The Friendship Circle of Peter of Celle." *Journal of Medieval History* 20 (1994): 237–60.

Haskins, Charles Homer. *The Renaissance of the Twelfth Century*. Cambridge: Harvard University Press, 1927.

Henry of Ghent. *Quodlibetal Questions on Moral Problems*. Edited by Roland J. Teske, S.J. Milwaukee: Marquette University Press, 2005.

Heyking, John von. "Taming Warriors in Classical and Early Medieval Political Theory." In *Ethics, Nationalism, and Just War: Medieval and Contemporary Perspectives*, edited by Henrik Syse and Gregory M. Reichberg, 11–35. Washington, D.C.: Catholic University of America Press, 2007.

Holmberg, John, ed. *Das "Moralium dogma philosophorum" des Guillaume de Conches*. Uppsala: Almqvist & Wiksell, 1929.

Housely, Norman. "Aeneas Silvius Piccolomini, Nicolas of Cusa, the Crusade: Conciliar, Imperial, and Papal Authority." *Church History* 86 (2017): 643–67.

Howaston, M. C., and Ian Chilvers, eds. *The Concise Oxford Companion to Classical Literature*. Oxford: Oxford University Press, 1993.

Izbicki, Thomas M., Gerald Christianson, and Philip Krey, eds. *Reject Aeneas, Accept Pius*. Washington, D.C.: Catholic University of America Press, 2006.

Izbicki, Thomas M., and Cary J. Nederman, eds. *Three Tracts on Empire*. Bristol: Thommes Press, 2000.

James, M. R. *Two Ancient English Scholars*. Glasgow: Jackson, Wylie, 1931.

James of Viterbo. *De regimine christiano*. Edited by R. W. Dyson. Leiden: Brill, 2009.

John of Paris. *On Royal and Papal Power*. Edited by J. A. Watt. Toronto: Pontifical Institute of Mediaeval Studies, 1971.

John of Salisbury. *Frivolities of Courtiers and Footprints of Philosophers*. Translated by Joseph B. Pike. Minneapolis: University of Minnesota Press, 1938.

———. *Metalogicon*. Translated by J. B. Hall. Turnhout: Brepols, 2013.

———. *Policraticus*. Edited by C. C. J. Webb. 2 vols. Oxford: Oxford University Press, 1909.

———. *Policraticus: Of the Frivolities of Courtiers and the Footprints of Philosophers*. Translated by Cary J. Nederman. Cambridge: Cambridge University Press, 1990.

———. *The Statesman's Book of John of Salisbury*. Translated by John Dickinson. New York: Knopf, 1927.

Jones, Chris. "John of Paris: Through a Glass, Darkly?" In *John of Paris: Beyond Royal and Papal Power*, edited by Chris Jones, 1–10. Turnhout: Brepols, 2015.

Kallen, Gerhard. *Aeneas Silvius Piccolomini als Publizist*. Cologne: Petrarca-Haus, 1939.

Kallendorf, Craig. "Ciceronianism." In *Oxford Bibliographies—Renaissance and Reformation*. DOI: 10.1093/obo/9780195399301-0314.

Kapust, Daniel. "Advenit Cicero." *Contemporary Political Theory* 17 (2018): 164–70.

———. "Cicero on Decorum and the Morality of Rhetoric." *European Journal of Political Theory* 10 (2011): 92–112.

———. "Ecce Romani!" *Political Theory* 45 (2017): 705–19.

Kaye, Joel. *A History of Balance, 1250–1375: The Emergence of a New Model of Equilibrium and Its Impact on Thought*. Cambridge: Cambridge University Press, 2014.

Keeline, Thomas. *The Reception of Cicero in the Early Roman Empire: The Rhetorical Schoolroom and the Creation of a Cultural Legend*. Cambridge: Cambridge University Press, 2018.

Kempshall, Matthew S. *The Common Good in Late Medieval Political Thought*. Oxford: Oxford University Press, 1999.

———. "*De re publica* I.39 in Medieval and Renaissance Political Thought." In *Cicero's Republic*, edited by

J. G. F. Powell and J. A. North, 99–135. London: Institute of Classical Studies, 2001.

———. *Rhetoric and the Writing of History*. Manchester: Manchester University Press, 2011.

Kennedy, Geoff. "Cicero, Roman Republicanism and the Contested Meaning of *Libertas*." *Political Studies* 62 (2014): 488–501.

Kennedy, George A. "Cicero's Oratorical and Rhetorical Legacy." In May, *Brill's Companion to Cicero*, 482–501.

Keohane, Nannerl O. *Philosophy and the State in France*. Princeton: Princeton University Press, 1980.

Keyes, Mary. *Aquinas, Aristotle, and the Promise of the Common Good*. Cambridge: Cambridge University Press, 2006.

Kisch, Guido. *Enea Silvio Piccolomini und die Jurisprudenz*. Basel: Helbing & Lichtenhahn, 1967.

Laarhoven, Jan van. "Thou Shall NOT Slay a Tyrant." In *The World of John of Salisbury*, edited by Michael Wilks, 319–41. Oxford: Blackwell, 1984.

Labarrière, Jean-Louis, ed. "Le *Songe de Scipion* de Cicéron et sa tradition." *Les Études Philosophiques* 99 (2011): 451–562.

Lachaud, Frédérique. *L'éthique du pouvoir au Moyen Âge*. Paris: Classiques Garnier, 2010.

Lagarde, George de. "Une adaptation de la politique d'Aristote au XIVᵉ siècle." *Revue Historique de Droit Français et Étranger*, 4th ser., 11 (1932): 227–69.

———. *Le Defensor pacis*. Louvain and Paris: Nauwelaerts, 1970.

———. *La naissance de l'esprit laïque au déclin du Moyen Âge*. 2 vols. Saint-Paul-Trois-Châteaux: Éditiones Béatrice, 1934.

Lapidge, Michael. "The Stoic Inheritance." In *A History of Twelfth-Century Western Philosophy*, edited by Peter Dronke, 81–112. Cambridge: Cambridge University Press, 1988.

Las Casas, Bartolomé de. *Apologética historia sumaria*. Edited by Edmundo O'Gorman. 2 vols. Mexico City:

Universidad Nacional Autónomia de México, 1967.

———. *De unico vocationis modo omnium gentium.* Edited by Agústin Millares Carlo. Mexico City: Fondo de Cultura Económica, 1942.

———. *Una disputa o controversia.* In *Tratados.* 2 vols. Mexico City: Fondo de Cultura Económica, 1965.

———. *Historia de las Indias.* Edited by Agústin Millares Carlo. 3 vols. Mexico City: Fondo de Cultura Económica, 1951.

———. *In Defense of the Indians.* Translated by Stafford Poole. DeKalb: Northern Illinois University Press, 1974.

———. *Tratado comprobatorio del imperio soberano.* In *Tratados.* 2 vols. Mexico City: Fondo de Cultura Económica, 1965.

Latini, Brunetto. *The Book of the Treasure.* Edited by Paul Barnette and Spurgeon Baldwin. New York: Garland, 1993.

———. *Li livres dou tresor.* Edited by Paul Barnette and Spurgeon Baldwin. Tempe: Arizona Center for Medieval and Renaissance Studies, 2003.

———. *Li livres dou tresor.* Edited by F. J. Carmody. Berkeley: University of California Press, 1947.

———. *La rettorica.* Edited by Stefania D'Agata D'Ottavi. Kalamazoo, Mich.: Medieval Institute, 2016.

———. *La rettorica.* Edited by Francesco Maggini. Florence: Felice le Monnier, 1968.

Lee, Alexander. *Humanism and Empire: The Imperial Ideal in Fourteenth-Century Italy.* Oxford: Oxford University Press, 2018.

Lee, Hwa-Yong. *Political Representation in the Later Middle Ages.* New York: Peter Lang, 2008.

Leibeschütz, Hans. *Mediaeval Humanism in the Life and Writings of John of Salisbury.* London: The Warburg Institute, 1950.

Lencek, Rado L. "Humanism in the Slavic Cultural Tradition." In *Renaissance Humanism,* edited by Albert Rabil,

2:345–76. 3 vols. Philadelphia: University of Pennsylvania Press, 1988.

Leone, Marialucrezia. "Moral Philosophy in Henry of Ghent." In *A Companion to Henry of Ghent,* edited by Gordon A. Wilson, 274–314. Leiden: Brill, 2011.

Lewis, Ewart. "The 'Positivism' of Marsiglio of Padua." *Speculum* 38 (October 1963): 541–82.

Maass, Richard W. "Political Society and Cicero's Ideal State." *Historical Methods* 45 (2012): 79–92.

MacKendrick, Paul. *The Philosophical Books of Cicero.* London: Duckworth, 1989.

Macrobius. *Commentary on the Dream of Scipio.* Edited by William Harris Stahl. New York: Columbia University Press, 1952.

Maiolo, Francesco. *Medieval Sovereignty: Marsilius of Padua and Bartolus of Saxoferrato.* Delft, The Netherlands: Eburon, 2007.

Marsilius of Padua. *The Defender of Peace.* Edited by Alan Gewirth. New York: Columbia University Press, 1956.

———. *The Defender of the Peace.* Edited by Annabel Brett. Cambridge: Cambridge University Press, 2005.

———. *Defensor pacis.* Edited by Richard Scholz. Hannover: Hahn, 1932.

Martin, Janet. "John of Salisbury as Classical Scholar." In *The World of John of Salisbury,* edited by Michael Wilks, 179–201. Oxford: Blackwell, 1984.

Martindale, Charles A. "Introduction: Thinking Through Reception." In Martindale and Thomas, *Classics and the Uses of Reception,* 1–13.

Martindale, Charles A., and Richard F. Thomas, eds. *Classics and the Uses of Reception.* Oxford: Blackwell, 2006.

Maso, Stefano. *Grasp and Dissent: Cicero and Epicurean Philosophy.* Turnhout: Brepols, 2015.

May, James M., ed. *Brill's Companion to Cicero: Oratory and Rhetoric.* Leiden: Brill, 2002.

McGinn, Colin. *Truth by Analysis: Names, Games, and Philosophy.* Oxford: Oxford University Press, 2012.

McGuire, Brian Patrick. *Friendship and Community: The Monastic Experience, 350–1250.* Kalamazoo, Mich.: Cistercian Press, 1988.

McIlwain, C. H. *The Growth of Political Thought in the West: From the Greeks to the End of the Middle Ages.* New York: Macmillan, 1932.

Mews, Constant J. "The Latin Learning of Christine de Pizan in the *Livre de paix.*" In *Healing the Body Politic: The Political Thought of Christine de Pizan,* edited by Karen Green and Constant J. Mews, 61–80. Turnhout: Brepols, 2005.

Miethke, Jürgen. *De potestate papae: Die päpstliche Amtskompetenz im Widerstreit der politischen Theorie van Thomas von Aquin bis Wilhelm von Ockham.* Tübingen: Mohr Siebeck, 2000.

Millor, W. J., and C. N. L. Brooke, eds. *The Letters of John of Salisbury.* Vol. 2: *The Late Letters (1163–1180).* Oxford: Clarendon Press, 1979.

Millor, W. J., H. E. Butler, and C. N. L. Brooke, eds. *The Letters of John of Salisbury.* Vol. 1: *The Early Letters (1153–1161).* London: Thomas Nelson and Sons, 1955.

Mitchell, R. J. *The Laurels and the Tiara: Pope Pius II, 1458–1464.* London: Harvill Press, 1962.

Moore, R. I. *The First European Revolution, c. 975–1215.* Oxford: Blackwell, 2000.

Moreno-Riaño, Gerson. "John of Paris, Private Property, and the Study of Medieval Political Thought." In *John of Paris: Beyond Royal and Papal Power,* edited by Chris Jones, 225–37. Turnhout: Brepols, 2015.

———. "Marsilius of Padua's Forgotten Discourse." *History of Political Thought* 29 (2008): 441–60.

———, ed. *The World of Marsilius of Padua.* Turnhout: Brepols, 2006.

Moreno-Riaño, Gerson, and Cary J. Nederman, eds. *A Companion to Marsilius of Padua.* Leiden: Brill, 2012.

Mulcahy, Daniel G. "The Hands of Augustine but the Voice of Marsilius." *Augustiniana* 21 (1971): 457–66.

———. "Marsilius of Padua's Use of St. Augustine." *Revue des Études Augustiniennes* 18 (1972): 180–90.

Muldoon, James. *Empire and Order: The Concept of Empire, 800–1800.* New York: St. Martin's Press, 1999.

———. "Nicholas of Cusa, the Papacy, and World Order: Vision and Reality." In *Inventing Modernity in the Middle Ages, c. 1100–c. 1550,* edited by Bettina Koch and Cary J. Nederman, 172–90. Kalamazoo, Mich.: Medieval Institute, 2018.

———. *Popes, Lawyers, and Infidels: The Church and the Non-Christian World, 1250–1550.* Philadelphia: University of Pennsylvania Press, 1979.

Mulieri, Alessandro. "Against Classical Republicanism: The Averroist Foundations of Marsilius of Padua's Political Thought." *History of Political Thought* 40 (2019): 218–45.

Mulve, Leidulf. "'The Revolt of the Medievalists': Directions in Recent Research on the Twelfth-Century Renaissance." *Journal of Medieval History* 32 (2006): 231–52.

Munk-Olsen, Birger. "L'humanisme de Jean de Salisbury: Un cicéronien au 12ᵉ siècle." In *Entretiens sur la renaissance du 12ᵉ siècle,* edited by Maurice de Gandillac and Édouard Jeauneau, 53–69. Paris: Moutons, 1968.

Murphy, James J., and Michael Winterbottom. "Raffaele Regio's 1492 *Quaestio* Doubting Cicero's Authorship of the *Rhetorica ad Herennium*: Introduction and Text." *Rhetorica* 17 (1999): 77–87.

Myers, Henry. *Medieval Kingship.* Chicago: Nelson-Hall, 1982.

Naegle, Giesela. "Ratgeber des Königs und Würdenträger der Kirche: Wissen und Macht bei Jean Juvénal des Ursins, Enea Silvio Piccolomini und Nikolaus van Kues." *Quaestiones Medii Aevi Novea* 22 (2017): 251–77.

Najemy, John. *A History of Florence, 1200–1575.* Oxford: Blackwell, 2006.

Nederman, Cary J. "The Aristotelian Doctrine of the Mean and John of

Salisbury's Concept of Liberty." *Vivarium* 24 (1986): 128–42.

———. "Aristotelianism and the Origins of 'Political Science' in the Twelfth Century." *Journal of the History of Ideas* 52 (1991): 179–94.

———. "Character and Community in the *Defensor Pacis*: Marsiglio of Padua's Adaptation of Aristotelian Moral Psychology." *History of Political Thought* 13 (1992): 377–90.

———. "Community and Self-Interest: Marsiglio of Padua on Civil Life and Private Advantage." *Review of Politics* 65 (2003): 395–416.

———. "A Duty to Kill: John of Salisbury's Theory of Tyrannicide." *Review of Politics* 50 (1988): 365–98.

———. "Friendship in Public Life During the Twelfth Century: Theory and Practice in the Writings of John of Salisbury." *Viator: Medieval and Renaissance Studies* 38 (2007): 385–97.

———. *John of Salisbury*. Tempe, Ariz.: Medieval and Renaissance Texts and Studies, 2005.

———. *Lineages of European Political Thought: Explorations Along the Medieval/Modern Divide from John of Salisbury to Hegel*. Washington, D.C.: Catholic University Press of America, 2009.

———. "The Meaning of 'Aristotelianism' in Medieval Moral and Political Thought." *Journal of the History of Ideas* 57 (1996): 563–85.

———. *Medieval Aristotelianism and Its Limits: Classical Traditions in Moral and Political Philosophy, 12th–15th Centuries*. Collected Studies Series 565. London: Ashgate/Variorum, 1997.

———. "The Puzzle of the Political Animal: Nature and Artifice in Aristotle's Political Theory." *Review of Politics* 56 (Spring 1994): 283–304.

———. Review of *The Defender of the Peace*, edited by Annabel Brett. *Political Studies Review* 4 (2006): 328–29.

———. "Rhetoric, Reason, and Republic: Republicanisms—Ancient, Medieval, and Modern." In *Renaissance*

Civic Humanism, edited by James Hankins, 247–69. Cambridge: Cambridge University Press, 2000.

Nederman, Cary J., and Karen Bollermann. "'The Extravagance of the Senses': Epicureanism, Priestly Tyranny, and the Becket Problem in John of Salisbury's *Policraticus*." *Studies in Medieval and Renaissance History*, 3rd ser., 8 (2011): 1–25.

Nederman, Cary J., and Catherine E. A. Campbell. "Priests, Kings and Tyrants: Spiritual and Temporal Power in John of Salisbury's *Policraticus*." *Speculum* 66 (1991): 572–90.

Nederman, Cary J., and Mary Elizabeth Sullivan. "The Polybian Moment: The Transformation of Republican Thought from Ptolemy of Lucca to Machiavelli." *European Legacy: Toward New Paradigms* 17 (2012): 867–81.

———. "Reading Aristotle Through Rome: Republicanism and History in Ptolemy of Lucca's *De regimine principum*." *European Journal of Political Theory* 7 (2008): 223–40.

Nelson, Eric. *The Greek Tradition in Republican Thought*. Cambridge: Cambridge University Press, 2004.

Nicgorski, Walter, ed. *Cicero's Practical Philosophy*. Notre Dame: Notre Dame University Press, 2012.

———. *Cicero's Skepticism and His Recovery of Political Philosophy*. New York: Palgrave Macmillan, 2016.

Nicholas of Cusa. *The Catholic Concordance*. Edited by Paul Sigmund. Cambridge: Cambridge University Press, 1991.

———. *Opera omnia*. Vol. 14, *De concordantia catholica*. Edited by Gerhard Kallen. Hamburg: Felix Meiner, 1959–65.

Nussbaum, Martha. "Duties of Justice, Duties of Mutural Aid: Cicero's Problematic Legacy." *Journal of Political Philosophy* 8 (2000): 176–206.

Oakley, Francis. *The Emergence of Western Political Thought in the Latin Middle Ages*. 3 vols. New Haven: Yale University Press, 2010–15.

———. *Politics and Eternity: Studies in the History of Medieval and Early-Modern Political Thought.* Leiden: Brill, 1999.

O'Daly, Irene. *John of Salisbury and the Medieval Roman Renaissance.* Manchester: Manchester University Press, 2018.

O'Donovan, Oliver, and Joan Lockwood O'Donovan, eds. *From Irenaeus to Grotius: A Sourcebook in Christian Political Thought.* Grand Rapids, Mich.: Eerdmans, 1999.

Olivieri, Luigi. "Teoria Aristotelica dell'opinione e scienze politica in Marsilio da Padova." *Medioevo* 5 (1979): 223–35.

Oresme, Nicole. *Le livre de éthiques d'Aristote.* Edited by Albert D. Menut. New York: G. E. Stechert, 1940.

———. *Le livre de politiques d'Aristote.* Edited by Albert D. Menut. Transactions of the American Philosophical Society, n.s., 60, part 6. Philadelphia: American Philosophical Society, 1970.

———. *Le livre de yconomique d'Aristote.* Edited by Albert D. Menut. Philadelphia: American Philosophical Society, 1957.

Otto of Freising. *The Two Cities: A Chronicle of Universal History to the Year 1146 A.D.* Edited by Austin P. Evans and Charles Knapp. New ed. New York: Columbia University Press, 2002.

Pagden, Anthony. *The Fall of Natural Man: The American Indian and the Origins of Comparative Ethnology.* Cambridge: Cambridge University Press, 1982.

———. *Lords of All the World.* New Haven: Yale University Press, 1995.

Partner, Peter. *Renaissance Rome, 1500–1559.* Berkeley: University of California Press, 1976.

Pawlak, Mieszko. "Teoria prawa Marsyliusza z Padwy." *Politeja* 39 (2015): 5–23.

Pelagius, Alvarus. *Status et Planctus Ecclesiæ.* Edited by Miguel Pinto de Meneses. 8 vols. Lisbon: Instituto Nacional de Investigação Científica, 1988–98.

Pennington, Kenneth. "Bartolomé de Las Casas and the Tradition of Medieval Law." *Church History* 39 (1971): 149–61.

Pennington, Kenneth, and Wolfgang P. Müller. "The Decretists: The Italian School." In *The History of Medieval Canon Law in the Classical Period, 1140–1234: From Gratian to the Decretals of Pope Gregory IX,* edited by Wilfied Hartmann and Kenneth Pennington, 121–73. Washington, D.C.: Catholic University of America Press, 2008.

Perelli, Luciano. *Il peniero politico di Cicerone.* Florence: La Nuova Italica, 1990.

Pez, Berhard, ed. *Thesaurus anecdotorum novissimus.* Augsburg, 1721–29.

Pezzini, Domenico. "The Sermons of Aelred of Rievaulx." In Dutton, *Companion to Aelred of Rievaulx,* 73–97.

Piccolomini, Aeneas Silvius. *De ortu et auctoritate imperii Romani.* In "Der Briefwechsel des Eneas Silvius Piccolomini," edited by Rudolph Wolkan. *Fontes Rerum Austriacarum* 67 (1912): 6–24.

Pighius, Albertus. *Hierarchiae ecclesiastica assertio.* Cologne, 1551.

Post, Gaines. *Studies in Medieval Legal Thought: Public Law and the State, 1100–1322.* Princeton: Princeton University Press, 1964.

Powell, J. G. F., ed. *Cicero the Philosopher.* Oxford: Oxford University Press, 1995.

Powell, J. G. F., and J. A. North, eds. *Cicero's Republic.* London: Institute of Classical Studies, 2001.

Previté-Orton, C. W. "The Authors Cited in the *Defensor pacis.*" In *Essays in History Presented to R. L. Poole,* edited by H. W. C. Davis, 405–20. Oxford: Clarendon Press, 1927.

Ptolemy of Lucca. *On the Government of Rulers / De regimine principum.* Edited by James M. Blythe. Philadelphia: University of Pennsylvania Press, 1997.

Quillet, Jeannine. "L'aristotélisme de Marsile de Padoue." *Miscellanea Mediaevalia* 2 (1963): 696–706.

———. "L'aristotélisme de Marsile de Padoue et ses rapports avec l'averroïsme." *Medioevo* 5 (1979): 81–142.

———. "Community I: Community, Counsel, and Representation." In *The Cambridge History of Medieval Political Thought*, edited by J. H. Burns, 520–72. Cambridge: Cambridge University Press, 1988.

———. *La philosophie politique de Marsile de Padoue*. Paris: J. Vrin, 1970.

Rabil, Albert. "The Significance of 'Civic Humanism' in the Interpretation of the Italian Renaissance." In *Renaissance Humanism: Foundations, Form, and Legacy*, edited by Albert Rabil, 3:141–74. 3 vols. Philadelphia: University of Pennsylvania Press, 1988.

Radford, Robert T. *Cicero: A Study in the Origins of Republican Philosophy*. Amsterdam: Rodopi, 2002.

Rand, E. K. *Cicero in the Courtroom of St. Thomas Aquinas*. Milwaukee: Marquette University Press, 1946.

Remer, Gary. *Ethics and the Orator: Political Morality and the Ciceronian Tradition*. Chicago: University of Chicago Press, 2017.

Renna, Thomas J. "Aristotle and the French Monarchy, 1260–1130." *Viator: Medieval and Renaissance Studies* 9 (1978): 309–24.

Reynolds, L. D., and H. G. Wilson, *Scribes and Scholars: A Guide to the Transmission of Greek and Latin Literature*. 4th ed. Oxford: Oxford University Press, 2013.

Rifkin, Lester. "Aristotle on Equality: A Criticism of A. J. Carlyle's Theory." *Journal of the History of Ideas* 14 (1953): 276–83.

Rolfe, John C. *Cicero and His Influence*. Boston: Marshall Jones, 1923.

Rouse, Mary A., and Richard H. Rouse. *Authentic Witnesses: Approaches to Medieval Texts and Manuscripts*. Notre Dame: Norte Dame University Press, 1981.

Rouse, Richard. "Survival of the Latin Classics." In *Texts and Transmissions*, edited by Larry Reynolds, 54–142. Oxford: Clarendon Press, 1983.

Rubinstein, Nicolai. "Political Theories in the Renaissance." In *The Renaissance: Essays in Interpretation*, edited by André Chastal, 153–200. London: Methuen, 1982.

Sabine, George H. *A History of Political Theory*. 3rd ed. London: Harrap, 1937.

Saccenti, Riccardo. *Debating Medieval Natural Law*. Notre Dame: University of Notre Dame Press, 2016.

Sastre, Gerado López. "National Prejudice and Religion in the Toleration Debate Between Bartolomé de Las Casas and Juan Ginés de Sepúlveda." In *Religious Toleration: "The Variety of Rites" from Cyrus to Defoe*, edited by John Christian Laursen, 75–92. New York: St. Martin's Press, 1999.

Schabel, Christopher, ed. *Theological Quodlibeta in the Middle Ages: The Fourteenth Century*. Leiden: Brill, 2007.

Schmidt, James. "A Raven with a Halo: The Translation of Aristotle's *Politics*." *History of Political Thought* 7 (1986): 295–319.

Schulze-Busacker, Elisabeth. *Le didactique profane au Moyen Âge*. Paris: Classiques Garnier, 2012.

Scott, Joanna V. "Influence or Manipulation? The Role of Augustinianism in the *Defensor pacis* of Marsigilio of Padua." *Augustinian Studies* 9 (1978): 59–79.

Seagrave, S. Adam. "Cicero, Aquinas, and Contemporary Issues in Natural Law." *Review of Metaphysics* 62 (2009): 491–523.

Segall, Hermann. *Der "Defensor pacis" des Marsilius von Padua: Grundfragen der Interpretation*. Wiesbaden: Franz Steiner Verlag, 1959.

Sherman, Claire Richter. *Imaging Aristotle: Verbal and Visual Representation in Fourteenth-Century France*. Berkeley: University of California Press, 1995.

Sigmund, Paul. "The Influence of Marsilius of Padua on XVth-Century Conciliarism." *Journal of the History of Ideas* 23 (1962): 395–402.

———. *Nicholas of Cusa and Medieval Political Thought*. Cambridge: Harvard University Press, 1963.

Silk, Mark. "John of Salisbury and the Civic Utility of Religion." In *History in the*

Comic Mode: Medieval Communities and the Matter of Person, edited by Rachel Fulton and Bruce W. Holsinger, 128–42. New York: Columbia University Press, 2007.

———. "Numa Pompilius and the Idea of Civil Religion in the West." *Journal of the American Academy of Religion* 72 (2004): 863–96.

Skinner, Quentin. *The Foundations of Modern Political Thought*. 2 vols. Cambridge: Cambridge University Press, 1978.

———. "The Limits of Historical Explanation." *Philosophy* 41 (1966): 179–215.

———. "Meaning and Understanding in the History of Ideas." In *Visions of Politics*, vol. 1, *Regarding Method*, 57–89. Cambridge: Cambridge University Press, 2002.

———. "Political Philosophy." In *The Cambridge History of Renaissance Philosophy*, edited by C. B. Schmitt and Quentin Skinner, 387–452. Cambridge: Cambridge University Press, 1988.

Smith, Gregory Bruce. *Political Philosophy and the Republican Future: Reconsidering Cicero*. Notre Dame: University of Notre Dame Press, 2018.

Sol, Thierry. *Fallait-il tuer César: L'argumentation politique de Dante à Machiavel*. Paris: Delloz, 2005.

Somerville, Robert, and Bruce Brasington, eds. *Prefaces to Canon Law Books in Latin Christianity*. New Haven: Yale University Press, 1998.

Steel, Catherine, ed. *The Cambridge Companion to Cicero*. Cambridge: Cambridge University Press, 2013.

———. *Cicero, Rhetoric, and Empire*. Oxford: Oxford University Press, 2002.

Straumann, Benjamin. *Crisis and Constitutionalism: Roman Political Thought from the Fall of the Republic to the Age of Revolution*. Oxford: Oxford University Press, 2016.

Struve, Tilman. *Die Entwicklung der organologischen Staatsauffassung im Mittelalter*. Stuttgart: Hiersemann, 1978.

———. "The Importance of the Organism in the Political Theory of John of Salisbury." In *The World of John of Salisbury*, edited by Michael Wilks, 303–17. Oxford: Blackwell, 1984.

Sturner, Wolfgang. "Adam und Aristoteles im 'Defensor pacis' des Marsilius von Padua." *Medioevo* 6 (1980): 379–95.

Stuurman, Siep. *The Invention of Humanity: Equality and Cultural Difference in World History*. Cambridge: Harvard University Press, 2017.

Sullivan, Mary Elizabeth. "The Bonds of Aristotelian Language Among Medieval Political Thinkers." In *Communities of Learning*, edited by Constant J. Mews and John N. Crossley, 213–28. Turnhout: Brepols, 2011.

———. "Political Science and Paradigms in Medieval Europe." *Midsouth Political Science Review* 14 (2013): 1–17.

Syros, Vasileios. *Marsilius of Padua at the Intersection of Ancient and Medieval Traditions of Political Thought*. Toronto: University of Toronto Press, 2012.

Terraciano, Kevin. "The Spanish Struggle for Justification in the Conquest of America: Tolerance and Intolerance in Early Writings on Spanish America." In *Religious Toleration: 'The Variety of Rites' from Cyrus to Defoe*, edited by John Christian Laursen, 93–126. New York: St. Martin's Press, 1999.

Testard, Maurice. *Saint Augustin et Cicéron*. 2 vols. Paris: Études Augustiniennes, 1958.

Theng, Andrew A. K. "Why Did John of Paris Write *De potestate regia et papali*? A Reconsideration." In *John of Paris: Beyond Royal and Papal Power*, edited by Chris Jones, 151–91. Turnhout: Brepols, 2015.

Thierry of Chartres. *Commentarius super De inventione*. In *The Latin Rhetorical Commentaries by Thierry of Chartres*, edited by Karin M. Fredborg, 45–215. Toronto: Pontifical Institute of Mediaeval Studies, 1988.

Thomson, Rodney M. *William of Malmesbury*. Woodbridge, U.K.: Boydell Press, 1987.

Tierney, Brian. "Aristotle and the American Indians—Again: Two Critical Discussions." *Cristianesimo nella Storia* 12 (1991): 295–322.

———. *Religion, Law, and the Growth of Constitutional Thought, 1150–1650.* Cambridge: Cambridge University Press, 1982.

Tobin, R. B. "The Cornifician Motif in John of Salisbury's *Metalogicon.*" *History of Education* 13 (1984): 1–6.

Todorov, Tzvetan. "Toleration and the Intolerable." In *The Morals of History*, translated by Alyson Waters, 141–57. Minneapolis: University of Minnesota Press, 1995.

Toeste, Marco. "The Naturalness of Human Association in Medieval Political Thought Revisited." In *La nature comme source de la moral au Moyen Âge*, edited by Maaike van der Lugt, 113–88. Florence: SISMEL Edizioni del Galluzzo, 2014.

Toiavanen, Juhana. "Beasts, Human Beings, or Gods? Subjectivity in Medieval Political Philosophy." In *Subjectivity and Selfhood in Medieval and Early Modern Philosophy*, edited by Jari Kaukua and Tomas Ekenberg, 181–98. Cham, Switzerland: Springer, 2016.

Troilo, Erminio. "L'averroismo di Marsilio da Padova." In *Marsilio da Padova: Studi raccolti nel VI centenario della morte*, edited by Aldo Cecchini and Norberto Bobbio, 44–77. Padua: CEDAM, 1942.

Truax, Jean. *Aelred the Peacemaker: The Public Life of a Cistercian Abbott.* Collegeville, Minn.: Liturgical Press, 2017.

Tuck, Richard. *Philosophy and Government, 1572–1651.* Cambridge: Cambridge University Press, 1993.

Ubl, Karl, ed. *Die Schriften des Alexander von Roes und des Engelbert von Admont.* Vol. 2. Wiesbaden: Harrassowitz Verlag, 2004.

Ullmann, Walter. *Medieval Political Thought.* Harmondsworth, U.K.: Penguin, 1965.

Vasoli, Cesare. "La 'Politica' di Aristotele e la sua utilizzazione de parte di Marsilio de Padova." *Medioevo* 5 (1979): 237–57.

Vickery, Paul. *Bartolomé de Las Casas: Great Prophet of the Americas.* New York: Paulist Press, 2006.

Viroli, Maurizio. *For Love of Country: An Essay on Patriotism and Nationalism.* Oxford: Oxford University Press, 1995.

Voigt, Georg. *Enea Silvio Piccolomini als Papst Pius der Zweite und sein Zeitalter.* 3 vols. Berlin: de Gruyter, 1857–63.

Wagner, Henry R. *The Life and Writings of Bartolomé de Las Casas.* Albuquerque: University of New Mexico Press, 1967.

Ward, John O. Ward. *Ciceronian Rhetoric in Treatise, Scholion and Commentary.* Turnhout: Brepols, 1995.

———. *Classical Rhetoric in the Middle Ages: The Medieval Rhetors and Their Art, 400–1300, with a Manuscript Survey to 1500 CE.* Leiden: Brill, 2018.

———. "The Date of the Commentary on Cicero's *De inventione* by Thierry of Chartres (ca. 1095–1160?) and the Cornifician Attack on the Liberal Arts." *Viator: Medieval and Renaissance Studies* 3 (1972): 219–73.

———. "What the Middle Ages Missed of Cicero, and Why." In *Brill's Companion to the Reception of Cicero*, edited by William H. F. Altmore, 307–26. Leiden: Brill, 2015.

Watanabe, Morimichi. *The Political Ideas of Nicholas of Cusa with Special Reference to De concordantia catholica.* Geneva: Droz, 1963.

Widmer, Berthe. *Enea Silvio Piccolomini in der sittlichen und politischen Entscheidung.* Basel: Helbing & Lichtenhahn, 1963.

Williams, John R. "The Authorship of the *Moralium dogma philosophorum.*" *Speculum* 6 (1931): 392–411.

———. "The Quest for the Author of the *Moralium dogma philosophorum*, 1931–1956." *Speculum* 32 (1957): 736–47.

Wilson, Gordon A., ed. *A Companion to Henry of Ghent.* Leiden: Brill, 2011.

Witt, Ronald. *In the Footsteps of the Ancients: The Origins of Humanism from Lovato to Bruni*. Leiden: Brill, 2000.

Wittgenstein, Ludwig. *Philosophical Investigations*. Translated by G. E. M. Anscombe. 3rd ed. New York: Macmillan, 1968.

Wood, Ellen M. "The State and Popular Sovereignty in French Political Thought: A Genealogy of Rousseau's 'General Will.'" *History of Political Thought* 4 (Summer 1983): 281–315.

Wood, Neal. *Cicero's Social and Political Thought*. Berkeley: University of California Press, 1988.

Young, Charles R., ed. *The Twelfth-Century Renaissance*. Huntington, N.Y.: Krieger, 1977.

Ypma, E. "Recherches sur la carrière et la bibliothèque de Jacques de Viterbe." *Augustiniana* 24 (1972): 247–82.

Zarecki, Jonathan. *Cicero's Ideal Statesman in Theory and Practice*. London: Bloomsbury Academic, 2014.

INDEX OF WORKS CITED

INDEX OF PROPER NAMES

INDEX OF SUBJECTS